The experience of migration, a key factor in the shaping of modern Arabic literature, has taken new, unprecedented dimensions in the last decades. Drawing on the finest scholarship in several fields, the contributions of this volume explore multiple representations of the migrant in both contemporary Arabic and Arab American literature, and discuss their role in shaping new forms of transcultural and transnational identities, thus providing the reader valuable insights into a most recent literary production as well as into the deep changes it reveals in the social and political contexts these literary works represent.

Richard Jacquemond, *Professor of Modern Arabic Literature, Aix-Marseille Université, France*

The Migrant in Arab Literature

This edited book offers a collection of fresh and critical essays that explore the representation of the migrant subject in modern and contemporary Arabic literature and discuss its role in shaping new forms of transcultural and transnational identities. The selection of essays in this volume offers a set of new insights on a cluster of tropes: self-discovery, alienation, nostalgia, transmission and translation of knowledge, sense of exile, reconfiguration of the relationship with the past and the identity, and the building of transnational identity. A coherent yet multi-faceted narrative of micro-stories and of transcultural and transnational Arab identities will emerge from the essays: the volume aims at reversing the traditional perspective according to which a migrant subject is a non-political actor.

In contrast to many books about migration and literature, this one explores how the migrant subject becomes a specific literary trope, a catalyst of modern alienation, displacement, and uncertain identity, suggesting new forms of subjectification. Multiple representations of the migrant subject inform and perform the possibility of new post-national and transcultural individual and group identities and actively contribute to rewriting and decolonizing history.

Martina Censi is Assistant Professor of Arabic Language and Literature at the University of Bergamo (Italy). She is a member of the Équipe de Recherche Interlangue (ERIMIT) at the University of Rennes 2 (France). In her research, she deals with literary representations of the body, processes of the construction of masculinity and femininity, and migration with a special focus on contemporary Arabic novel. She has published the book *Le Corps dans le roman des écrivaines syriennes contemporaines: Dire, écrire, inscrire la différence* (2016) and other articles about modern and contemporary Arabic literature.

Maria Elena Paniconi is Associate Professor of Arabic Literature at the University of Macerata. She is interested in the rise of the Arab novel and in the dialectics among literary genres during the Arab *Nahḍa*. She has written articles and essays in the *Journal of Arabic Literature* and *Oriente Moderno* on nahḍawī authors and co-edited with Jolanda Guardi the special issue of *Oriente Moderno*, "Nahḍa Narratives". She wrote the entries on Ṭāhā Ḥusayn and Muḥammad Ḥusayn Haykal for the third edition of the *Encyclopedia of Islam*. Her book *Bildungsroman and the Arab Novel: Egyptian Intersections* (Routledge 2023) explores a corpus of Egyptian canonical novels featuring young protagonists in their path toward adulthood, through the lens of international Bildungsroman.

Routledge Advances in Middle East and Islamic Studies

23 **Dissident Writings of Arab Women**
Voices Against Violence
Brinda Mehta

24 **Higher Education Revolutions in the Gulf**
Globalization and Institutional Viability
Fatima Badry and John Willoughby

25 **Knowledge Production in the Arab World**
The Impossible Promise
Sari Hanafi and Rigas Arvanitis

26 **Palestinian Culture and the Nakba**
Bearing Witness
Hania A.M. Nashef

27 **Orientalism, Zionism and Academic Practice**
Middle East and Islam Studies in Israeli Universities
Eyal Clyne

28 **The Migrant in Arab Literature**
Displacement, Self-Discovery and Nostalgia
Edited by Martina Censi and Maria Elena Paniconi

29 **Bildungsroman and the Arab Novel**
Egyptian Intersections
Maria Elena Paniconi

30 **Narratives of Dislocation in the Arab World**
Rewriting *Ghurba*
Edited by Nadeen Dakkak

For more information about this series, please visit: www.routledge.com/middleeaststudies/series/SE0728

The Migrant in Arab Literature

Displacement, Self-Discovery and Nostalgia

Edited by
Martina Censi and Maria Elena Paniconi

Routledge
Taylor & Francis Group
LONDON AND NEW YORK

First published 2023
by Routledge
4 Park Square, Milton Park, Abingdon, Oxon OX14 4RN

and by Routledge
605 Third Avenue, New York, NY 10158

Routledge is an imprint of the Taylor & Francis Group, an informa business

British Library Cataloguing-in-Publication Data
A catalogue record for this book is available from the British Library

Library of Congress Cataloging-in-Publication Data
Names: Censi, Martina, editor. | Paniconi, Maria Elena, editor.
Title: The migrant in Arab literature : displacement, self-discovery and nostalgia / edited by Martina Censi and Maria Elena Paniconi.
Description: Abingdon, Oxon ; New York, NY : Routledge, 2023. |
Series: Routledge advances in Middle East and Islamic studies |
Includes bibliographical references and index.
Identifiers: LCCN 2022021969 | ISBN 9780367135881 (hardback) |
ISBN 9781032303994 (paperback) | ISBN 9780429027338 (ebook)
Subjects: LCSH: Emigration and immigration in literature. |
Immigrants in literature. | Exiles in literature. |
Arabic literature–History and criticism.
Classification: LCC PJ7519.E54 M54 2023 |
DDC 892.7/09352691–dc23/eng/20220712
LC record available at https://lccn.loc.gov/2022021969

ISBN: 978-0-367-13588-1 (hbk)
ISBN: 978-1-032-30399-4 (pbk)
ISBN: 978-0-429-02733-8 (ebk)

DOI: 10.4324/9780429027338

Typeset in Times New Roman
by Newgen Publishing UK

This book is dedicated to Adelina Sejdini and to all migrant women who struggle daily, with their bodies, against exploitation, oppression, and violence.

Contents

List of Contributors xi
Acknowledgements xiii

Introduction 1
MARTINA CENSI

1 Migrating to and in Europe Beyond the Nahḍawī and Modernist Paradigm: *Mudun bi-lā nakhīl* by Ṭāriq al-Ṭayyib and *Taytanikāt Ifrīqiyya* by Abū Bakr Khāl as Novels of Forced Migration 12
MARIA ELENA PANICONI

2 Transcultural Identities in Two Novels by Ḥanān al-Shaykh 28
MARTINA CENSI

3 The Body and the Migrating Subject in the Gulf: *Daqq al-ṭabūl* by Muḥammad al-Bisāṭī 52
CRISTINA DOZIO

4 Writing Arabic in the Land of Migration: Waciny Laredj from *Ḥārisat al-ẓilāl: Dūn Kīshūt fī al-Jazā'ir to Shurafāt baḥr al-shamāl* 69
JOLANDA GUARDI

5 Resistant Assimilation and Hometactics as Decolonial Practices: The Stories of Leilah and Ibrahim in *The Orange Trees of Baghdad* 83
SHIMA SHAHBAZI

6 The Negotiation of Identity in Laila Halaby's *Once in a Promised Land* and *West of Jordan* 103
SARA ARAMI

7 "Smotherland" Speaks: Syrian Refugee Identity in the Spaces Between Media and Literature 123
ROULA SALAM

8 The Global Migration Context and the Contemporary Iraqi Novel 151
IKRAM MASMOUDI

Epilogue 175
MARIA ELENA PANICONI

Index 184

Contributors

Sara Arami is a temporary lecturer at the Jean Monnet University in Saint-Etienne and a member of SEARCH (Savoirs dans l'Espace Anglophone: Représentations, Culture, Histoire). She completed her PhD at the University of Strasbourg (France). Her research interests involve questions around the subjects of identity, diaspora, nationality, femininity, cartography, and the body.

Martina Censi is Assistant Professor of Arabic Language and Literature at the University of Bergamo (Italy). She is a member of the Équipe de Recherche Interlangue (ERIMIT) at the University of Rennes 2 (France). In her research, she deals with literary representations of the body, processes of the construction of masculinity and femininity, and migration with a special focus on contemporary Arabic novel. She has published the book *Le Corps dans le roman des écrivaines syriennes contemporaines: Dire, écrire, inscrire la différence* (Brill, 2016) and other articles about modern and contemporary Arabic literature.

Cristina Dozio is Assistant Professor of Arabic Language and Literature at the University of Milan, Italy. Her research interests are modern and contemporary Arabic literature, humour, popular culture, urban literary representation, and literary translation. Her book *Laugh Like an Egyptian: Literary Humour in the Contemporary Egyptian Novel* (DeGruyter Mouton, 2021) examines the interplay of humour, satire, and aesthetic innovations. She translates Arabic fiction into Italian.

Jolanda Guardi teaches Arabic Language and Literature at the University of Turin (Italy). Her research focuses on dynamics of intellect and power in Arabic literature (with a focus on Algeria) and gender issues. She is a member of the University Autonoma de Barcelona SIMREF's Scientific Board. She is Series Editor (novels and poetry translated from Arabic) for the Italian publishing house Jouvence and Scientific Director of ILA Arabic Certificate Program (Milan, Italy).

Ikram Masmoudi is Associate Professor of Arabic at the University of Delaware. She is the author of *War and Occupation in Iraqi Fiction*

(Edinburgh University Press, 2015). She has also published numerous journal articles and is currently working on a new book project, *Imaginings of Apocalypse*, in Arabic.

Maria Elena Paniconi is Associate Professor of Arabic Literature at the University of Macerata. She is interested in the rise of the Arab novel and in the dialectics among literary genres during the Arab *Nahḍa*. She has written articles and essays in the *Journal of Arabic Literature* and *Oriente Moderno* on nahḍawī authors. She has written *Bildungsroman and the Arab Novel: Egyptian Intersections* for Routledge (2023).

Roula Salam is a lecturer and a curriculum developer at the University of Alberta (Edmonton, Alberta, Canada). She teaches and develops language, literature, and cultural communication courses at the undergraduate and graduate levels and mentors teachers in training. She is also a certified Arabic–English translator and is currently President of the Association of Translators and Interpreters of Alberta.

Shima Shahbazi is a sessional lecturer and tutor at the University of Sydney and Western Sydney University in Sydney, Australia. She graduated with a PhD in Comparative Literature and International Studies in 2019 from the University of Sydney. Her research focuses on memoirs and autobiographies of migrant women with Middle Eastern backgrounds as well as on decolonial epistemologies. She is currently writing her monograph, *Reading Between Borders*, which focuses on Iranian and Iraqi women's narratives of border crossing.

Acknowledgements

This volume originated in 2016, from a panel entitled "The migrating subject: Displacement, self-discovery and nostalgia" that we organized within the 13th SeSaMO (Society for Middle Eastern Studies) Conference about "Migrants: Communities, Borders, Memories, and Conflicts", at the University of Catania (Italy). The panel, which involved women scholars from different backgrounds, was an important opportunity for exchanging ideas and investigating the character of the migrant, increasingly pervasive in contemporary Arabic literature. In this regard, our gratitude goes to Mirella Cassarino and Samuela Pagani, who helped us to animate and broaden the discussion with their support and questions. We also thank Lucia Sorbera for suggesting scholars interested in the topic. The richness and methodological diversity of the papers, as well as the relevance and urgency of the topic, encouraged us to think about a book. The publication project took several years, and it has been realized with the support of an international network of scholars. It is not a coincidence that it turned out to be a female-signed book, precisely because migrants and women share an "eccentric" and "peripheral" positioning with respect to dominant discourses, that is mirrored, we believe, in the analyses and assessments developed by the authors. Our sincerest and deepest gratitude, therefore, goes to our "travelling companions" who contributed to this volume and patiently accompanied us in the adversities of this long journey by sharing their valuable work. We are especially grateful to Routledge's anonymous peer reviewers who, with their precious advice, helped us to refine the project and better focalize the subject matter and the methodological approach. Many thanks, finally, to miriam cooke and Richard Jacquemond for being the first readers of the manuscript.

Each of us also has personal travel companions who have joined on this exciting path.

Martina Censi is grateful to Miloud Gharrafi, who has been a precious resource in the domain of Arabic literature on migration and a generous presence with whom to discuss and share reflections on the topic. A special thank goes to the équipe de recherche ERIMIT at the University of Rennes 2 (France) for their support in the organization of a journée d'étude on "Le sujet migrant dans la littérature arabe" and of an international conference, co-organized with Miloud Gharrafi, about the "Poétique du récit migratoire". These moments of intense scientific exchange contributed in various ways to the achievement of this book. Censi would also address her gratitude to the Department of Foreign Languages, Literatures and Cultures of the University of Bergamo (Italy) for funding her research project on the "Representations of the Migrant Subject in Contemporary Arabic Literature", giving her the opportunity to deepen this boundless field of studies. Sincere thanks to the colleagues Zaïneb Ben Lagha, Laurence Denooz, Safaa Monqid, and Elisabeth Vauthier who, in various ways, have been helpful in this long research path through the involvement in various academic initiatives. Finally, special thanks go to the students of Arabic literature at the University of Bergamo who, through their presence, their questions, and observations, continually give new life to the literary texts analysed in class.

Maria Elena Paniconi thanks the Institut für Orientalistik at the University of Vienna, where her research began during an internship in 2016. She addresses her gratitude to the writer and friend Tarek al-Tayyeb for releasing some interesting interviews and for helping her, during several meetings, to better understand his intellectual journey and stylistic choices. Paniconi also thanks the Istituto Storico Parri of Bologna and the ITALINT Master's programme, provided by the Department of Humanities at the University of Macerata (Italy) and directed by Edith Cognigni, for offering her the space to reflect, during lectures and seminar activities, on the theme of the migrant subject in the Arabic novel. Finally, the translator Barbara Benini and all the colleagues with whom she was able to exchange ideas and perspectives on the subject are also warmly thanked.

To conclude, we especially wish to thank all the women and men writers who, through their writings, carry on an indispensable work of resistance against all forms of homogenization and invisibility.

Introduction

Martina Censi

In his study *The Figure of the Migrant* (2015), Thomas Nail defines the 21st century as the century of migration and argues that the condition of "being a migrant" is becoming more widespread since spatial, social and economic mobility is generally on the rise. Migrants constitute an important component of society that is closely entwined with its transformation and evolution. For a long time, the theme of migration has been the focus of an important and composite branch of inter and multi-disciplinary studies involving experts in history, economics, statistics, geography, sociology, anthropology, post-colonial studies, etc. Apart from being a phenomenon at the centre of our daily lives and the political agenda, migration entails calling into question a series of fixed categories that have now become obsolete and inappropriate for analysing reality. More specifically, the concepts of nation, belonging and identity may no longer be considered as monocultural, closed and homogeneous, but should be reconsidered in terms of processuality, heterogeneity and openness. The political figure that inevitably demolishes these categories of thought is the migrant, who simultaneously implies social expulsion and the prospect of an alternative narrative for the politics of inclusion. However, migrants are still represented in dominant cultural discourses as non-political subjects, antithetical to the modern concept of "citizen" (Balibar, 2010), for the very reason that identity and belonging are still considered in terms of *stasis*. As Nail explains:

> The first problem is that the migrant has been predominantly understood from the perspective of *stasis* and perceived as a secondary or derivative figure with respect to place-bound social membership. Place-bound membership in a society is assumed as primary; secondary is the movement back and forth between social points.
>
> (Nail, 2015, 3)

Therefore, from this point of view, it is the very characteristics of mobility and change that characterize the identity of the migrant, rendering him or her a non-normative subject who jeopardizes the order of society and of the nation state.

DOI: 10.4324/9780429027338-1

In his analysis, with a philosophical slant, Nail sheds light on how the label "migrant" covers various subjects who share different types of mobility, resulting from very different conditions that may lead to diametrically opposed consequences: "For some, movement offers opportunity, recreation, and profit with only a temporary expulsion. For others, movement is dangerous and constrained, and their social expulsions are much more severe and permanent" (Nail, 2015, 2). In Nail's study, the types of movement or force – not only spatial, but also economic and social – become the variable allowing the classification of the different figures of the migrant, who, in his opinion, are ranked between two extremes: that of the tourist and that of the vagabond (Nail, 2015, 3).

Mobility and change are closely intertwined with the processual dimension of the migrant's identity, which means overcoming the idea that this figure belongs to a fixed, homogeneous and monocultural category. In actual fact, this was already a key theme of numerous studies undertaken in the 1980s and 1990s, such as *Orientalism* by Edward Said (1978), *The Location of Culture* by Homi Bhabha (1994) and *Questions of Cultural Identity* (Hall, Du Gay, 1996), a collection of essays dedicated to analysing cultural identity and written by various scholars who try to reconsider identity beyond existentialist paradigms by appreciating its cultural and discursive components.

Following on from this approach, more recently we have witnessed the development of a specific interest in the transcultural and transnational components of identity, other intrinsic elements in the figure of the migrant. These factors are also analysed in the literary field, as in the study *Transcultural Identities in Contemporary Literature* (Nordin et al., 2013), which is dedicated to the recontextualization of the concept of culture "from a transcultural perspective, emphasizing transnational and transmigrant networks as crucial factors in redefinitions of collective and individual identities" (Nordin et al., 2013, xii). In order to do this, authors from different geographical, linguistic and cultural contexts are taken into consideration and their works are analysed from a transcultural point of view. In this regard, the editors insist on the fact that "The incorporation of transculturality and related concepts into the analysis of literary works is relatively recent. […] Yet, to date, only a few studies dealing with these themes in specific contexts have been produced" (Nordin et al., 2013, xi).

Literature, and particularly narratives of migration, exile, diaspora and self-displacement, offer new opportunities for understanding the political and social agency of migrant subjects. Besides providing a literary representation of migrant subjects, whose identities are characterized by transcultural and transnational identities and multi-tier citizenship (Yuval-Davis, 1997), contemporary literary narratives of migration deconstruct the dominant national narrative and suggest alternative and non-essentialist forms of identity and belonging. This aspect also emerges in two recent studies in the literary field by Jopi Nyman: *Home, Identity, and Mobility in Contemporary Diasporic*

Fiction (2009) and *Displacement, Memory, and Travel in Contemporary Migrant Writing* (2017). In the first, the author focuses on the concepts of diaspora and hybridity in a selection of texts of contemporary migrant literature and states that:

> By focusing on stories of mobility and identity construction, diasporic writing delves into the globalized world of transnationalisms, hybridity, and mobile identities. Although migrancy and exile have always been central in literary production in general and modernism in particular, as the examples of Joseph Conrad, James Joyce, Thomas Mann, Richard Wright, and Bessie Head show, more recent postcolonial writing by authors such as Salman Rushdie, Caryl Phillips, and Emine Sevgi Özdamar calls into question fixed understandings of the issues of home, identity, and nation by crossing cultural, linguistic, and national boundaries and transforming formerly homogeneous cultures and societies.
>
> (Nyman, 2009, 10)

The need to overcome fixed understandings of identity and nation is also at the core of a second study by Nyman, in which the focus is more specifically on the theme of "migration and the cultural encounters and transformations that it generates, with particular reference to both fictional and autobiographical texts" (Nyman, 2017, 2).

The same theoretical reflection on the concepts of identity, belonging and nation are also found in the studies dedicated to Arabic literature of migration, the key theme of this book. Some of these studies have been dedicated to the production of the Arab American *Mahjar* literati of the 20th century – from Amīn Rīḥānī, to Jubrān Khalīl Jubrān (Kahlil Jibran) and Mīkhāʾīl Nuʿayma – which developed a series of tropes related to the migratory experience, contributing to the shaping of a modern Arab sensibility linked to a sense of loss, alienation and displacement and often framed in a nostalgic reading of the past. Others consider the more recent literary production of Arab American and Arab British intellectuals written in English. On this matter, a study with a historical perspective by Evelyn Shakir (1996) is a pioneering work that pinpoints three phases in the production of these literati: early period (1900–1920s), middle period (1930s–1960s), recent period (1970s–today). The work *Immigrant Narratives: Orientalism and Cultural Translation in Arab American and Arab British Literature* by Waïl S. Hassan (2011) belongs to this trend, taking into consideration Arab American and Arab British writers starting from the first generation of the *Mahjar* literati of the 20th century up until the present day. By means of a postcolonial and "translational" approach, Hassan deals with how the migration experience has modelled the literary production of Arab American and Arab British immigrant authors and contributed to forming its own canons. In his opinion, most of these writers adopt the position of "cultural translator who claims a privileged position to interpret the Arab world to American or British readers", and he adds, with a warning, that "Such interpretation is always conducted through the prism of Orientalism, a hegemonic frame of reference that cannot be avoided, and is always framed, whether explicitly or implicitly, by the politics of empire" (Hassan, 2011, xii). Among the works dedicated to the production of Arab American writers of the 20th and 21st centuries, we also find the studies by Steven Salaita, *Modern Arab American Fiction: A Reader's Guide* (2011), and Carol Fadda-Conrey, *Contemporary Arab-American Literature: Transnational Reconfigurations of Citizenship and Belonging* (2014). Another stream has also developed within this vein dedicated to the production of women writers, as demonstrated, for example, by the various works of Lisa Suhair Majaj and the volume *Contemporary Arab American Women Writers: Hyphenated Identities and Border Crossing* (2007) by Amal Talaat Abdelrazek.

The migrant subject – characterized by his/her complex location, transnational and transcultural identity, alienation, outsiderness and self-discovery – is also a central theme in modern and contemporary literature written in Arabic. Critics are showing growing interest in this important literary vein involving the narrative genre above all. In the introduction to the edited volume *Al-Hijra fī al-adab al-ʿarabī al-muʿāṣir* (2016), the editor, Miloud Gharrafi, affirms that, until now, a large proportion of the studies on Arab migration literature has mainly pivoted around *adab al-mahjar*, the works of Syrian-Lebanese writers who settled in America at the turn of the 20th century. The first half of the 20th century was characterized by the emergence of another important literary vein regarding migration towards Europe which, as Gharrafi points out, concentrates on the character of the student and the intellectual (Gharrafi, 2016, 5). At the centre of works such as Tawfīq al-Ḥakīm's *ʿUṣfūr min al-Sharq* (Bird of the East, 1938), Yaḥyā Ḥaqqī's *Qindīl Umm Hāshim* (The Lamp of Umm Hashim, 1944) and *al-Ḥayy al-Lātīnī* (The Latin Quarter, 1953) by Suhayl Idrīs, we find the figure of the young migrant, usually from the élite classes of his country of origin, who migrates towards the European metropolises – especially London and Paris – to complete his education and whose attitude swings from the idealization of Europe to the crisis of identity. On this matter, one of the first works placing the crisis of the intellectual Arab following his contact with Europe at the centre of the plot is *Adīb* (A Man of Letters, 1935) by Ṭāhā Ḥusayn. This type of production sets migration in a postcolonial context and re-examines in different ways the power relations between the colonizer and the colonized and explores, in particular, the Arab world–Europe vector, giving life to a series of representations of "European otherness" in which Europe is depicted as a synecdoche of modernity. These representations of Europe have long been seen by critics through the lens of "East–West encounters", borrowing the paradigm of the clash between East and West civilizations (El-Enany, 2006). However, as Lorenzo Casini et al. (2013) claim, these same references to Europe may be interpreted as a strategy, adopted by the authors of the novels, to question and criticize some of the ways of representing Arab modernity as a synonym of the European lifestyle.

The novel *Mawsim al-hijra ilā al-shimāl* (Season of Migration to the North, 1966), by the Sudanese writer Ṭayyib Ṣāliḥ, represents a turning point, as it is considered a sort of deconstruction of the idealization of Europe pursued during the Nahḍa, by overthrowing the colonial violence, which is no longer endured by the colonized but introjected and actively exerted on the European other, represented by the female characters. The protagonist, a Sudanese man who has emigrated to London to do a doctorate, exerts forms of psychological and physical violence on his lovers, who belong to different social classes, leading two of them to commit suicide, while he himself will murder his wife. Published in 1966, *Mawsim al-hijra ilā al-shimāl* seems to stand in contrast to the turning point of 1967, which

> marked a dramatic shift in Arabic literary narratives of travel to and exile in Europe. [...] These are transformed through a focus on social and political oppression in the Arab world operating alongside an idealization of Europe. [...] exile and travel literature in the post-1967 period tends to idealize European spaces and re-centre the east–west categories that had long been part of this genre.
>
> (Sellman, 2018, 757–758)

Starting from this period, one of the themes at the centre of Arabic literature of migration is that of the return, which becomes an opportunity to represent the homeland through an idealization of Europe, seen as a politically and socially more advanced dimension, but always within the "East vs West" binomial, or through the lens of nostalgia. *Cultural Identity in Arabic Novels of Immigration: A Poetics of Return* (2020), by Wessam Elmeligi, is a study dedicated to the theme of return, which is explored starting from the concept of cultural identity. The identity of the migrant is seemingly modelled by his/her relationship with the motherland, which may lead to an idealization of the same and a resulting sense of alienation and extraneousness in the land of immigration. The impossibility of finding a place in the new society may lead to a consequent desire to return – perceived as either a triumph or a loss – which becomes a distinguishing trait of the characters populating the novels analysed by Elmeligi, which range in time from 1935 to 2010.

According to Gharrafi, too, the 1970s represent a turning point in Arabic literature of migration as it sees the emergence of a new type of migrant, the migrant worker, both documented and undocumented, who is no longer headed exclusively towards Europe, but towards the Gulf countries. From the beginning of the 1970s, in Morocco alone, about 60 novels have been published centring on this new type of migrant (Gharrafi, 2016, 6). Here, the question of identity is no longer played out according to the "East–West" binomial (understood in the sense of "Arab countries" vs "Europe"), but the "Arab–Arab" binomial. The pioneering work on this literary vein concerning migration towards the Gulf is *Rijāl fī al-shams* (Men in the Sun, 1963) by Ghassān Kanafānī, while Hani Elayyan (2016) devotes himself to a comparative analysis of three more recent Arab novels again on the same theme: Ibrāhīm Naṣr Allāh's *Barārī al-ḥummā* (Prairies of Fever, 1985), Ibrāhīm ʿAbd al-Majīd's *Al-Balda al-ukhrā* (The Other Place, 1990) and Saʿūd al-Sanʿūsī's *Sāq al-bāmbū* (The Bamboo Stalk, 2012). Elayyan concentrates on the figure of Arab expats and underlines that

> Naṣrallāh and ʿAbdalmagīd have delineated the expatriation experience and highlighted the discrepancy between the expats' expectations of brotherhood, which originated from their belief in the dominant pan-Arab ideology, and the reality of existence in societies that had social configurations that did not necessarily privilege Arab expats.
>
> (Elayyan, 2016, 87)

The changing figure of the migrant in contemporary Arabic literature is also noted by Johanna Sellman in her study "A Global Postcolonial: Contemporary Arabic Literature of Migration to Europe" (2018), which pinpoints a turning point starting from the 1990s when "Arabic literature of migration to Europe has increasingly foregrounded the perspectives of refugees, asylum seekers and undocumented migrants" (Sellman, 2018, 752). This literary production includes the so-called *harraga*[1] novels from the Maghreb that "feature undocumented Mediterranean crossings and tell stories of those who choose to embark on them" (Sellman, 2018, 752). This type of narration is also found in sub-Saharan African literatures and other Arabic literatures. Included in these narrative works about forced and undocumented migration we also find literary narrations about asylum seekers in Europe, which, although they "do not typically focus on journeys or crossings, they share a focus on writing borderlands; that is, spaces outside normative citizenship" (Sellman, 2018, 752). In her recent book *Arabic Exile Literature in Europe: Defamiliarizing Forced Migration* (2022), Sellman analyses contemporary Arabic literature of forced migration in the 21st century, focusing on exile literature in Europe, written from the perspective of refugees, asylum seekers, undocumented migrants, and others subaltern subjects who are situated outside normatively defined citizenship. In this case, the focus is not on mobility in itself, but on the place taken by the migrant in the country of immigration and how it affects his/her individual and collective identity, leading to a necessary reconsideration of the normative forms of citizenship based on exclusion. Between the 1990s and 2000s, we witness a shift in focus from the character of the political exile to that of the refugee, in relation to the change in the socio-political context, and the spread of mass migration. As a distinguishing trait of this new literature of migration, Sellman identifies a move away from the colonial and postcolonial dimension and the consequent exploration of "new aesthetics and modes of representing migration in a global context" (Sellman, 2018, 754), where the portrayal of the European metropolis also changes, no longer being idealized by means of the East–West paradigm, but understood as a globalized dimension of multiple cultural encounters. This more recent refugee literature contributes to the deconstruction of the idealized and aesthetic vision of exile as a privileged condition and "catalyst for change" (Halabi, 2017, 97), a legacy of romantic and modernist poetry. On this point, as Zeina Halabi observes in her book *The Unmaking of the Arab Intellectual: Prophecy, Exile and the Nation* (2017), the role of literature proves to be crucial for the very fact that it reallocates the experience of migration and exile within specific historical, material and political conditions, avoiding any abstraction or idealization that inevitably leads to the desubjectification of the migrant.

Starting from the active and performative role of literature in re-conferring centrality to the specific nature of each human experience, the contributions of this edited volume explore multiple representations of the migrant in contemporary Arabic literature and discuss their role in shaping new forms of transcultural and transnational identities. The essays in this work are devoted to the analyses of writings by contemporary authors from all over the Arab world, analysed through a multi-disciplinary approach. In contrast to many books about migration and literature, this one explores how the migrant subject becomes a specific literary trope, a catalyst of modern alienation, displacement and uncertain identity, suggesting new forms of subjectification. Multiple representations of the migrant inform and perform the possibility of new post-national and transcultural individual and group identities and actively contribute to decolonizing and re-writing history.

While several works have been dedicated to the literature produced by Arab authors in diaspora that discuss, from a postcolonial point of view, how Arab immigrant writers reflect on their identity, on their role as cultural translators and on the production of new subjectivities in a migratory context, our volume will attempt to recast the role of the migratory experience at the core of literary sensibility itself, going beyond every idealized representation of hybridity and focusing on the material component of each individual experience. Literature does not simply represent the historical experience of Arab migration. Migration becomes a specific literary trope with great impact on the formation of taste, genres and cultural experiences in the Arab world, and the migrant becomes a specific character. In this selection of studies on writings in Arabic and English by authors of Arab origin, each essay deals with the ways in which Arab literary production contributes to our understanding of how new strategies of individual and collective subjectification are performed through writing in a world greatly affected by social and political movement and change.

Each chapter offers a set of new insights on a cluster of tropes: self-discovery, alienation, nostalgia, transmission and translation of knowledge, sense of exile, reconfiguration of the relationship with the past and identity and the building of transnational identities. A coherent yet multi-faceted narrative of micro-stories and of transcultural and transnational Arab identities will emerge: the volume aims to reverse the traditional perspective according to which a migrant subject is a non-political actor. On the contrary, our aim is to re-position migration and migrant subjects at the core of the political discourse, by highlighting the performative aspects fostered by literary tropes such as displacement, migration and forced migration. In the first chapter, Maria Elena Paniconi discusses the new portrayals of migrant subjectivities in two novels depicting two forced migrations: *Mudun bi-lā nakhīl* (Cities Without Palms, 1992) by Ṭāriq al-Ṭayyib and *Taytanikāt Ifrīqiyya* (African Titanics, 2008) by Abū Bakr Khāl. The novels are analysed considering a recent study on migration by Nail (2015) that puts the spotlight back on the migrant's political subjectivity. At the same time, this analysis will highlight how the political dimension of the Earth system takes shape, reacting to human actions as well, in the current climate crisis. In her analysis of these novels, Paniconi distances herself from a viewpoint that regards the situation of permanence and citizenship as "standard", and thus migration as an extraordinary phenomenon.

Chapter 2, by Martina Censi, is devoted to transcultural identities among the universe of characters in two novels by the Lebanese writer Ḥanān al-Shaykh, who lives in London. The novels in question are *Misk al-ghazāl* (The Gazelle's Musk, 1988) and *Innahā London yā ʿazīzī* (This Is London, My Dear, 2001). In these two works, al-Shaykh deals with two different experiences of migration that had a strong impact on Arab societies during the 1980s and 1990s, one being migration towards the Gulf countries and the other towards European metropolises. Although they were published more than ten years apart, there appears to be a dialogue between the novels in the way of representing the effects of migration on the characters' identity and for the narratological and stylistic choices adopted in the texts. The analysis centres on the path to identity undertaken by the characters at the heart of these two polyphonic novels, bearing in mind the relationship between identity, space and body and referring to the notion of transcultural identity.

Migration from the Gulf is the focus of Chapter 3, where Cristina Dozio examines *Daqq al-ṭabūl* (Drumbeat, 2006), by the Egyptian Muḥammad al-Bisāṭī, as a contemporary novel that shapes the migrant's identity in the Gulf with a mixture of realism and fantasy. The native population of a nameless Emirate is sent to France when the national football team qualifies for the World Cup, leaving the country in the hands of labour migrants. Through close textual analysis, this contribution explores the novel's thematic and narrative strategies, focusing on the relationship between peers (in this case migrants and outsiders) in a transnational context, and the impact of displacement on the body and gender relations. Finally, storytelling emerges as a tool for both self-discovery and survival.

Chapter 4, by Jolanda Guardi, is devoted to two novels by the Algerian author Waciny Laredj (Wāsīnī al-Aʿraj) settled in Paris: *Ḥārisat al-ẓilāl. Dūn Kīshūt fī al-Jazāʾir* (The Shadows' (She)Guardian: Don Quixote in Algiers, 1996) and *Shurafāt baḥr al-shimāl. Amṭār Amstirdām* (North Sea's Balconies: Amsterdam Rains, 2001). In *The Shadows' (She)Guardian*, the protagonist has his tongue and his penis cut, symbolizing the loss of speech and desire. After discussing this loss, an outline is given of the intellectual path of the author, who has chosen to trespass physically on the border in order to maintain his "tongue", and to migrate with it; then, Guardi focuses on the novel *North Sea's Balconies*, where the author deals with the intellectuals' *manfā* (broadly translated as "exile") from their own country. Laredj, in fact, succeeds in remaining an Arabic writing author despite living abroad and avoids being included in the so-called migration literature discourse. In doing so, he subverts the discourse about migration literature and transforms his writing into a powerful tool to question migration in Western discourse.

In Chapter 5, Shima Shahbazi draws on feminist phenomenology and uses an intersectional methodology to study Leilah Nadir's *The Orange Trees of Baghdad* (2014), which mostly reflects on the post-2003 invasion of Iraq, from the perspective of a half Iraqi, half British woman who has never been to Iraq but perceives of Iraq as her homeland. Focusing on multiple voices in this memoir, Shahbazi aims to show how three different generations of an Iraqi family practise homemaking and create a sense of belonging to "home" before, during and after the 2003 invasion of Iraq. The author studies the intersections of homeland, identity and politics, using *The Orange Trees of Baghdad* as a good example of second-generation migrant life writing.

The negotiation of identity in two novels by the Arab American writer Laila Halaby is at the core of Sara Arami's analysis, in Chapter 6. Born to a Jordanian father and an American mother in Beirut, Laila Halaby belongs to the new generation of Arab American women writers. This chapter focuses on her *Once in a Promised Land* (2007) and *West of Jordan* (2003), in order to demonstrate how Halaby uses fiction to question the stereotypes of gender and nationality, making it her mission to challenge the ossified image of a sexed and racialized female body. She not only contests the role of women's bodies in representing the national culture but also questions the Western view of that body, a view that fixes Middle Eastern women in the position of a passive victim of traditional oriental patriarchy and religious practices. By doing so, she replies to the growing need – especially after 9/11 – for a redefinition of Arab American women's subjectivities from their own discursive positions, and a representation of the complexities of identity and belonging they entail as a way of soliciting understanding and a "place" for their non-conformist presence(s).

The active role of literature in the deconstruction of objectified and stereotyped representations of migrants and refugees is at the centre of Chapter 7 by Roula Salam. The analysis, which discusses depictions of the Syrian crisis, juxtaposes channels of mainstream and artistic media with pre-revolutionary and revolutionary Syrian Arab literature to focus on questions of voice and Syrian identity. The chapter begins by outlining some of the troublesome issues underlying the representation of refugees and then analyses how both mass media and artistic media, in their reaction to the crisis, tend to position refugees within a controlled space where they are objectified; attention is also paid to how such representation may silence refugees' sociocultural and historical narratives through practices such as museumification and framing. The final part of the chapter, which presents a contrast to depictions of the visual narratives imposed by the dominant culture, illustrates how pre-revolutionary and revolutionary narratives by Syrian authors allow distinctly Syrian identities to emerge and argues that this is a crucial step for reasserting identity and giving voice to important sociocultural Syrian narratives at risk of being silenced.

The book closes with an analysis of the global migration context and the contemporary Iraqi novel by Ikram Masmoudi, in Chapter 8, which discusses narratives of migration experiences, articulating the migrant subjectivity as depicted in three contemporary Iraqi novels published after 2003. Masmoudi investigates and traces the changes affecting the aesthetics and politics of representing migration from a postcolonial modernist perspective to a global context characterized by perennial wars, border violence and xenophobia. The analysis and discussion of these novels demonstrate the shift from the postcolonial to the global in the main areas of interest, including the trope of cultural encounter and the idea of return. Today, migration experiences of Iraqis are triggered by the trauma of the continuing violence at home and shaped by the politics of increased border control, rejection and disillusion.

By examining a wide range of narrative literary texts by male and female writers originating from various parts of the Arab world and adopting a multi-disciplinary approach, combining textual analysis with media studies, trauma studies, migration studies, gender studies, comparative literature, migrant and refugee studies, cultural studies and postcolonial studies, the book aims to analyse the migrant subject as a literary trope suggesting new systems of knowledge and of subjectification. The novels' characters embody new and fluid models of transnational, transcultural and gender identities, refusing to conform to collective norms based on a criterion of "inclusion vs exclusion" and exposing the inadequacy of old static categories of "identity", "membership" and "nation".

Note

1 This is a colloquial Arabic term referring to the migrants' practice of burning their documents prior to crossing the border in order to hide their nationality.

References

ʿAbd al-Majīd, I. (1990) *Al-Balda al-ukhrā*. London: Dār Riyāḍ al-rayyis.

Abdelrazek, A.T. (2007) *Contemporary Arab American Women Writers: Hyphenated Identities and Border Crossing*. Youngstown, NY: Cambria Press.

Balibar, E. (2010) Antinomies of Citizenship. *Journal of Romance Studies*, 10(2), 1–20.

Bhabha, H. (1994) *The Location of Culture*. London: Routledge.

Casini, L., Paniconi, M.E., Sorbera, L. (2013) *Modernità arabe. Nazione, narrazione e nuovi soggetti nel romanzo egiziano*. Messina: Mesogea.

El-Enany, R. (2006) *Arab Representations of the Occident: East–West Encounters in Arabic Fiction*. London: Routledge.
Elayyan, H. (2016) Three Arabic Novels of Expatriation in the Arabian Gulf Region: Ibrāhīm Naṣrallāh's *Prairies of Fever*, Ibrāhīm 'Abdelmagīd's *The Other Place*, and Sa'ūd al-San'ūsī's *Bamboo Stalk*. *Journal of Arabic and Islamic Studies*, 16, 85–98.
Elmeligi, W. (2020) *Cultural Identity in Arabic Novels of Immigration: A Poetics of Return*. Lanham, MD: Lexington Books.
Fadda-Conrey, C. (2014) *Contemporary Arab-American Literature: Transnational Reconfigurations of Citizenship and Belonging*. New York: New York University Press.
Gharrafi, M. (ed.) (2016) *Al-Hijra fī al-adab al-'arabī al-mu'āṣir*. Oujda: Manshūrāt kulliyat al-ādāb wa-l-'ulūm al-insāniyya.
Halabi, Z. (2017) *The Unmaking of the Arab Intellectual: Prophecy, Exile and the Nation*. Edinburgh: Edinburgh University Press.
Hall, S., du Gay, P. (eds) (1996) *Questions of Cultural Identity*. London: SAGE.
Hassan, W.H. (2011) *Immigrant Narratives: Orientalism and Cultural Translation in Arab American and Arab British Literature*. Oxford: Oxford University Press.
Nail, T. (2015) *The Figure of the Migrant*. Redwood City, CA: Stanford University Press.
Naṣr Allāh, I. (1985) *Barārī al-ḥummā*. Beirut: Arab Research Organization.
Nordin, I.G., Hansen, J., Llena, C.Z. (eds) (2013) *Transcultural Identities in Contemporary Literature*. Amsterdam: Rodopi.
Nyman, J. (2009) *Home, Identity, and Mobility in Contemporary Diasporic Fiction*. Amsterdam: Rodopi.
Nyman, J. (2017) *Displacement, Memory, and Travel in Contemporary Migrant Writing*. Leiden: Brill.
Said, E. (1978) *Orientalism*. New York: Pantheon Books.
Salaita, S. (2011) *Modern Arab American Fiction: A Reader's Guide*. New York: Syracuse University Press.
Ṣāliḥ, Ṭ. (1966) *Mawsim al-hijra ilā al-shamāl*. Beirut: Dār al-'awda.
Al-Samman, H. (2015) *Anxiety of Erasure: Trauma, Authorship, and the Diaspora in Arab Women's Writings*. New York: Syracuse University Press.
San'ūsī, S. (2012) *Sāq al-bāmbū*. Beirut: al-Dār al-'Arabiyya li-l-'ulūm Nāshirūn.
Sellman, J. (2018) A Global Postcolonial: Contemporary Arabic Literature of Migration to Europe. *Journal of Postcolonial Writing*, 54(6), 751–765.
Sellman, J. (2022) Arabic Exile Literature in Europe: Defamiliarizing Forced Migration. Edinburgh: Edinburgh University Press.
Shakir, E. (1996) Arab-American Literature. In A.S. Knippling (ed.) *New Immigrant Literatures in the United States: A Sourcebook to Our Multicultural Literary Heritage*. Westport: Greenwood Press, 3–18.
Yuval-Davis, N. (1997) Women, Citizenship and Difference. *Feminist Review*, 57, 4–27.

1 Migrating to and in Europe Beyond the Nahḍawī and Modernist Paradigm

Mudun bi-lā nakhīl by Ṭāriq al-Ṭayyib and *Taytanikāt Ifrīqiyya* by Abū Bakr Khāl as Novels of Forced Migration

Maria Elena Paniconi

Introduction: The Trope of Migration in Changing Contexts

The enduring theme of migration to and in Europe lies at the foundation of both the late-*Nahḍa* Arabic novel (Ziyād, 2012, 23) and the more experimental novels of the 1960s and 1970s (Badawi, 1993; Hassan, 2017, 148). These works have long been read by literary critics as a sort of reification of the "East–West encounter", and therefore as depicting Europe through the eyes of the protagonist and the dimension of the relationships established within the context of migration (El-Enany, 2006). The last decade saw the rise of a critical approach more inclined to view the theme of migration not so much as a realistic description of the phenomenon of migration to Europe by Arab students or workers but, first and foremost, as a narrative trope allowing authors to develop the idea of a modern subject. In these writings, Europe – far from being the *portrait* of an objective reality – is a discursive *construction* onto which authors projected elements of the ideological and identity debate underway at the time they wrote their novels (Casini, 2013; Casini, 2018).

In the canonical *nahḍawī* novels (for example, in *ʿUṣfūr min al-sharq* by Tawfīq al-Ḥakīm, *Adīb* by Ṭāhā Ḥusayn, *Qindīl Umm Hāshim* by Yaḥyā Ḥaqqī, *Duktūr Ibrāhīm* by Dhū-l-Nūn Ayyūb), the youths migrating to Europe distance themselves from their families of origin, define their own self, experience the tension of a family structure portrayed as a "traditional" family, and try to take their place in a new world: Europe, portrayed instead as a synecdoche of modernity. Jeff Shalan claims that "the modern Arabic novel developed in conjunction with a specifically nationalist mode of thought, and that it was instrumental not only in the dissemination of that thought, but in its very formation as well" (Shalan, 2002, 213). More specifically, we might consider the trope of the student migrating to Europe as one of the main axes around which the nationalist imaginary mentioned by Shalan was built. Thus, the description of the other European and the – partial or total – setting

DOI: 10.4324/9780429027338-2

of the plot in Europe were, in this phase, functional to a codification of the national narrative language.

In the later novels of the 1960s and 1970s, known as "migration and exile literature", the classic trope of the student on a study mission abroad is joined by political or economic migrants. In these more recent novels, migration and exile are, in turn, a metaphor for an existential exile caused by the historical failure of fundamental ideologies such as Pan-Arabism. Within the social and political condition of the post-*Naksa* Arab world, authors and intellectuals found themselves "exiled" from their own history (Halabi, 2017, 98–130) thus, themes of migration or exile come to depict the contemporary debate on modernity, historical legacy, and prospects of the nation-state at a time of profound political crisis. One thing these writings – that is, the novels of the *nahḍawī* migration and, subsequently, the exile and alienation novels of the late 1960s and 1970s – have in common is the predominance of the issue of identity of the migrant, often defined in national, linguistic, and cultural terms. Paradoxically, this identity would be defined and described precisely *thanks* to the themes of detachment, of exile, of the expropriation of identity.

Starting from the 1990s, a new "literature of migration" in Arabic began emphasising the viewpoints of the refugees, the asylum seekers, the migrants who did not *choose* to migrate but who were *forced* to do so for economic, political, or war reasons (Sellman, 2018, 254–256). Known as novels of "forced migration" (Sellman, 2018, 759–762), these works push the migrants' quest for identity and interaction with the context of arrival into the background, focusing instead – within the layout of the construction of meaning of the novels – on the actual experience of migration. The stories centre on the coastal gathering points of migrants, on borderlands, on the crossings – whether over the desert in pick-up trucks or buses, on ships or makeshift vessels – endured by the migrants.

By means of various narrative techniques, the plots of these novels showcase the migrants' attempts to reach Europe by makeshift means and the – at times violent – refoulement carried out by the law enforcement agencies in charge of "containing" the impact of migration by applying anachronistic laws (Mezzadra, 2013). Examples of novels about migration are *Safīnat Nūḥ* by Khālid al-Khamīssī (Noah's Arch, 2009) or *Majnūn sāḥat al-ḥurriya* (The Madman of Freedom Square, 2009) by Ḥasan Blāsim. These contemporary novels, especially the ones describing the Moroccan and Algerian migrations, are also defined as "*Harraga* literature", from the Moroccan term *harraga* ("to burn"), which refers to the practice of burning identification papers before crossing the Mediterranean so as to avoid repatriation, while also becoming a symbolic act of burning one's identity prior to the crossing (Sellman, 2018, 752). Examples of this trend are *Hashīsh* by Yūsuf Fāḍil (Hashish, 2000) or *Layla Ifrīqiyya* (An African Night, 2010) by Muṣṭafā Laghtīrī – both Moroccan authors.

While the "*Harraga* literature" or novels of "forced migration" began to take shape in the 1990s, the transformation of the migration theme had already appeared in 1980s novels or short stories. Indeed, once considered a literary trope linked to national identity viewed in terms of cultural specificity and political self-determination, it became a "post-national" theme, avoiding the control of a nation-state narrative by then perceived by many as problematic (Ouyang, 2013, 225–226). Examples foretelling a migratory experience told in post-national terms are the short stories *Bi-l-amsi ḥalamtu bi-ka* (Last Night I Dreamt of You) by Bāhā' Ṭāhir (1980), or the short story *1964*, included in the collection *Aisha* by Ahdaf Soueif (1983).[1]

In both stories, the protagonist migrates to a European country where there is no closely knit "community" – in cultural, social, or political terms – in which to integrate. "I knew there was no hidden world, no secret society from which I was barred. There was just – nothing" (Soueif, 1983, 39), to quote the protagonist of *1964*, faced with the failure of her expectations when the much-anticipated Valentine's Day dance turned into a fiasco. And the narrator says of one of the characters in *Bi-l-amsi ḥalamtu bi-ka*: "Ten years had passed since he had started working in a bank, he had even obtained citizenship ... yet he felt lost" (Ṭāhir, 1980, 12–13).[2] The protagonists of these two stories are unable to experience either "integration" into the society hosting them or, on the other hand, a rediscovered identity as a consequence of the migratory experience as occurs in the *nahḍawī*/modernist tradition. In both cases, the subject's interior feeling of alienation is pervasive and mirrors the weaknesses of the national narrative. Ṭāhir and Soueif's stories are among the first to deliberately overcome the "developmental" paradigm characterising the migratory experience in the *nahḍawī* novel – a paradigm where migration was generally synonymous with striving towards a more modern and liberal context within which a political and social set-up would ensure an improvement in the living conditions of migrants.

At times, novels of colonial and postcolonial migration to non-Arabic speaking areas are also based on the model pinpointed by Dawes as the "coming-of-age narrative" – that is, the telling of the passage from a world deprived of human rights to a world that instead offers them (Dawes, 2018, 50–53). Externally, this passage takes the shape of a journey of personal growth, thus creating an intersection between novel of migration and the classic coming-of-age formula. According to Slaughter, this literary form is the one that throughout history innervated the spreading of the topic of human rights to extra-European contexts, ultimately becoming the literary equivalent of the "Human Rights Law":[3]

> The narrative homology between human rights and the *Bildungsroman* is not merely fortuitous; both articulate a larger discourse of development that is imagined to be governed by natural laws and that is historically bound to the modern institutions and technics of state legitimacy.
>
> (Slaughter, 2017, 93)

According to Slaughter, in particular, the developmental discourse articulated by both the Human Rights Law and *Bildungsroman* assumes the laws and structure of the nation-state as "natural", pointing to it as the best possible sociopolitical organisation that modern humanity can aspire to. The fact that in several postcolonial novels the process of obtaining citizenship takes the shape of the natural "transforming" of youth into adult (Dawes, 2018, 94) only confirms the homology mentioned by Slaughter.

The two stories by Ṭāhir and Soueif referred to earlier do not show a progressive journey to citizenship, instead demystifying – whether by means of disillusioned language (Soueif) or an anguished *rêverie* (Ṭāhir) – the very idea of citizenship and identity. With the Arabic novel of "forced migration", which unfolded mainly in the decade following the abovementioned stories, the developmental discourse at the foundation of the *nahḍawī* novel (and in any case present on the horizon of the postcolonial novel) is further destabilised. The aim of this chapter is to analyse the new portrayals of migrant subjectivities in two novels depicting two forced migrations: *Mudun bi-lā nakhīl* (Cities Without Palms, 1992) by Ṭāriq al-Ṭayyib e *Taytanikāt Ifrīqiyya* (African Titanics, 2008) by Abū Bakr Khāl. The novels are analysed in light of a recent study on migration by Nail (2015) that puts the spotlight back on the migrant's political subjectivity. At the same time, this analysis will also highlight how the political dimension of the Earth-system takes shape, also reacting to human actions, in the current climate crisis (Latour, 2018). In the wake of the abovementioned studies, we have decided to distance ourselves from a viewpoint that hypothesises the situation of permanence and citizenship as "standard" and that, instead, hypothesises migration as an extraordinary phenomenon.

As underscored by Sellman, literature should not be interpreted from a sociological point of view, yet it helps create a collective imaginary that communicates with sociological observation (Sellman, 2018, 755). Therefore, while the novels have not been interpreted solely according to their documentary and sociological interest, this chapter will identify and analyse the elements suited to giving readers a new idea of the identity of the migrant.

The analysis will help emphasise how novels of "forced migration" break away from the developmental migration underlying several *nahḍawī* and modernist novels to release the identity of the migrant from the hidden meanings implied in the previous narrations. In particular, we will emphasise the shifting nature of migrants in the novels of forced migration, where their identity is constantly redefined, also depending on the bodies that control the "borders" of the nation-states and, therefore, define and determine the migrants' status (Nyman, 2017, 18). However, migrants are not merely "defined" by external factors; they are also active subjects in their own right. This can be inferred by the choices made during the journey (bearing in mind that these people were originally forced to migrate against their will), by their adaptive skills and by the decisions made along the way.

Migrating Subjects/Shifting Masks

In *Mudun bi-la Nakhīl* – henceforth *Mudun* – Ṭāriq al-Ṭayyib's[4] successful first novel told in the first person, we find the story of 19-year-old Ḥamza, who leaves behind his village in Sudan and his mother and his two younger sisters to travel across Egypt, Italy, France, Belgium, and the Netherlands before returning to Sudan (Hassan, 2017, 428–429). A clandestine traveller, Ḥamza resigns himself to doing seasonal jobs with no kind of protection, and, as we shall see, his return to the village when his migration comes to an end will not, as hoped, improve his life or that of his family. In *Taytanikāt Ifrīqiyya* by Abū Bakr Khāl[5] – henceforth *Taytanikāt* – we find the voice of Abdar, both protagonist and narrator, who tells of his own trip from Sudan and Eritrea to Tunisia. The narrative voice allows for other types of narrative inserts that act as "traces" of the passage of other routes and other lives aside from Abdar's.

Abdar's journey begins on a pick-up truck with a group of other migrants and turns into a desperate desert crossing ("everything looks different, the dunes move") within reach of the Hambata[6] to reach the Libyan coast. Several of his travelling companions die along the way. Upon arriving in Tripoli, Abdar meets his companions for the remainder of the migration, including Terhas, a young Eritrean woman who will share several stages of the journey with the protagonist. But as they wait to put out to sea on a makeshift vessel from Tripoli, they are dispersed by the Libyan gendarmerie. So Abdar, Terhas, and four other migrants travel on foot to Tunisia, where they are eventually arrested, leading to Abdar's repatriation. Though not autobiographical per se, these novels centre on migratory journeys that, especially in Khāl's case, parallel the author's true experience. The two novels describe the situations, itineraries, and encounters experienced by the migrants with vivid realism. Though generally keeping to the codes of realism, the two stories analysed here also set in motion narrative strategies such as de-familiarisation, testimonial narration and, especially in Khāl, narrative inserts as texts within the text. The two protagonists' past experiences and actions are always included, and recalibrated each time, within the framework of the natural environment, which takes on a central, proactive role in both novels.

In his book *Down to Earth*, Bruno Latour invites us to rethink alternative models to "local" and "global" categories in the wake of the climate crisis, asserting the need to welcome nature's proactive quality in the placement of people in it and, consequently, in determining what is "local" and what is "global" (Latour, 2018, 25–32). According to Latour, nature is able to act and *react* to society. In other words, it is not a powerless background completely controlled by humans but, rather, plays a leading role in our lives and decisions. In their specific plots and in the network of impressions and imaginaries they build, both *Mudun bi-lā nakhīl* by Ṭāriq al-Ṭayyib and *Taytanikāt Ifrīqiyya* by Abū Bakr Khāl assign nature the central role, as if, in Latour's words, "the decor, the wings, the background, the whole building have come on stage and are competing with the actors for the principal role" (Latour, 2018, 43).

Indeed, the beginning of *Mudun* describes the bleak drought and famine that strike the village that the main character, Ḥamza, feels forced to leave. In *Taytanikāt*, migration *is* in and of itself a sort of natural phenomenon that attacks the human race, taking root especially in young people: it is "a pandemic, a plague" (Khaal, 2014, 3) and, thus, like all forces of nature, impossible to control or stem. The two authors, therefore, trace the migratory phenomenon back to a natural context and describe it as a direct consequence of an environmental crisis, a natural phenomenon equal to a flood:

> The desert keeps growing, and sorrow, not rain, is all that comes to us. Drought and disease, agony and death: we are the dying, the living dead.
> (Eltayeb, 2009, 2)

> Migration came flooding through Africa, a turbulent swell, sweeping everything along in its wake. None of us knew when or how it would end. We simply watched, dumbfounded, as the frenzy unfolded. From all across the continent came mournful lamentations: "Africa will soon be no more than a hollow pipe where the wind plays melodies of loss".
> (Khaal, 2014, 3)

In both novels, the act of migrating is described as a reaction to a natural emergency. Furthermore, neither protagonist develops a migratory plan of their own; indeed, both decide to set out without planning their journey and without worrying much about the road that lies ahead. Instead, they seem more worried about what they are leaving behind, as appears clearly in this glimpse into Ḥamza's thoughts:

> I call to my mother and tell her that I have made up my mind about something, and briefly explain my plan to leave. She sadly bows her head and silently looks at the ground for a while – I think she is going to cry. … I visit my silent city: I go to the graves to bid them farewell. I am not sure how long I stay here. For once I do not sing. I simply sit there, lost in my memories. Suddenly I realize that I am leaving tomorrow. I think less about the road ahead and about what will become of me than I do about leaving my mother and two young sisters alone in the village.
>
> Perched on top of a palm tree, a crow caws loudly and startles me. The palm has lost its fronds – I cannot bear to watch it die like this. I was its sole keeper. … we have shared so many memories, the palm and I, and now it is dying, silently dying while the crow caws on its barren summit, announcing its dominion over the palm's ruined kingdom.
> (Eltayeb, 2009, 14–15)

Ḥamza barely has time to bid farewell to his past in that land: a farewell that passes through the graves of the people who once lived there and the palm tree that, as we see in lots of poetry and prose of the Arabic literary tradition, is something more than a mere fruit tree – it is a landmark of memory.[7] Similarly, migration is described as something that Abdar, the protagonist and narrator of *Taytanikāt*, undergoes without, on the face of it, having any say in the matter:

> I was plucked from Eritrea, swept across the Sudanese border and on into Libya, in the dark of night. I was lost, and almost perished in the desert, before slipping through into Tunisia. I remember feeling as though I was fated forever to continue my ceaseless roaming, and that I would never again escape the endless road.
>
> (Khaal, 2014, 4)

In Khāl's writing, therefore, migration is a "plague" or a "bug", a mysterious "bell" "calling one and all to its promise paradise" (Khaal, 2014, 3). These early pages already showcase what will prove to be the specific features of Khāl's narrative language that is, the continuous intrusion between two dimensions: reality and highly imaginative writing, interwoven with oral stories and legends collected by Abdar. Both protagonists become migrants against their will, and both of them – another feature shared by the two novels – will adapt to the various situations and conditions encountered along the way, wearing a different mask each time: that of political refugee, smuggler, economic migrant, aspiring refugee, migrants without papers. The masks worn by Ḥamza and Abdar on their respective journeys foretell the mutable nature of the migrant described by Nail (Nail, 2015). The migrant has multiple identities and is called by multiple names: Abdar in *Taytanikāt* has dozens of *laqab*, or nicknames:

> in Khartoum I was known as Awacs (The Airborne Warning and Control System) because I's refuse to go to bed at night until I'd garnered every last useful scrap of information from the world of immigrant smuggling, by land, sea and air … . In Eritrea, my birthplace, I was al-Shamman, Arabic word for Sniffer, thanks to a so-called friend who spread it around that enjoyed sniffing petrol-soaked rags … that nickname soon superseded my original childhood one of Ambsa, the Tigré word for Lion.
>
> (Khaal, 2014, 15–16)

The loss of his own name inflicted on Ḥamza in *Mudun* acts as a counterpoint to this proliferation of names:

> The long and hopeless walk through the city has left me out of breath. It is incredibly hot, so much so that the pavement has eaten up my sandals, which are now stinging the soles of my feet. I move to the shade to escape this torment. … A tall young man suddenly appears in front of me … . He addresses me:

"How are you, my friend?"
"Not that well, as you can see. I'm exhausted – this heat is killing me."
"I can tell from your accent that you are not from the city."
"No, I'm not. I'm from a village called Wad al-Nār, hundreds of miles from here."

He closes his eyes and repeats what he has just heard, as if trying to remember something. Wad al-Nār, Wad al-Nār, what family are you from?

"You don't even know the name of my village, so how would you know the name of my family?"
"You are a light-hearted one, son of Nār!"[8]
"My name is Ḥamza."
"Your name is not important. Tell me who you're looking for."
(Eltayeb, 2009, 26)

The process of multiplication of identities in Khāl and, by contrast, of loss of identity al-Ṭayyib, are emblematic of the narrative techniques that are the hallmarks of these writings: accumulation in Khāl (Luffin, 2012a, 60–63), dispossession in al-Ṭayyib.[9] Several times, fate blindly distributes the "identity masks" to be put on – for example when a mistake made by the Tunisian gendarmerie allows Abdar and his four travelling companions to cross the border between Libya and Tunisia:

> we walked across the street with calm, even steps, waving cheerly at the driver. I felt a great rush of joy. Surely we were through the worst.
> At that moment, however, a booming voice rang out: "Hey you! [...] Where're you lot from?" the man barked. He was standing at the entrance of the police station. My mind went blank.
> "Eritrea. I'm from Eritrea."
> "Mauritania?" The policeman yelled.
> "Yes," I replied. My voice a little louder.
> "Alright then! On your way, Mauritanian!"
> (Khaal, 2014, 89)

In Europe, where the final part of *Mudun* is set, it is the passing of time rather than moving in space that changes the identity features of the migrants, for example turning a seasonal worker into an illegal immigrant.

> My first month in France ends, and with it my legal period of stay. Now, in my second month, I am illegal just like all the rest. I walk the streets like a rat, and whenever I see a police car or an officer's uniform. I scurry into the first alley I can find, or rush into a shop at random – I ask for soap at the butcher's and for bread at the bookstore. I have heard about

> what happens when you get caught; I would be forced to spend the night in prison and would then be deported back to Sudan, while all my money sits in a bank here in France.
>
> (Eltayyeb, 2009, 78–79)

The Escape-Plot in *Mudun bi-lā nakhīl*, Storytelling, and Interweaving of Stories in *Taytanikāt*

In both novels, the protagonist embarks on his migratory experience alone, but soon enters into a series of trans-regional crossings where he encounters other migrants. Ḥamza in *Mudun* leaves Sudan (specifically, a small Sudanese village) heading for Omdurman. From there, he will migrate towards Cairo, where he will suddenly decide to migrate to Europe, passing through Italy, France, Belgium, and the Netherlands before returning to Sudan. His journey only lasts a year and five months. After crossing the border between Belgium and the Netherlands "clandestinely", and after realising that he has heard from his family only once despite having sent them money several times, Ḥamza decides to return to his village to ascertain the fate of his mother and sisters. The style is spare, marked by the frenzied pace of Ḥamza's departures, arrivals and new leave-takings. As previously mentioned, *Mudun* is always narrated in the first person and in the "historic present"; this element adds vividness and draws readers into the space-time horizon of the action. The novel's table of contents showcases the order of his movements, stage by stage:

- From the Village
- To the City
- To Another City
- To Other Cities
- To the Village

The chapter titles, read as a whole and in the tension that is created between "Village" and "City", seem to recall the duality between city and countryside that spans all Arabic literature and organises the emerging of a narrative canon (Selim, 2004). Interestingly, migration to and in Europe is also not defined in so many words but, rather, as "To Other Cities", thus helping to represent Omdurman, or Cairo, as "cities" equivalent to the European capitals Ḥamza stops in during his brief journey through Europe. Even in the narrator-Ḥamza's thoughts, observations, and fleeting descriptions, the only place he calls "home" is his village, which he knows like the back of his hand, humanising its palm trees – as we saw previously – before bidding them farewell as he prepares to leave. With reference to the cities – whether Omdurman or Cairo, or the European cities – Ḥamza always gives voice to his state of alienation. He asks himself: "God, what will I do in this enormous city"? (Eltayyeb, 2009, 25), or notes that "Each neighbour resembles the other" (Eltayyeb, 2009, 27). All of Ḥamza's movements are accompanied by the image of the city-labyrinth, or of the inhospitable city. In Omdurman, Ḥamza experiences an interlude of "stability": after some initial difficulties, he manages to open a small stall and, later on, is hired by a shopkeeper to handle sales alongside his young wife. Ḥamza has an affair with the woman, who gets pregnant. Ḥamza's stay in the Sudanese city thus becomes a new situation to flee from, and so, after obtaining a permit, he arrives in Cairo via ship ("To Another City"). Here he relies on temporary and illegal jobs – notably joining a group of clothing smugglers who shuttle between Cairo and the free-trade area of Port Said. He finally manages to obtain a travel visa and, in the hopes of escaping a future of uncertainty, travels to Europe via ship, departing legally from the Port of Alexandria.

In Rome, the feeling of alienation that has always accompanied the protagonist's arrival in cities emerges with greater intensity: Ḥamza loses his suitcase of interwoven palm fronds, leaving it on the platform as he gets on the wrong train (Eltayyeb, 2009, 70–71). In this situation of total deprivation, that single object represented a landmark of his inner geography. Once he has lost the last memento of the palm trees of Wad al-Nār, Ḥamza's story grows more and more similar to an escape: a succession of European cities and seasonal jobs is interspersed with references to "lost" objects and stolen money, sometimes inflicted on the migrants by their own travelling companions. In the end, Ḥamza is found without papers and arrested at the Amsterdam airport (Eltayyeb 2009, 84).

After a brief detention, Ḥamza rewinds his journey, keeping a tight grip on his amulet ("the only thing I have left from Wad al-Nār"; Eltayyeb, 2009, 84) as he backtracks. Upon arrival, however, he discovers that an outbreak of cholera has killed most of the villagers, including his mother and younger sisters. The ending is, so to speak, bitterly ironic in that it invalidates the reasons Ḥamza had migrated in the first place. The newly completed journey undertaken with the aim of helping his family therefore shows its bitter consequences of total loss and cruel irony. Only one live palm tree remains standing, once a symbol of his home and now a gravestone before which to sit and mourn. Ḥamza's grief has the flavour of archaic poetry and his words are those of the tragic heroes facing their destiny: "I sit down on it, and face the ruins of the village (*ḥuṭām al-qarya*)" (Eltayyeb, 2009, 89). To sum up, we could say that the model of the escape-plot novel is the foundation driving the narration of *Mudun*: indeed, Ḥamza's movements are triggered by his finding himself forced into a position or a situation, like when he feels stuck in the village of Wad al-Nār, or when he undergoes his most critical sequence of events in Omdurman: "I have arrived at a crossroads, caught between the wreckage of the past and an aimless future, while the present slowly, mercilessly gnaws on my living flesh" (Eltayyeb, 2009, 47).

As for Abdar's journey in *Taytanikāt*, with its series of unforeseen events, returns and false starts, it resembles travelling through a maze. Interestingly, *Taytanikāt* also has a "circular" plot and a retroactively ironic ending, which appears to invalidate the entire journey undertaken by the protagonist. However, Khāl's novel is founded on very different textual mechanisms compared to *Mudun*. Less frenzied in its rhythm, less "linear", the narration unfolds by incorporating several subplots and texts within the text that span Abdar's story.

Khāl's world is inter-Eritrean first and foremost, with several characters of Eritrean origin (albeit with different ethnic and religious affiliations) who are on good terms with one another, seemingly setting aside any discord ensuing from the civil war (Luffin, 2012a, 60). In a liberating story, before his death during the desert crossing at the start of the novel, the character of Asgedom relives the trauma of the war and, facing certain death, appears to realise the folly of a fratricidal war for the first time:

> We were identical ... the lot of us ... our features, our clothes ... even our weapons were the same ... and we all knew the enemy's language ... and when we fought in the dark ... their army would attack each other ... and we'd fight each other too ... we buried their dead beside ours ... because we couldn't tell them apart. ... They did the same.
>
> (Khaal, 2014, 33)

Secondly, Khāl describes an inter-African and cosmopolitan world made up of people from "Eritrea, Sudan, Somalia, Ghana and Liberia" (Khaal, 2014, 43), who intersect in the makeshift lodgings and various gathering points that form along the Mediterranean coastline while waiting for the many people smugglers to organise the departing groups. Here people wait, feverishly consult the weather reports, strike up relationships that can prove incredibly strong, consider alternative possibilities and routes in case of variations. The journey narrated by Abdar is structured around these junctions and intersections between the migratory routes of the most diverse individuals. Compared to al-Ṭayyib's story, therefore, Khāl's story centres more on the idea of "community" and seems to be pervaded by an underlying trust in the people who end up becoming travelling companions. The narrative voice detects their *pietas* in the midst of death, when the first victims are claimed by the "maze" (*matāha*) of the desert and the "red death" (*al mawt al-aḥmar*), or death from thirst. The tragic crossing of the sea of sand, a sort of "narrative double" of the real sea (Luffin, 2012a, 61), destabilises the common reader, who finds him or herself reflecting, perhaps for the first time, on the dangers and journeys that sub-Saharan migrants undergo *before* embarking on the various "*taytanic*".

The ironic name given to these makeshift rafts, inflatable dinghies, or fishing boats departing from the coasts of migrants also disorients the readers who, alongside a tale of desperation and death, find the irony with which the migrants exorcise their fear of death. Chief among the voices and stories collected by Abdar are the words of Maluk, his Liberian friend and travelling companion whose tragic end is disclosed in the very first pages. Maluk never lets go of his guitar or his stories: he tells of the exploits of his grandfather, "Maluk the First", who once set off to rescue his wife, kidnapped by local pirates, and of the "adventures of Kaji", an imaginary character who lives in Maluk's notebook and is dealing with a grandson who has decided to migrate. Maluk also sets his poems to music and tells stories about Liberia and his fiancée, killed in the war: Khāl's narrative choice here is to "project typographically the disjunction between the narrator's semi-realist account and the artistic commentary by italicising the inset stories and poems, many by Malouk" (Wilson, 2017, 7).

Maluk's stories and the ones about Kaji in his notebook, along with all the other stories contained in *Taytanikāt*, make up several pieces of a larger storyline that envelops the individuals to become a network, a sort of "ancient and heterogeneous" map of the people who, over the years, have defied their own geography, setting sail like "Maluk the Second". In Maluk's case, the boat sank, leaving no survivors. The event is reconstructed in detail at the end of the novel, which describes the reasons why the inexperienced 'Alī took the helm of the boat, the first leaks, the first dead bodies piled up on the bridge, and finally the last days spent starving and dying of thirst, adrift in international waters under the indifference of oil tankers that watch the migrants dying one by one (Khaal, 2014, 107–111). But Maluk's words and stories do not sink with him. They live on in Abdar; they enlarge and expand his identity, becoming in turn a sort of "amulet" – like the one given to Ḥamza by his mother to protect him from misfortune, like the one that Maluk himself hoped to find prior to his departure, in a poem collected and revived by Abdar:

Without an amulet
I slid through the guarded gates
Crawling like a worm
Trough barbs and wire
Swallowed by salty swamps
Surrounded by desert dogs
I ran on
Between wicked trees
Clawing at my clothes
While rain lashed me
I watched my legs
Sink into graves of clay
Dissolving into watery floods
I crossed
But now I must find an amulet
To cross
Straits of fire
Towards continents of snow.

(Khaal, 2014, 101)

The ending describes how the narrator-protagonist Abdar and Terhas are escorted back to the border by Tunisian authorities and repatriated, following a brief period of detention during which they were mistreated and tortured. Like in *Mudun*, the ending of *Taytanikāt* shows the mocking smile of an ironic fate: Abdar is forced to repatriate just as he was forced to leave in the first place, while Maluk – the only one of the group of migrants to "escape" the police roundup – manages to leave Tunis only to meet his death. At the end of the story, Abdar wonders if the real reason for his migration was actually to meet Maluk and to collect his tales, his talisman of interwoven verses and stories.

Conclusions

While *Mudun* sheds light on the subjectivity of an individual migrant (Ḥamza), in *Taytanikāt* we witness the construction of an inter-subjectivity of the migrants – a feature that represents a further deviation from the *nahḍawī* and modernist migratory literature of the early 20th century and the 1960s and 1970s. This inter-subjective dimension replaces the prevailing – and often racialised (identity is white) – idea of a subjective identity derived from the contrast with an "otherness" perceived as culturally superior or inferior. Instead, Khāl reconstructs a migrant identity that is community-based, transversal, and non-racialised. These "imagined communities" acted upon by the migrants and recounted by Abdar are the protagonists of this novel, starting from the beginning of the crossing, in the desert that moves and "speaks" like a human being (Khaal, 2014, 31), and ending with his repatriation.

As previously mentioned, neither Ḥamza nor Abdar *choose* to migrate; they are forced to do so by an emergency that expels them from the place where they were born and raised, opening a new space-time. As in most tragedies, these characters defy their preordained fate and the geography familiar to them. The sense of tragedy surfaces and is detonated in the circular plots of the novels, and especially in the two retroactive endings that question the choices, perspectives, and narration of forced migration. The protagonists who dared to defy their fate and their familiar, everyday geographies find themselves "cheated" by that very fate and brought home almost against their will, just as against their will they had left.

In *The Figure of the Migrant*, Nail explains how, in migratory circulation, movement turns into counter-movement, and how the migratory flow is continually folds back onto itself (Nail, 2015, 28). Once again, albeit without calling for a derivative and sociological-documentary analysis, we could, however, observe how the migratory paths mapped out by the authors examined offer a plastic depiction of *Kinopolitics* – that is, the spontaneous politics of movement theorised by Nail. Ḥamza and Abdar's backwards movement along the migratory *telos* is a sort of admission of defeat, with migration showing itself in all its futility.

In conclusion, these two novels can be hypothesised as examples of the "forced migration novel" that, despite their structural differences, tend to demystify the traditional "progressive" *nahḍawī* literature of migration to and in Europe, on the one hand, and to demystify the "developmental rhetoric" of "human rights literature", on the other, though sharing a few of its aspects. Both novels make use of the tools of the imagination to regain possession of functions "normally" performed by the national government. The reconstruction of the memory of those who migrate to Europe put in place by the narrator of *Taytanikāt* and the story of Ḥamza's desperate attempt to migrate to protect his destitute family are not only plots; they are also starting points for a series of narratives that present themselves as "authentic" in the face of a falsified national narrative. Abū Bakr Khāl's magical realism and Ṭāriq al-Ṭayyib's frenzied prose mark a necessary return to the narrated word, necessarily "raised" from the plane of individual experience and, instead, reshaped on the basis of a collective reality, shared by subjects who are marginalised and anonymous in the public discourse. To sum up, these novels make use of different rhythms, narrative models, and viewpoints to portray two tragic and contemporary heroes who – equipped with a physical amulet like Ḥamza, or with an amulet interwoven with verses and stories like Maluk – defy the geography of the familiar to venture into the unfamiliar. Diverging from outmoded models of migration narratives, the two authors likewise choose unfamiliar languages to radically question the concepts of "identity", "home", and "nation".

Notes

1 Originally written in English and only later translated into Arabic, *1964* by Soueif (1983) is a story inspired by the author's own migratory experience. The tones of the story are realistic. *1964* is part of the collection *Aisha*, where all the stories revolve around the main character – Aisha herself – who was raised in London before returning to Egypt. From the very first lines of *1964*, migration is viewed as an experience where gender, class, and race intersect: the protagonist's identity is thus complicated, questioned, and not strengthened by her migratory experience. Aisha grows up in her "diaspora" according to social rules dictated by class and gender and, in part, by the further class awareness represented by the "academic diaspora" to which her parents belong. At school, the girl experiences a sort of double isolation, because her behaviour and fluent English set Aisha apart from the stereotype of Arab migrant: "with my prim manners and prissy voice they wouldn't want me for a friend anyway. I was a misfit" (Soueif, 1983, 31). *Last Night I Dreamt of You* by Bāhā᾽ Ṭāhir, on the other hand, is pervaded by disturbing tones and resembles a *rêverie* in a foreign land. The story is based on the meeting between the anonymous main character, an Arab youth in a snow-covered European country, and a local girl. After a few chance meetings, the two get to know each other, but the resistance and inexplicable feelings the youth rouses in the girl lead to growing tension and incommunicability.

2 My translation.

3 The homology between Human Rights Law and *Bildungsroman* is explained in detail in the chapter "Human Rights, the *Bildungsroman* and the Novelization of Citizenship" (Slaughter, 2017, 86–139).
4 Born in Cairo to Sudanese parents in 1959 and living in Vienna since 1984, Ṭāriq al-Ṭayyib is one of the best-known and most-translated authors of the Arab diaspora.
5 Abū Bakr Khāl is an Eritrean author who currently lives in Denmark. A former fighter in the ELF, he lived in Libya until 2011. He had published three novels before *Taytanikāt*: *Rā'iḥat al-silāḥ* (The Scent of Arms, 2005); *Birkintiyya. Arḍ al-mar'a al-ḥakīma* (Barkantiyya: Land of the Wise Woman). For this author's literature, see Luffin (2012a).
6 "Hambata" is a dialectal Sudanese Arabic word used by the author to refer to groups of bandits who attack the vehicles of passers-by, often clandestine migrants heading for the coast (Luffin, 2012a, 61).
7 In Ṭāhā Ḥusayn's novel *Adīb*, for example, the protagonist's departure for Europe is marked by a visit he pays to the palm trees in his village and to the verses that Muṭīʿ b. Iyās, a poet who lived between the end of the Umayyad period and the beginning of the Abbasid period, wrote in honour of this tree in his poem: "On Two Palms of Ḥulwān".
8 Ḥamza's village is called Wad al-Nār, thus the young man calls him "son of Nār".
9 In a May 2016 interview, the author himself told me that he had worked on this novel "by subtraction", reducing its volume during the final revision.

References

al-Ṭayyib, Ṭ. (2006) *Mudun bi-lā nakhīl*. Cairo: al-Ḥaḍāra li-l-nashr.

al-Ṭayyib, Ṭ. (1992) *Mudun bi-lā nakhīl*. Cairo: al-Ḥaḍāra li-l-nashr.

Badawi, M.M. (1993) Perennial Themes in Modern Arabic Literature. *British Journal of Middle Eastern Studies*, 20(1), 3–19.

Casini, L. (2018) New Perspectives on the European Woman Trope in the Arabic Novel. A concise Study of the Egyptian Case. *Le forme e la storia*, 11(2), 227–241.

Casini. L., Paniconi, M.E., and Sorbera, L. (2013) *Modernità Arabe. Nazione, narrazione e nuovi soggetti nel romanzo egiziano*. Messina: Mesogea.

Colucci, M. (2018) *Storia dell'immigrazione straniera in Italia. Dal 1945 ai nostri giorni*. Roma: Carocci.

Dawes, J. (2018) *The Novel of Human Rights*. Cambridge (MA): Harvard University Press.

El-Enany, R. (2006) *Arab Representations of the Occident: East–West Encounters in Arabic Fiction*. London and New York: Routledge.

Eltayeb, T. (2009) *Cities Without Palms*. Cairo: The American University in Cairo Press.

Halabi, Z. (2017) *The Unmaking of the Arab Intellectual: Prophecy, Exile and the Nation*. Edinburgh: Edinburgh University Press.

Hassan, W.S. (ed.) (2017) *The Oxford Handbook of Arab Novelistic Tradition*. Oxford: Oxford University Press.

Khaal, A.B. (2014) *African Titanics*. Translated by Charis Bredin. London: Darf Publishers.

Khaal, A.B. (2008) *Taytanikāt Ifrīqiyya. Dār al-Sāqī?, Bayrūt*

Latour, B. (2018) *Down to Earth: Politics in the New Climatic Regime*. Translated by Catherine Porter. Cambridge, UK: Polity.

Luffin, X. (2012a) "Les Romans d'Abû Bakr Hâmid Kahhâl. Littérature nationale, littérature Universelle", *Études Littéraires Africaines*, 33, 55–61.

Luffin, X. (2012b) L'épanouissement d'une littérature en langues locales: Tigrigna, tigré et arabe. *Études Littéraires Africaines*, 33, 17–27.
Mezzadra, S. (2013) *Border as Method, or, the Multiplication of Labor*. Duke: Duke University Press.
Nail, T. (2015) *The Figure of the Migrant*. Stanford: Stanford University Press.
Nyman, J., (2017) *Displacement, Memory, and Travel in Contemporary Migrant Writing*. Leiden: Brill.
Ouyang, W. (2013) *Politics of Nostalgia in the Arabic Novel: Nation-State, Modernity and Tradition*. Edinburgh: Edinburgh University Press.
Selim, S. (2004) *The Novel and the Rural Imaginary in Egypt, 1880–1985*. New York and London: Routledge – Curzon.
Sellman, J. (2018) A Global Postcolonial: Contemporary Arabic Literature of Migration to Europe. *Journal of Postcolonial Writing*, 54(6), 751–765.
Shalan, J. (2002) Writing the Nation. *Journal of Arabic Literature*, 33(3), 211–247.
Slaughter, J. (2007) *Human Rights, Inc.: The World Novel, Narrative Form and International Law*, Fordham: Fordham University Press.
Soueif, A. (1983) *Aisha*. London: Jonathan Cape.
Ṭāhir, B. (1980) *Bi-'l-amsi ḥalamtu bi-ka*. Cairo: Ha'ya al-Miṣriyya al-'āmma li-'l-kitāb.
Wilson, J. (2017) Novels of Flight and Arrival: Abu Bakr Khaal's *African Titanics* (2014 [2008]) and Sunjeev Sahota's *The Year of the Runaways* (2015). *Postcolonial Text*, 12(3–4), 1–14.
Ziyād, Ṣ. (2012) *al-Riwāya al-'arabiyya wa-l-tanwīr: qirā'a fī namādhij mukhtāra*. Beirut: Dār al-Fārābī.

2 Transcultural Identities in Two Novels by Ḥanān al-Shaykh

Martina Censi

Introduction

Migration, in its many different forms, is the distinguishing feature of our times and shapes contemporary societies in the era of globalization. For the migrant, it is a dramatic event and one of loss, but it may also be a key to a better future. It redefines relationships between the individual and the community and implies new ways of experiencing space and time that are reflected inexorably on the identity, rendering the migrant a political subject who eludes the static categories typical of the nation state. Seen increasingly in its processual dimension and as being in the making, identity is no longer considered as a fixed and unalterable, monocultural entity that the individual "possesses" and that characterizes him or her unequivocally and definitively in the eyes of others. Recent studies in the literary field, such as those by Nyman (2009 and 2017) and Nordin et al. (2013), highlight the transcultural dimension of identity, which changes according to the relationship established by the individual with others and with space.

The theme of the dialectical relationship between space and identity is widely explored in contemporary literary narratives dedicated to migration. It also characterizes the literary production in Arabic – not only nowadays, but also at the turn of the 19th and 20th centuries – which is dedicated to the narration of the migratory experience in its most varied forms. Belonging to this genre is part of the narrative production of the Lebanese author Ḥanān al-Shaykh (b.1945), who represents, in some of her works, the effects of displacement on the characters' identity. This occurs, for example, in two of her important novels – *Misk al-ghazāl*[1] (The Gazelle's Musk, 1988) and *Innahā London yā ʿazīzī*[2] (This Is London, My Dear, 2001) – that we have chosen as the focus of our analysis. A 13-year gap separates the writing of these two novels, which are in dialogue with each other to represent the effects of migration on the identity of the characters. They find themselves fighting to fit into two very distant and very different cosmopolitan realities:[3] one is an unspecified city in the Gulf in *Misk al-ghazāl* and the other is London in *Innahā London yā ʿazīzī*.[4] In this chapter, we will concentrate on analysing the path of identity undertaken by the characters at the centre of these two polyphonic

DOI: 10.4324/9780429027338-3

novels, bearing in mind the relationship between identity, space and body and referring to the notion of transcultural identity.

The Writing of Ḥanān al-Shaykh, between "Decentration" and Polyphony

Ḥanān al-Shaykh belongs to a line of female authors who have long been excluded from the literary canon, or kept on the side-lines, even though their novels occupy a central position in the production of contemporary Arabic narrative. The importance of Ḥanān al-Shaykh's writings is linked to both the issues dealt with and the narrative techniques adopted. The first stage of her literary production belongs to the current characterizing the Lebanese novel from 1975 onwards, dedicated mainly to representing the civil war (1975–1990), a dramatic experience that contributes to legitimizing the novel as a literary genre at the centre of the canon.[5] During the civil war, female authors acquired increasing visibility in the literary field. Indeed, the movement of the so-called Beirut Decentrists was formed, the name coined by miriam cooke (cooke, 1987), alluding to the "eccentric" and "marginal" position from which the women observe and describe the war, and whose members include Ḥanān al-Shaykh as well as Emily Naṣr Allāh, Etel ʿAdnān, Laylā ʿUsayrān, Claire Jebeyli and Ghāda al-Sammān.

The writing of Ḥanān al-Shaykh not only refers to the Lebanese context but also transcends national boundaries, concentrating on issues of a social nature such as the position of women in Arab countries, the impact of the patriarchal system on social organization and the issue of migration and integration, often using what are considered to be "marginal" characters such as women, transvestites and homosexuals. In so doing, al-Shaykh shows that she maintains her "decentralized" position even in the novels in which she does not deal with the civil war, making it a privileged point of view from which to question and deconstruct the monolithic representation of reality advanced by the hegemonic discourse. The transnational calling of al-Shaykh's writing is reflected in the spatial framework of her novels, which feature multiple settings including not only Lebanon and other Arab countries but also European metropolises such as London.

The desire to represent "the margins" and to give voice to eccentric individuals is achieved through a series of narratological and stylistic choices that permeate her writing, becoming one of the author's key characteristics. We refer, for example, to the attention given to the female dimension, which is widely explored in her novels, highlighting the intersections between the variables of sex, gender, social class and nationality and how they act on the characters' individual and collective identity. Polyphony is, without doubt, one element that distinguishes Ḥanān al-Shaykh's poetics and is accomplished in a narration that often has multiple and varying focuses, thanks to which each character can express his or her own point of view about reality. Another particular feature is the attention given to the body – especially in the sphere of intimacy and sexuality – as it is presented as a symbolic space for the individual's search for identity, in his/her perpetual dialectic with the other and with society.

Al-Shaykh was born in Beirut in 1943,[6] in the conservative Muslim district of Ras al-Nabaa. Her mother left the family to go and live with her lover, arousing scandal in the district and marking the life of her daughter, who would dedicate a book to her.[7] Ḥanān stayed with her father, attended a religious primary school for girls and, during her secondary school, met the feminist writer Laylā Baʿalbakī, her geography teacher, who had a strong influence on her, especially after she read her novel-manifesto about women's emancipation, *Anā aḥyā* (I Live, 1958). At the age of 16, al-Shaykh was already publishing essays in some national newspapers. From 1963 to 1966, she moved to Egypt to study at the American College for Girls in Cairo, where she wrote her first novel, *Intiḥār rajul mayyit* (Suicide of a Dead Man), which was only published in 1970. The novel was inspired by a real love story that the authoress had with a much older man. One of the distinguishing features of her writing is, indeed, the intertwining of fiction and autobiographical elements, which are also present in the novels at the centre of this chapter. Following her experience in Cairo, al-Shaykh returned to Lebanon and started working for television and for the newspaper *Al-Nahar*, and she got married. In 1976, after the outbreak of the Lebanese civil war, she moved to Saudi Arabia with her husband and two daughters and remained there for seven years. In 1982, she moved to London, and in 1988 she published *Misk al-ghazāl*, her fourth novel based on her experiences of life in Saudi society. *Innahā London yā ʿazīzī* was published in 2001 and deals with the theme of migration in multi-ethnic London, where the writer herself settled.

Al-Shaykh's multiple belonging pervades her writing, transcending national boundaries, and it is representative of the multi-dimensionality of the contemporary Arab novel: national, subnational, pan-Arabic and transnational (Hassan, 2017, 6–7). One of the main themes of her works is, in fact, the crisis of the nation and the consequent need to rethink individual and collective identities as shifting and fluid.[8] This is demonstrated through the transnational settings of her works and the transculturality of the universe of fiction. The works of al-Shaykh encourage a reflection on not only Arab societies but also a series of categories involving all contemporary societies, such as those of gender, culture, identity, belonging and nation.

Transcultural Space and Identity in Two Novels by Ḥanān al-Shaykh

In *The Gazelle's Musk* and *This Is London, My Dear*, the two novels forming the focus of our analysis, al-Shaykh deals with two different experiences of migration that have had a strong impact on Arab societies during the 1980s and 1990s. In *The Gazelle's Musk*, the theme is migration towards the Gulf countries, which involved people from various parts of the world, not only Arab states, in search of better job opportunities during the time of the oil boom and when the real-estate market in the area was in rapid expansion. On the contrary, in *This Is London, My Dear*, the writer concentrates on Arab migration towards European metropolises, more specifically London, to escape the traumatic experiences of poverty, war and persecution, in order to rediscover a lost freedom.

Although a 13-year gap separates the publication of these two works and they are set in very different contexts, they have numerous points in common and are, in a certain sense, in dialogue with one another, not only as far as the universe of characters is concerned, but also for a series of textual elements and narrative techniques. These two novels do not exactly fit into the post-1967 trend of the Arab novel, characterized by "a re-emergence of pronounced east-west binaries" that, as Sellman explains, "are transformed through a focus on social and political oppression in the Arab world operating alongside an idealization of Europe" (Sellman, 2018, 757). They also stand out from the narratives about forced migration, centred on "subjectivities born of mass migration" (Sellman, 2018, 751), that started to develop in the field of Arab fiction in the 1990s and today represent an important literary trend. The theme of migration at the heart of these two novels does not, in actual fact, deal with the same characters as those present in Arab novels about forced migration, or the so-called refugee literature, which are filled with characters such as asylum-seekers who rely on traffickers and undertake dangerous journeys in order to reach the European mirage. Although the characters in both *The Gazelle's Musk* and *This Is London, My Dear* have fled from an Arab country because of wars or poverty, they reach their destination via legal channels. Al-Shaykh does not focus on a specific character or exclusively on the more underprivileged classes but describes a broader spectrum of migrants, some of whom even belong to the middle and upper classes.

Following a recent landmark classification of contemporary Arab literature on the topic of migration, in these two works, al-Shaykh goes beyond the postcolonial approach to the narration of migration in order to set it in a global context. On this point, Sellman specifies that:

> the shift from the postcolonial to the global pivots on an understanding of the postcolonial as an experience of continuing domination exerted by a former colonial nation on the one hand, and a conception of the global, where domination and inequities are more diffuse and migration patterns less clearly charted, defined as much by points of transit (Paynter 2018) as points of arrival.
>
> (Sellman, 2018, 754)

Al-Shaykh draws attention to the attempt made by various migrant subjects to fit into their countries of destination, where they are exposed to different types of injustice and forms of domination, according to variables such as gender, social class, ethnicity and religious affiliation. The writer does not just set experiences of migration in a global context but represents the transcultural dimension, and one way of doing so is by choosing the polyphonic novel, filled with a multitude of characters who are all quite different from each other. Therefore, these two works may be classified as belonging to the trend characterizing the narrative production of the last three decades which, as Nordin et al. explain, is increasingly suffused with an interest for transcultural experiences:

> Imaginative literature offers a powerful means of exploring transcultural experience and grappling with the challenges it poses to individuals and societies alike. The very act of reading literary texts is potentially a transcultural experience, in that it invites the reader to identify with the perspectives of fictional characters from unfamiliar geographical locations, as well as from a variety of cultural and social backgrounds. Many literary works published over the past three decades reflect a preoccupation with transcultural encounters against the background of globalization and increased migration. Literary criticism, in turn, can make a valuable contribution to understandings of transculturality and the re-conceptualization of collective and individual identities. By viewing fictional representations of contemporary reality as crucial cultural manifestations, literary criticism can elucidate how individuals experience contemporary social changes and experience a heightened sense of "inner transculturality."
>
> (Nordin et al., 2013, ix)

In *The Gazelle's Musk* and *This Is London, My Dear*, the characters' search for identity takes place in a constant interaction with both the internal and external space in which the migrants live. The relationship with the external environment is very different in the two novels, as the spatial organization of the Gulf societies, and in particular of Saudi Arabia – where the plot of *The Gazelle's Musk* is presumably set, given the writer's biographical experience – is based on the strict division between private and public space, where the woman is granted only limited access to the latter. In *This Is London, My Dear*, by contrast, the external space plays a significant role in the metamorphosis of the characters' identity, as they do not limit themselves to interacting within the protective walls of their apartments.[9]

The central role of space emerges right from the very titles of the two novels, metaphorically in *The Gazelle's Musk* and more explicitly in *This Is London, My Dear*, where the dimension of the metropolis permeates the narration.[10] *The Gazelle's Musk* is a title that, in itself, conveys traces of a contradictory reality, divided between tradition and uninhibited progress, a characteristic typical of the Gulf countries. The title refers to a substance extracted from a gland of the gazelle that is reputed to have aphrodisiac properties. This substance appears only once in the novel but acquires a symbolic value as a distinctive element of the Bedouin setting and of the traditions and customs of the desert of which it has remained a token, despite the disruption of the landscape and the sudden establishment of a globalized and sedentary society. The question of identity, which is central to the novel, affects not only individuals but also spaces. Thanks to her personal experience in this place that abounds with contradictions, Ḥanān al-Shaykh lays bare a simulacrum of the Gulf through the tale of four women who speak directly in the first person and whose stories interweave.

The novel is set right at the very start of the building boom during which unrestrained urbanization tried to subdue the desert and delete the authenticity of a place linked to the essentially nomadic world of the Bedouins.[11] This reality came into being, as a political entity, in the 1970s, with the subdivision into various states, following the exportation of oil and natural gas. The struggle between two movements played out in the area emerges in the novel. On one side, there is the frenetic movement of the so-called progress, related to money, that takes shape through the violent appropriation of the land, with the nonstop construction of buildings, luxury hotels, housing and shopping centres, leading to an unrelenting upheaval of the natural landscape. It concerns a movement linked to the predator-like presence of foreigners – driven exclusively by the exploitation of the land's resources – who aim to leave as soon as possible, to return home rich and build a future elsewhere. On the other side, there is the autochthonous dimension linked to nature, the rhythms of the desert and the Bedouin traditions that risk being cancelled forever. This struggle for identity taking place on the land has an unequivocal impact on the characters who live there.

In *This Is London, My Dear*, the privileged space, as emerges from the title, is London. Here the lives of the four main characters converge by chance on a plane from Dubai. As Hanadi Al-Samman explains:

> These characters are leaving frustrated projects of a personal and financial nature behind in Dubai, heading to London with dreams of resettling and making a fresh start. Amira, who usually sells her escort services to Arab men on Edgware Road in London, is disappointed at the knowledge that her services in Dubai are no longer needed because of the competition of blond and skinny Russian women entertainers. The transvestite Samir leaves a wife and five kids behind, and hopes that in London he can finally be free to come out of the closet. Nicholas, the British citizen, is the only one whose trip from Dubai culminated in success and satisfaction after he brokered the sale of rare Indian artifacts to a wealthy sheikh in Oman. But the novel's portrayal of how "routes produce roots" centers on the story of Lamis. Following her divorce from a wealthy Iraqi husband in London, whom she was forced to marry at a young age, Lamis had returned to Dubai to live with her immigrant parents and to start a dried flower arrangement business. However, after facing the trouble of having her shipment of dried poppies confiscated as contraband at the

> Emirate customs' office, Lamis abandons the whole project of replanting her roots in the Arab world and returns to London.
>
> (Al-Samman, 2015, 197–198)

Although the narration is in the third person, there is an internal and varying focus, and so the events are filtered by all the characters – as occurs in *The Gazelle's Musk*, too. The first spatial link between the two novels seems to be established, symbolically, by the plane trip itself – a typical "in-between" place (Bhabha, 1994) – from the Gulf area, the setting of *The Gazelle's Musk*, to the metropolis of London. As in *The Gazelle's Musk*, in *This Is London, My Dear*, the characters have different backgrounds, gender, sexual orientation and social class and their relationship with London is contradictory: on one hand, it represents a special place where, not without sufferance, they can express a part of their identity that is censored elsewhere; on the other hand, as Fischer explains, "the protagonists struggle to find places for themselves in a city where global relations of economic, political, and social power marginalize them" (Fischer, 2004, 108).

In the two novels, the relationship with the space underlines the transcultural nature of the characters' identity, "resulting from diverse cultural encounters" (Nordin et al., 2013, ix), which differs from the concepts of multiculturality and interculturality:

> These latter concepts have been used to describe the multiplicity of forms of cultural life that coexist within a specific society. […] the concept of transculturality fosters an inclusive, rather than exclusive, understanding of culture as characterized by differences; it emphasizes the need for groups to identify common ground among cultures, and the need for the individual to acknowledge the foreign within oneself in order to be able to comprehend others.
>
> (Nordin et al., 2013, x)

In al-Shaykh's two novels, the characters' transcultural identity represents an alternative both to complete assimilation into the dominant culture of the country of arrival and to the adherence to a homogenous monocultural national identity. The state of dispossession[12] that they experience – and that they try to overcome – does not derive so much from the need to have to choose between two distinct cultural realities, but rather from the fluid and multifaceted nature of their identity resulting from different cultural encounters.

At the centre of the plot of *The Gazelle's Musk* are four female protagonists of different origin and social background, who find themselves living in a city of the Gulf and whose stories intersect. These women are Suhā, who is Lebanese, Tamar, an Arab of Turkish origin, Suzanne the American, and Nūr, an Arab of Bedouin origin. The novel develops around four separate narrations in which each character speaks, creating a polyphonic work that puts forward various points of view on the same reality, thus contributing towards a deconstruction of a monolithic representation of the real. Narrated by women, the male characters are described from the female points of view and, therefore, represented through "the other", as a result of a true reappropriation of the word and, consequently, a takeover of reality. The different narrations revolve around the daily lives of these four women, who share a boring life, solitude, oppression and the inaccessibility to outdoor space. This reality in which the women live is characterized by the presence of numerous boundaries, first and foremost the spatial one, which is apparent in the clear division between the places accessible to men and those accessible to women. Another boundary is represented by class, which is a decisive factor in a society built on economic inequality and the exploitation of labour on an ethnic basis.

The novel begins with the character of Suhā, who shares autobiographical features with the writer. She is an educated, upper-middle class Lebanese woman who has moved to the Gulf from Beirut, both to escape from the Lebanese civil war and to accompany her husband, who had to move for reasons of work. They have a school-age son whose name is ʿUmar. Used to working and having her own economic independence and freedom of movement, Suhā detests life in the Gulf, where she cannot stand the boredom, the lack of activity and uselessness of her days, the impossibility to work, the solitude and the shallowness of the meetings with other women, even though they often represent the only opportunity for her to leave the apartment and go to a place other than the one delineated by the four walls of her home. Coming from an educated, open and dynamic background, like that of Beirut, Suhā is not able to adapt to life in the Gulf, and her whole narration is permeated with sufferance and frustration. In many passages, the focus is on the landscape, whose identity is subject to continuous upheaval following the oil boom.

In the description of what she sees on her arrival in the Gulf, Suhā represents the very collision between two opposing souls: the one linked to the "authentic" nature of the desert and the one violently introduced to satisfy the needs of the "foreigners" whose only concern is to exploit the oilfields:

> Our hotel was luxurious although whoever designed it had been unsuccessful, obviously seeing things through foreign eyes and wanting to create his own idea of Arab architecture and furnishings, with the result that wealth superseded taste in every room. The picture windows looked out on to distant lights, and in the daytime I saw a big harbour and a sturdy bridge. Who'd said that we were in the desert here, when all the trappings and institutions of city life were to be found in abundance? Not much time passed before I realized I'd been mistaken: I was neither in the desert nor in a city.
>
> The desert was only a place to be explored; even getting to know its natives was an experience like something out of a tourist brochure and they themselves were ill at ease with anything but … tents and camels and sand. Those in the city, meanwhile, were in conflict with whatever came

> to them from beyond the desert. Every aircraft that landed on their sands brought something that frightened them and that they didn't want to know about because it didn't spring out of their own arid land. But these aircraft carried people and their different civilizations and they couldn't afford to reject them because the incomers were the ones who knew the secrets of the desert, almost as if they had been created in its belly and knew where the black liquid was and how to turn it into door handles and bathtaps made of gold.
>
> (al-Shaykh, 1992, 30–31)[13]

This passage clearly shows how the crisis of identity involves the external space first of all and then reflects on the individual sphere. The territory is portrayed as an entity suffering a predatory invasion by a mass of people of different origins, who are disgorged incessantly from the planes and have neither respect for nor interest in desert life. Suhā is painfully aware of the violence taking place on the land as a result of the unrestrained building work that is trying to delete the desert, and whose result is contradictory. This condition is reflected by the location of the character herself, who affirms "I was neither in the desert nor in a city" (*mā kuntu fī al-ṣaḥrā' wa-lā fī al-madīna*; al-Shaykh, 1988, 30), in order to represent her own instability. Apart from her observation regarding the effect of the human activity on the desert and the resulting destruction, Suhā's words reflect a judgement on the type of human being perpetrating such an action, a human being who, as we read in the first lines of the passage, confuses wealth with "taste".

Being a woman, Suhā's access to outdoor space is extremely limited. To enable her to escape from the segregation, her husband provides her with a private chauffeur. The car constitutes a buffer space between private and public, which allows the protagonist to have a mediated relationship with the outdoors. In this sense, the role of the private car in *The Gazelle's Musk* seems analogous to that of the taxi for Lamīs in *This Is London, My Dear*. Here the taxi becomes a protective space chosen by the woman that allows her to reach places in the city far from her flat, but without having any direct interaction with others.

These two female characters have numerous points in common. Firstly, they seem to embody the author's point of view, also as a result of several autobiographical elements. Secondly, both Suhā and Lamīs experience a state of change with regard to their interaction with the external space, and this has a direct impact on their identity. After moving to the Gulf, Suhā seeks a socially acceptable way of gaining access to the outdoors, in a context where the presence of women in public spaces is strictly regulated. Lamīs returns to London having divorced her husband, a rich Iraqi whom she had been forced to marry by her family, who were of a lower class, in the aim of moving up in the world both socially and economically. After the marriage, Lamīs settles down in London with her husband, with whom she has a son, but life under the man's and the mother-in-law's oppressive control soon becomes unbearable. Despite pressures from her family, Lamīs decides to get divorced, and the novel begins with her return to London, after a brief stay in Dubai. Once off the plane, she makes her way to the flat that her ex-husband has left her, which is still full of boxes. From this moment on, Lamīs undergoes a process of change, during which she tries to free herself from her Arab identity, and that involves studying English, a love affair with Nicholas, an Englishman she met during the flight from Dubai, and her peregrinations across London by taxi: a space previously unknown to her and to which she had never before been granted access.

In *The Gazelle's Musk*, Suhā makes the most of the chauffeur placed at her disposal by her husband to visit the only places women and foreigners are allowed to go: luxury hotels, shopping centres and private homes. One day, she decides to go swimming in a hotel pool, and here she meets Nūr, an attractive young woman of Bedouin origin, who belongs to a very wealthy family and lives in an opulent home. Nūr soon reaches out to Suhā and invites her to her home. Having been abandoned by first her parents and then her husband, Nūr's life is characterized by loneliness, boredom and depression. When she was a child, her parents compensated for their absence with opulence and money and, at 16 years old, the girl asked her father to build her a house opposite the family home, and she settled in there with her nanny. She spends her days there riding around on a motorbike and organizing parties and events. She meets her first husband, who, like her, is rebellious and a lover of the good life, but soon she discovers that he is homosexual and that he married her only to respect social conventions and enjoy his affairs in secret. After divorcing her first husband, Nūr meets Ṣāliḥ, her second husband, who tries to rescue her from the emptiness of her life, which consists only of distractions and superficiality, and to escape from her miserable solitude. The man urges her to study and read and tries to establish a relationship with her based on sharing and conversation, but the gap between the married couple remains unbridgeable and is exacerbated by the contradictions and limitations of life in the Gulf.

Nūr's frustration and her unease are intensified by her pregnancy and the birth of her daughter. These events force the woman to curb her social life in order to take on the role that the community expects from her: that of wife and mother. Her lack of interest in the baby and in family life leads the husband to lose respect for his wife and to leave her permanently. Ṣāliḥ is almost always away on business, and Nūr takes advantage of this to go abroad and experience the freedom that she is not allowed at home, or at least not in public spaces. Only when the accounts of the unruly and wild lifestyle that she is leading in Europe reach her husband's ears and threaten his respectability does Ṣāliḥ decide to have her brought back home by force, and he confiscates her passport. In this way, Nūr loses her freedom of movement and lies abandoned like a forgotten object among the many luxurious objects in her house. In this sense, although Nūr is the only character of the novel who lives in the same place as she was born, she shares the condition of dispossession typical of those without a country and without citizenship. As a woman, she is, in fact, dispossessed of all her civil and political rights, and even in the private sphere, her every choice is subject to the will of others. It is during this phase of desperation that she finds her only way to salvation in Suhā. Initially, Suhā is fascinated by this reality, which represents a distraction from her boredom, and she describes the first visit to her friend's home as follows:

> Her house was like a peep-show where servants and nannies of different races milled around with children, gazelles and saluki dogs. A delicate perfume floated to meet me whenever I went through the door, and Arab and foreign music reverberated through the spacious rooms. Beautiful clothes, high fashion, the latest of everything – including the furniture and the chocolates she offered me, like Godiva from Belgium and Chantilly from Lebanon – mangoes and pineapples from the Philippines. It was a large house with white marble everywhere and the trees in the garden visible through the windows, acting as a buffer between the house and the desert. [...] There were two video machines in the huge sitting-room. The furniture was used to divide the room into three sections. Her daughter and Umar and some other children were shouting and screaming as they fought satellites on the video screen. Female friends and relations of Nur watched stars like Dalida and the Egyptian Nellie on television, and the Filipino men-servants sang and called to each other with loud whistles. Dogs wandered in, wrestled with the children, and wandered out. Budgerigars and canaries and green and white parrots hopped around their aviaries talking to one another. There was a big aquarium alive with different sea creatures. When the friends and relations got bored they would come over to Nur and me and then I wondered which of them to talk to or look at. Some of them were enveloped in abayas and veils and had henna patterns on their hands, while others wore clothes in the latest styles and colours; their jewellery was either embossed Bedouin gold or modern international designer style. Which magazine should I flick through? It seemed as if all the world's magazines, and the magazines produced by all the big international stores, were there on the table.
>
> (al-Shaykh, 1992, 39–40)

As with the description of the landscape of the Gulf, here too the space is characterized by the coexistence of various contradictory elements that form, in a certain sense, a transcultural space, where the limits between cultural and national belonging are transcended. Yet, rather than expressing potentiality, this aspect is reduced to a condition of accumulation and ostentation that once again seems to exemplify an area where material wealth is considered a founding value. However, the ostentation of pomp counterbalances the political administration governed by authoritarian regimes that deny fundamental rights and exercise an invasive form of censorship, separating public from private spaces and limiting the freedom especially of women and disadvantaged classes. All these contradictions are displayed within this heterogeneous space, populated by the various female members of the Gulf society. Here women of high social class find themselves – some fully veiled, others flaunting the latest designer clothes – next to servants of various nationalities.

Initially, Nūr's house is a distraction, but Suhā soon becomes bored by it and starts to distance herself from her friend. Nūr, however, is obsessed with Suhā, who she considers to be the only person capable of staying by her side and alleviating her unbearable sensation of emptiness and solitude. As a result, she starts contacting her spasmodically, until she manages to persuade her to come to her house once again, under the pretence that she needs to be consoled and wants to ask for advice about how to rekindle her relationship with her husband. At this point, Nūr draws Suhā into a sexual relationship that, rather than being the result of a free choice, stems from the same condition of dispossession. This is an answer to a reality based on appearances and on the presence of a series of spatial and normative boundaries, in which it is difficult to forge relationships with others, whether male or female. The body becomes the symbolic location of the struggle between collectivity and the individual. In the public sphere, the body is disciplined; it is part of a network of regulations that give it meaning. In the private sphere, the body tries to free itself from this normative wire-netting and take possession of the individual dimension and of desire.

Another character in *The Gazelle's Musk* who tries to free herself from the limitations linked to being a woman in the Gulf is Tamar. She is a lower-class Arab woman of Turkish origin, who has been repudiated by her husband and lives with her mother and son at her brother's house. The flat in which Tamar lives is a sort of microcosm inhabited by an extended family, a traditional institution for anyone coming from a conservative environment, in which women do not have free access to the outside world. Tamar's narration, which is always in the first person, begins with the fight that she is waging to convince her brother to allow her to attend lessons at a cultural institute, where Suhā works as a teacher. It is here that the two women meet and become friends. Tamar is immediately fascinated by Suhā's clothes and her nonchalant manner, which clearly derives from an environment that is entirely different to her own, and by the fact that she wears her hair down. To get permission to leave the house and go to the Institute, Tamar starts a hunger strike. However, her brother allows her to go thanks mainly to the help of Tamar's sister-in-law, who threatens her husband with a sex strike, becoming a sort of modern-day Lysistrata. Intent on redeeming herself for her passive role as repudiated wife under her brother's care, another of Tamar's projects is to open a beauty salon. The difficulties encountered in order to obtain the various permits and the money from the bank highlight the contradictions of a country in which women are not a legal entity, but must, by law, rely on a male tutor, even if he is much younger. This project also meets with success and Tamar manages to open the beauty salon, a strictly female space that offers a sample of the local society: here women of all ages, of different origins and social class, meet and are finally free – for the very reason that there are no males present – to show their bodies and pamper themselves.

The body also plays a key role in *This Is London, My Dear*, and it is linked to the characters' metamorphosis of identity, which is manifested externally even through transvestitism.[14] Samīr and Amīra, in particular, are two of the various characters who turn to this expedient. Samīr is a poor, young homosexual from Lebanon, who has left his wife and five children in Dubai. He lands in London, smuggling a monkey with him on the plane. Unknown to him, the monkey has been made to swallow a diamond that has to be delivered to a shady character who, in the end, swindles him. Until his arrival in London, Samīr's life is marked by his inability to live his non-heterosexual orientation freely. In his youth, when he was still in Lebanon, he was committed to a psychiatric hospital by his family to remedy his propensity for transvestitism and his homosexual desires. His wife seems to be unaware of the real sexual leanings of her husband, who takes advantage of the upheaval of the social context caused by the conflict during the civil war, in order to affirm his true identity: he moves from one part of Beirut to another dressed as a woman, taking food and cigarettes and dancing to entertain the militants. As a result, in the context of war, his identity manages to acquire a normative side that would otherwise have been denied to him. Once in London, Samīr finally feels free to start relationships with various young lovers and to cross-dress. The transcultural component of his identity is represented by the way he dresses, as explained by El-Ariss:

> Depicted as a "flamboyantly dressed man," wearing a Versace shirt and cowboy boots and looking like Klinger in Mash, Samir's transvestism is transcultural. It is shaped by the worlds of fashion and television from Lebanon to Italy to Hollywood, blurring the lines between East and West, native and foreign.
>
> (El-Ariss, 2013, 298)

Amīra, a Moroccan woman who has been living in London for many years, where she works as a prostitute in the Arab district of Edgware Road, also decides at some point to start disguising herself. Unlike the character of Samīr, the woman's metamorphosis is not driven by the need to give free rein to her desires but rather by her wish to win back social liberation. Amīra comes from a large and extremely poor Moroccan family that has never taken care of her. When she arrives in London, the woman makes prostitution her means of livelihood, but now that she has become older, she wants to obtain a sort of pension for her future, and she devises a plan to dress as a princess in order to trick rich Arab men who are in town on business. As Al-Samman explains, overcoming the boundaries between social classes is represented by the overcoming of the spatial boundaries between the suburbs and the city centre by means of the reappropriation of space:

her upward mobility project would involve leaving "'little Arabia' as the English call Edgware Road," and living in "the real London" of Bayswater Road in the midst of the Hyde Park and Marble Arch districts.

(Al-Samman, 2015, 202)

The metamorphosis from prostitute to princess – which is, moreover, reflected in her name "Amīra", which actually means "princess" – is reminiscent of the metamorphosis of the character Muʾmina in the play *Ṭuqūs al-ishārāt wa-l-taḥawwulāt* (Rituals of signs and transformations, 1994) by the Syrian playwright Saʿd Allāh Wannūs. Here the transformation occurs in reverse, involving a woman of high Damascene society at the end of the 19th century, who decides of her own free will to devote herself to the profession of prostitute. In the case of Amīra, it is her very condition of being uprooted, of moving to a different country, and her transcultural identity that offer her the opportunity to acquire a new identity, as emerges in the passage in which the woman visits a prestigious London dressmaker to choose a new dress:

> "I want a princess dress." [...] "Don't you like it?" "Sorry. It's lovely but it's too thick for a princess-line." "I don't want a princess-line. I want a dress a princess would wear." The princess she'd seen was so ordinarily dressed. [...]
>
> The salesgirl, despite her embarrassment at not recognising the Princess and not knowing her name, opened the door and bid the Princess a smiling goodbye. The fact that the salesgirl believed in her was proof to Amira that she appeared quite authentic. Nobody asked princesses for their identity documents. Everything was possible when you were abroad.
>
> (al-Shaykh, 2002, 111,113)[15]

The change of identity takes place through the change of dress: Amīra specifies that she does not want a dress with "a princess-line" (*qaṣṣat prinsīs*), but "a dress a princess would wear" (*fustānan ka-allatī tartadī-hi al-amīrāt*) (al-Shaykh, 2001, 123). In the second part of the passage, it becomes clear how, apart from the disguise, her change of identity is made possible thanks to the woman's uprooting: the land of emigration becomes a blank page on which she can outline the profile of her new identity. However, Amīra does not want to renounce her Arab background, which is what allows her to exploit the disguise to her advantage. Her victims are, in fact, wealthy Arab men staying in the luxury hotels of London, who the woman wants to swindle in order to obtain considerable sums of money. The theme of disguise highlights how the body – a reality that is at one and the same time physical, symbolical and social – is placed at the intersection between the individual and society. By modifying our body, we adapt our image in the eyes of others and, consequently, our social position, as occurs to the character Amīra, whose metamorphosis is triggered by her dressing up as a princess, a fictitious element, but one that has an effect on the reality and identity of the character and her social position. Her path seems to be in line with Butler's claim that fantasy is a kind of subversion of the norm (Butler, 2004).

As Jolanda Guardi explains (Guardi, 2018, 127–128), the concept of disguise can be used to interpret the character of Lamīs as well. She presents numerous traits in common with Suhā in *The Gazelle's Musk*. Following her divorce, Lamīs, in fact, tries desperately hard to blend into London society by cancelling out her Arab roots. For this purpose, one device used in the novel to represent such a metamorphosis is Lamīs's decision to learn English, and in order to perfect her accent, she turns to a mother tongue teacher:

> if you take lessons with me, it's not only your way of speaking that will change. The movements of your tongue, everything related to your voice and larynx will have to change their habits radically. But it's not just your pronunciation – It goes deeper than that. Arabic is your mother tongue – altering the way you speak affects your personality inside." "I understand." "I'd like to know why, after living here for thirteen years, you've decided you want to acquire an English accent. And why did you choose to come here, to England, rather than some other country in Europe?" "I came to London because I was going to marry an Iraqi, and he was already living here. But we're divorced now. I have a son here, who's still at school, and I've realised I want to assimilate. I need to look for work. I think having an English accent could be the key." "In other words, you've taken England as your second home." "No, as my first home. I left Iraq when I was twelve years old. I don't think I'll ever live there again."
>
> The teacher's final words of advice rang in her head like a bell: "Turn on the television. Go to the theatre or the cinema every night if you can, and talk to your English friends. Keep away from anything Arab, even in your mind. You should stop eating Arab dishes, because subconsciously you'll be saying their names."
>
> (al-Shaykh, 2002, 53–54)

This passage shows how Lamīs has chosen to blend into the English culture and how this process constitutes a form of dispossession of part of the character's identity that ultimately prevents her from finding her own standing. Of relevance are the imperative verbs appearing in the text that are used by the mother tongue teacher to give instructions to her student when she says "keep away (*ibta'dī*) from anything Arab, even in your mind" and "stop (*imtan'ī*) eating Arab dishes" (al-Shaykh, 2001, 81). The realm of language becomes a metaphor for the impossibility to incarnate the identity of the other unless by means of an imitation that distorts the original, as in "colonial mimicry" theorized by Homi Bhabha (Bhabha, 1984), and which becomes a sort of subordination of the colonized other. However, in various passages of the novel, London appears not only as an alienating place in which the migrants have to cancel their origins in order to acquire a standing, but also as a set of "contact zones" that, as Nyman explains, are sites "of mutual interaction rather than as mere sites of coercion" (Nyman, 2017, 2). The metropolis is a cosmopolitan dimension that offers the opportunity for cultural encounters without necessarily involving mobility:

> The ability of cultural encounters to engender new cultural phenomena and identities has received wide attention in recent years in postcolonial and transcultural studies. They and their formation have been addressed in various ways, including the more traditional focus on the colonizer–colonized encounter [...] several writers have seen such encounters as producing new identities that resist dominant and colonial hegemonies, as seen in the widespread use of such critical terms as Homi K. Bhabha's "colonial mimicry" and "hybridity". For Bhabha, cultural contacts and the experience of in-betweenness often felt by migrants and refugees generate new, hybrid identities that resist conventional categorizations and nationalisms.
>
> (Nyman, 2017, 2)

Although on the surface the relationship between Lamīs and Nicholas, the Englishman she met on the plane, seems to imitate the paradigm of the colonized and the colonizer, it proves to be more complicated and nuanced and should be interpreted in light of the concept of transcultural identity. By means of this relationship, al-Shaykh represents the link between migration, cultural encounters and the ensuing transformations of identity. It is not only Lamīs who incarnates a transcultural identity; Nicholas does, too. Even if he is English and lives mainly in London, for years he has been spending periods of time in Arab countries – especially in Oman – for business, being an expert on Islamic art and a dealer in this field. Initially, the attraction between the two characters is based on a series of mutual projections, as El-Ariss explains:

> she perceives him as the British man who will allow her to express her sexuality freely, and he sees her as the beautiful yet fragile Arab woman in need of protection. The two lovers struggle to overcome their cultural projections, leading the relation to a standstill.
>
> (El-Ariss, 2013, 298)

At first, Nicholas, and the people he sees, tend to view Lamīs mainly as an Iraqi refugee in London, or, in any case, they associate her with an Arab world that he knows in part and that fascinates him. On the other hand, Lamīs considers him to be the key to unlocking her new identity as a Londoner following the divorce from her husband. Moreover, in her relationship with Nicholas, Lamīs feels free for the first time in her life to enjoy a desire that had never featured in the relations she was forced to have with her husband. However, the love affair goes through a crisis when Nicholas insists on formalizing their union, asking her to go and live with him and to marry him. Lamīs refuses, as she is not ready, whether before the Iraqi community in London or in her homeland, to assert her new identity as a free woman, being released from the moral values and the regulations of her country of origin. Furthermore, Lamīs does not want to rely on Nicholas during her process of reconciliation with London; she wishes to do it alone. As a result, the man disappears without a trace. The theme of identity, therefore, is central in the writing of al-Shaykh, who is able to represent the two components – individual and collective – that are often at odds with each other.

Two characters in *The Gazelle's Musk* who, in certain respects, share the workings of the couple Lamīs and Nicholas and, like them, incarnate transcultural identity, are Suzanne and Muʿādh. Suzanne is a middle-aged American who has moved to the Gulf with her son and husband after he has accepted a job offer there. The move represents an opportunity for her to rediscover her femininity and sexual desire after a lack of any type of intimacy with her husband that has lasted for years. As a woman, Suzanne has now become invisible in American society: she is no longer young; she is overweight and does not comply with the aesthetic standards to which one must conform in order to be considered desirable in the United States. For her, moving to the Gulf results in a passage from the world of the invisible to that of the hyper-visible, becoming the object of the men's continual gaze. From feeling like a piece of scrap in her country of origin, Suzanne becomes the prize catch for all the local men, and she embarks on a series of casual flings. Her story begins with a visit to a traditional healer, from whom she wishes to obtain a cure that will relight Muʿādh, her Arab lover's passion for her. It is precisely here that the famous "gazelle's musk", the title of the book, appears. Muʿādh is the male character who is described in most detail in the novel, but always from a female point of view. He is Suzanne's second lover, who she met at her husband's workplace.

Through the affair between Suzanne and Muʿādh, al-Shaykh represents the attitude of the so-called expats (expatriates, Westerners) towards the local culture and population. In fact, Suzanne adopts a consumerist approach towards her lover, who becomes a real form of entertainment and, in a certain sense, ornamental. Muʿādh enables her to feel she has direct and privileged access to the local reality, so she can discover its secrets and peculiarities in a special way, similar to what Nicholas does for Lamīs in London. Al-Shaykh uses the character of Suzanne to provide a critical representation of that orientalist and colonialist vision that leads to the exoticization and the appropriation of the other, as if he or she were a strange and bizarre object to be observed and possessed. This process not only characterizes Suzanne's attitude towards Muʿādh but is also reciprocal, as he too is attracted to the woman for the very reason that she is American and conforms to an image only seen in films, songs and advertisements. Their relationship should be understood as a cultural encounter within a cosmopolitan dimension that, although based on appearance, leads to a change in the characters' identity. Muʿādh restores

Suzanne's femininity and, in return, thanks to him, the woman lives out her orientalist fantasies about the Gulf and re-emerges from the abyss of monotony and invisibility of her life as an American housewife. The start of their turbulent love affair is described as follows, from Suzanne's point of view:

> At the start I was convinced that he was acting: when he saw me without my clothes on, he gasped and struck his head with the palm of his hand, exclaiming bitterly, "Why did God create foreign women different?" When I asked him what his wife's body was like he didn't answer me, but passed his hand over my flesh saying, "It's like silk. Pure silk." When he let out a noise like a bull roaring I nearly laughed. He said I was like one of the houris whom God had prepared for true believers when they entered Paradise. He even grabbed my foot and smelt it, muttering, "More fragrant than sandalwood or incense." I started to laugh out loud then. I was relaxed. [...] He was like a man worshipping at a pagan shrine, uttering incantations, most of them incomprehensible to me. ... I thought to myself that he must have seen a lot of silent films: his black eyes almost made holes in the screen, or in my face. I had no idea of the reasons for his outburst of emotion until, nearly in tears, he asked me why I was laughing. I didn't tell him that it was his melodramatic admiration of my body and his manner of loving that I found so funny; I made do with saying that there was no need for him to talk and behave as he had been doing because I was quite happy with him. Later I realized that he wasn't acting and that he really meant it when he called me the Marilyn Monroe of the desert. If I gestured, sat still, walked along, I was exciting; if I spoke, there was someone picking up my words as if they were kisses. He wanted me on the sand, in an empty house, in the open desert, at an oasis, waiting till midnight and keeping a big stick near him in case anyone surprised us. He wanted me in a camel [...] tent [...] ; in my house, in the bathroom or in bed. I abandoned myself to glorying in my plumpness, not caring about the blue veins in my legs and thighs; I no longer wore a girdle: Maaz took hold of the folds of flesh as if he were snatching up gold in Ali Baba's cave.
>
> (al-Shaykh, 1992, 183–184)

In the passage, the image that both characters draw on to represent the other is transcultural: this emerges, for example, from the use of the expression "Marilyn Monroe al-ṣaḥrāʾ" (the Marylin Monroe of the desert; al-Shaykh, 1988, 139), combining an icon of American culture with a desert setting. Then a series of elements typical of a Bedouin setting are added and convey the idea of a mythical, ahistorical place, like "al-ṣaḥrāʾ bi-lā abwāb" (the desert without doors), "al-raml" (the sand), "al-wāḥa" (the oasis), "khiyam" (tent) (al-Shaykh, 1988, 139).

Muʿādh's "instrumental" purpose manifests itself, unequivocally, when, having regained her lover's attention, Suzanne tires of him. Even when she discovers that he is seriously ill with syphilis, she disappears and launches into a series of other affairs with men she meets by chance. When her husband's company goes bankrupt and Suzanne has to return to Texas, her reaction is one of desperation because she knows that once back in the United States that renewed sensation of becoming visible again will vanish:

> I was like a deposed beauty queen: the jury had turned on me and replaced me with a new queen, dragging off the crown, robe and shoes, wiping away the make-up and taking the sceptre from my hand, tearing the smile off my lips and even the memory of the past happiness out of my heart. [...] Going back to America was going back to being a speck among the millions, while here I felt aware of my importance every minute of the day; if I just said good morning in Arabic everybody praised me. What does a woman in her forties do in a country swarming with others like her when she's been used to being the one and only? Who'd look at a fat woman in her forties with a lisp which made her hard to understand? Who'd call her on the phone except someone who'd dialled a wrong number? In my mind was an image of my telephone ringing all the time irrespective of the hour, transmitting their crazy longing to me. I was an oasis, green and sparkling in this great drought. [...] I could picture exactly what was going to become of me: in the car on the way to the airport I would revert to being a woman with rather a round face, hair hanging on a podgy neck, two fat arms, slack breasts and a stomach protruding over two short fat legs.
>
> (al-Shaykh, 1992, 233–234)

The special position held by Suzanne in the Gulf depends precisely on her status as "expat", thanks to the transcultural identity she has assumed. Once back in her homeland, Suzanne will return to a condition of anonymity. Conversely, Suhā is unable to accept the contradictions of the place that she deems to have nothing exotic about it, and she decides to return to Lebanon with her son:

> I craned my neck, looking down. I could see the high walls around the town protecting it from the horrors of the sand. The desert came into view, looking as it had done the first time I saw it: sand and palm trees, a way of life that revolved around human beings without possessions or skills, who had to rely on their imaginations to contrive a way of making their hearts beat faster or even to keep them at a normal pace; to search unaided for a hidden gleam of light, and to live with two seasons a year instead of four.
>
> (al-Shaykh, 1992, 279–280)

Once again, space is characterized by a violent clash between urbanization and the desert, as shown by the co-presence of terms linked to the city architecture "sūr shāhiq" (high walls) that serve to protect it from "al-rimāl al-mukhīfa" (frightening sands) (al-Shaykh, 1988, 81–82). This contradiction organizing the space is reflected in the identity of the leading character, who feels, at one and the same time, to be assaulted by the violence of the desert but unable to accept the artificiality of the unscrupulous urbanization and decides, as a consequence, to return to her homeland. This impossibility of finding one's true place in the contradictory society of the Gulf also affects the character of Nūr.

Instead, in *This Is London, My Dear*, despite the difficulties, the characters manage to find their own place in the metropolis, without having to renounce their origins in so doing. As Fischer explains:

> Al-Shaykh's characters manage to resist as they struggle against both the gendered and classed relations that have followed them from the Middle East and the orientalizing and economically marginalizing impulses of the imperial city. In *This is London, my dear*, Amira, Lamis, and particularly Samir find ways, which would not be available to them at "home," of constituting hybrid identities, which resist societal norms.
>
> (Fischer, 2004, 117)

In contrast to Fischer's claims, in our opinion, the character who, more than any other, finds that London is the place where she can fully express her subjectivity is Lamīs. Her path towards subjectivation occurs precisely through the interaction with space. When she is still married to her husband, she is almost completely barred from having access to the outside space of the city. Following her divorce, the woman experiences a sensation of displacement and anguish, but her desire to finally be able to discover the city where she lives leads her to leave her flat, using a taxi as a sort of buffer between the inside and outside world. In her analysis, Fischer clearly defines the process of change undergone by Lamīs's identity in her interaction with space:

> Like the flat she lives in, the taxi insulates her from direct interaction with London spaces. She tries to connect by taking English lessons to eliminate her Arabic accent and by distancing herself from her Middle Eastern friends as she enters the relationship with Nicholas. When she goes out, she does not experience herself as firmly located in space. Her sense of displacement is clear when she goes to the theater in the Strand and watches herself meeting Nicholas in the foyer and, once inside, finds herself watching "two plays, one on the stage, and the other acted out in her mind" (p. 179). Only when she is able to reconcile this split vision, which comes from her experience of displacement, is Lamis able to feel a sense of belonging in London and in the world, as well as within herself. This shift in perspective is enacted symbolically at the end of the novel when she finally convinces the officials at the British Telecom.
>
> (Fischer, 2004, 114–115)

Her ascent of the British Telecom tower, a building that the woman usually only sees from the window of her flat, represents the overcoming of the spatial confines between inside and outside and the chance to take possession symbolically of London by means of an all-encompassing view from above. The reconciliation with the space of the city is interrelated with the character's reconciliation with her own identity as she overcomes the division between her Iraqi and her London affiliation, in order to finally accept the fluidity of her transcultural identity. Only after this realization will Lamīs leave for Oman to look for Nicholas, and the novels closes with an open ending in which the woman is on a plane – once again an in-between, transnational space – just as in the incipit. Thus, al-Shaykh seems to leave a possibility for their relationship to continue. As a symbolic conclusion to the woman's process of identity change, her passport reappears, an element that is also present in the novel's incipit. At the beginning of the story, Lamīs loses her passport on the plane, and it is returned to her by Nicholas; in contrast, at the end of the book, the passport appears firmly in the woman's hands, as if she has at last re-found her identity and is no longer afraid to declare it. As Al-Samman explains about this novel:

> Unlike other diasporic narratives that introduced characters yearning to return to their homelands, these particular émigrés are settled physically in the diaspora but unsettled emotionally. They learn to negotiate the gains and losses of hyphenated identities, and to appreciate flexible citizenship, thereby forsaking homeland longings and engendering new belongings articulated through the "dialogic" relationship between roots and routes.
>
> (Al-Samman, 2015, 197)

Conclusion

Through the complex universe of the characters in these two novels, al-Shaykh joins the narrative production setting the experience of migration in a global and cosmopolitan context. The paths to identity followed by the characters contribute towards challenging "past definitions of collective and individual identities as essentially monocultural" and should, instead, be read in the light of the concept of transculturality, which "has often been adopted to describe the diverse and productive reality of processes of identity-formation that take place at cultural interfaces" (Nordin et al., 2013, ix). Therefore, the theme of transcultural identities proves to be central to these works and involves almost all the characters.

Al-Shaykh overcomes the idealization of Europe, which still distinguishes a part of the Arab literary production of the 20th century, in order to focus on two realities, the cities of the Gulf and that of London, which are characterized by what Nyman, quoting Ulrich Beck, defines as "'cosmopolitanism from below' (Beck, 2006, 103), where cultural encounters are part of the normal life of the contemporary world, rather than limited to the life of the globetrotting cosmopolitan elite" (Nyman, 2017, 3–4). The paths to identity of the characters in *The Gazelle's Musk* and *This Is London, My Dear* allow us to go beyond the concept of "cultural diversity", which Bhabha understands as "the representation of a radical rhetoric of the separation of totalized cultures that live unsullied by the intertextuality of their historical locations, safe in the Utopianism of a mythic memory of a unique collective identity" (Bhabha, 1994, 34).

The two spatial dimensions at the centre of *The Gazelle's Musk* and *This Is London, My Dear* are characterized by a strong mobility that challenges nationalisms and fixed identities, within narrations that demonstrate a multiple consciousness in terms of language, culture and religion. However, al-Shaykh does not only offer an idealized representation of the migratory experience and hybridity, solely in terms of an enrichment of identity; her narration "also contributes to the critique of such forms of postcolonial discourse that celebrate them as unproblematic ways of countering hierarchies and hegemonies" (Nyman, 2017, 1). This aspect emerges, above all, in *The Gazelle's Musk*, which is set in a reality where mobility – spatial, economic and of class – is often only apparent, being far more strictly regulated than in London, where deeply rooted forms of inequality linked to the capitalist system do exist but prove not to be as insurmountable as in the Gulf.

Notes

1 The novel has been translated into English under the title *Women of Sand and Myrrh* (1992). For a feminist criticism of the translation in English, starting from the very title of the book, see Hartman (2012).
2 The novel has been translated into English under the title *Only in London* (2002).
3 A recent study of cosmopolitanism in the Arab world is that of Elsayed and Webb (2020).
4 From now on, we will adopt our English translation of the titles of the novels.
5 As Felix Lang explains, starting from the second half of the 1970s, many Lebanese writers reacted to the shock of the civil war by making it the main theme of their novels, so much so that some critics – including the writer Ilyās Khūrī – consider it to be a true reason for legitimizing the novel as a prestigious literary genre (Lang, 2015).
6 Other sources give the author's date of birth as 1945.
7 Ḥ. Al-Shaykh (2005).
8 On this matter, see the study by Adams (2001).
9 For an analysis of the relationship between identity, home and family in the novel, reference should be made to Hout (2003).
10 On this point, please note the study by Fischer (2004), which deals precisely with the experience of migration towards the metropolis in the novel, and that of Boustani (2008), which analyses the representation of London as a land of refuge.
11 As far as the change in the area is concerned, following the arrival of the petrodollars, see, by way of an example, the study by Peterson (2016).

12 Reference here is to the concept of "dispossession" developed by Judith Butler and Athena Athanasiou, who define it as: "a term that marks the limits of self-sufficiency and that establishes us as relational and interdependent beings. Yet dispossession is precisely what happens when populations lose their land, their citizenship, their means of livelihood, and become subject to military and legal violence. We oppose this latter form of dispossession because it is both forcible and privative. In the first sense, we are dispossessed of ourselves by virtue of some kind of contact with another, by virtue of being moved and even surprised or disconcerted by that encounter with alterity. The experience itself is not simply episodic, but can and does reveal one basis of relationality – we do not simply move ourselves, but are ourselves moved by what is outside us, by others, but also by whatever "outside" resides in us" (Butler & Athanasiou, 2013, 3).

13 All the quotations have been taken from the English translation of the novel.

14 This aspect has been analysed by Guardi (2018) and El-Ariss (2013).

15 All the quotations are taken from the English translation of the novel.

References

Adams, A.M. (2001) Writing Self, Writing Nation: Imagined Geographies in the Fiction of Hanan al-Shaykh. *Tulsa Studies in Women's Literature*, 20(2), 201–216.

El-Ariss, T. (2013) Majnun Strikes Back: Crossings of Madness and Homosexuality in Contemporary Arabic Literature. *International Journal of Middle Eastern Studies*, 45, 293–312.

Baʿalbakī, L. [1958] (2010) *Anā aḥyā*. Beirut: Dār al-ādāb.

Beck, U. (2006) *The Cosmopolitan Vision*. Cambridge: Polity.

Bhabha, H. (1984) Of Mimicry and Man: The Ambivalence of Colonial Discourse. *October*, 28, 125–133.

Bhabha, H. (1994) *The Location of Culture*. London: Routledge.

Boustani, S. (2008) Terre d'exil, espace d'une identité en crise: essai sur le roman *Innahā London yā ʿazīzī* (*Londres mon amour*) de Hanan aš-Šayh. *Asiatische Studien*, 62, 1107–1123.

Butler, J. (2004) *Undoing Gender*. New York and London: Routledge.

Butler, J., Athanasiou, A. (2013) *Dispossession: The Performative in the Political*. Cambridge: Polity.

cooke, m. (1987) *War's Other Voices: Women Writers on the Lebanese Civil War*. Cambridge: Cambridge University Press.

Elsayed, H., Webb, A.K. (2020) Cosmopolitanism in the Arab World: Developments, Continuities and Changes Since the Arab Spring. *Middle East Journal of Culture and Communication*, 13, 123–130.

Fischer, S.A. (2004) Women Writers, Global Migration, and the City: Joan Riley's *Waiting in the Twilight* and Hanan Al-Shaykh's *Only in London*. *Tulsa Studies in Women's Literature*, 23(1), 107–120.

Guardi, J. (2018) Superare i confini. Trasgressione e travestimento in Ḥanān Al-Šayḫ *Innahā Lundun yā ʿazīzī*. *DEP Deportate, esuli, profughe*, 38, 123–136.

Hartman, M. (2012) Gender, Genre, and the (Missing) Gazelle: Arab Women Writers and the Politics of Translation. *Feminist Studies*, 38(1), 17–49.

Hassan, W.S. (ed.) (2017) *The Oxford Handbook of Arab Novelistic Tradition*. Oxford: Oxford University Press.

Hout, S. (2003) Going the Extra Mile: Redefining Identity, Home, and Family in Hanan al-Shaykh's *Only in London*. *Studies in the Humanities*, 30, 29–45.

Lang, F. (2015) *The Lebanese Post-Civil War Novel. Memory, Trauma and Capital*. London: Palgrave Macmillan.

Nordin, I.G., Hansen, J., Llena, C.Z. (eds) (2013) *Transcultural Identities in Contemporary Literature*. Amsterdam: Rodopi.

Nyman, J. (2009) *Home, Identity, and Mobility in Contemporary Diasporic Fiction*. Amsterdam: Rodopi.

Nyman, J. (2017) *Displacement, Memory, and Travel in Contemporary Migrant Writing*. Leiden: Brill.

Paynter, E. (2018) The Liminal Lives of Europe's Transit Migrants. *Contexts*, 17(2), 40–45.

Peterson, J.E. (ed.) (2016) *The Emergence of the Gulf States: Studies in Modern History*. London: Bloomsbury Academic.

Al-Samman, H. (2015) *Anxiety of Erasure: Trauma, Authorship, and the Diaspora in Arab Women's Writings*. New York: Syracuse University Press.

Sellman, J. (2018) A Global Postcolonial: Contemporary Arabic Literature of Migration to Europe. *Journal of Postcolonial Writing*, 54(6), 751–765.

Al-Shaykh, Ḥ. (1970) *Intiḥār rajul mayyit*. Beirut: Dār al-ādāb.

Al-Shaykh, Ḥ. (1988) *Misk al-ghazāl*. Beirut: Dār al-ādāb.

Al-Shaykh, Ḥ. [1988] (1992) *Women of Sand and Myrrh*. Translated by C. Cobham [e-book, Kindle edition]. New York: Anchor Books.

Al-Shaykh, Ḥ. (2001) *Innahā London yā ʿazīzī*. Beirut: Dār al-ādāb.

Al-Shaykh, Ḥ. [2001] (2002) *Only in London*. Translated by C. Cobham [e-book, Kindle edition]. New York: Anchor Books.

Al-Shaykh, Ḥ. (2005) *Ḥikāyatī sharḥun yaṭūl*. Beirut: Dār al-ādāb.

Wannūs, S. [1994] (2005) *Ṭuqūs al-ishārāt wa-l-taḥawwulāt*. Beirut: Dār al-ādāb.

3 The Body and the Migrating Subject in the Gulf

Daqq al-ṭabūl by Muḥammad al-Bisāṭī

Cristina Dozio

Introduction

The novel *Daqq al-ṭabūl* (Drumbeat, 2005) by the Egyptian Muḥammad al-Bisāṭī (1937–2012) starts with a challenging premise: the native population of a nameless Emirate is sent to France when the national football team qualifies for the World Cup, leaving the country in the hands of the labor migrants.[1] This unexpected, almost surreal event subverts the main tropes of migrant literature, since it is not the migrants who travel to reach their destination or return home, but the privileged citizens who leave their homes, enhancing self-discovery. Their absence opens a time window to explore the status of migrant workers, their mutual relations, and their interaction with the local population. Furthermore, this event makes it possible to question sexuality and gender relations, which are otherwise controlled by the local authorities and social norms. Even though no gender revolution happens, this novel stages some models of masculinity and femininity, embodying the disparity of resources that causes migration in a globalized context.

In these circumstances, the Gulf states have been a top destination for foreign workers from the neighboring Arab and Asian countries since the discovery of oil in the 1950s.[2] Lacking a local workforce, the Gulf states have been employing a large expatriate labor force in various sectors of the economy, government bureaucracy, and domestic work (Babar, 2017; IOM, 2004; Khalaf et al., 2015). Despite the sponsorship system (*kafāla*), this migration is not exempt of abuses and illegal recruitment. The presence of migrants is particularly impressive in the United Arab Emirates (UAE), where the citizens constitute less than 20% of the total population, which is around 9.4 million (UN DESA, 2017).

The presence of multicultural groups of expatriates raises some issues about the literary representation of the Self and the Other addressed, for instance, by the Kuwaiti writer Saʿūd al-Sanʿūsī (b. 1981) in *Sāq al-bāmbū* (The Bamboo Stalk, 2013). Awarded the International Prize for Arabic Fiction (IPAF), this novel has gained international recognition and has been examined for its thematic innovation: it follows the story of José/ʿĪsā, the son of a Kuwaiti citizen and a Filipino maid, who tries to find his place in the

DOI: 10.4324/9780429027338-4

world, traveling from the Philippines to Kuwait. In his analysis of this tale of repatriation, Elayyan suggests that the encounter with the Other – who is already part of the Kuwaiti society – allows the critical depiction of social contradictions alongside the construction of the national identity:

> Gulf people are minorities in their own countries. Thanks to oil, the prosperity and opportunity have attracted millions of people to the region, with the promise of riches and quick money. Although Gulf citizens have the lion's share of the wealth, they have to live with the fact of multiculturalism in many contexts. Even in their homes, they are met with foreign faces, languages, and religions. I argue that the Gulf writers have found realism as a suitable literary technique to make sense of diversity. Faced with the potential danger of melting in the mix, many Gulf writers choose realism as a way of capturing the details of their daily lives, of controlling the narrative through the reliable voice of the narrator.
>
> (Elayyan, 2016, 88)

Starting from *Sāq al-bāmbū*, it would be interesting to further explore the representation of migration and multiculturalism in Gulf literature (Michalak-Pikulska, 2012; Tijani, 2009; Tijani, 2014), which nevertheless goes beyond the scope of this chapter.

Egypt in the Gulf, the Gulf in Egypt

The other side of the coin – equally understudied so far – is represented by tales of expatriation to the Gulf. To better contextualize al-Bisāṭī's novel, it is worth mentioning some Egyptian novels that are representative of this narrative trend over the decades, a literary representation that often originates from the author's personal experience.[3] A classic in this respect is *al-Balda al-ukhrā* (The Other Place, 1990) by Ibrāhīm ʿAbd al-Majīd (b. 1946), awarded the Naguib Mahfouz Medal for Literature in 1996. Partly based on the author's experience in Saudi Arabia, it follows an Egyptian teacher of English traveling to the wealthy monarchy to economically help his family; there he experiences alienation and has some hallucinated encounters with the local and expatriate characters, before going back home when his mother dies. Elayyan (2016) argues that *al-Balda al-ukhrā* harshly criticizes the political and economic policies after the end of pan-Arabism by staging the clash between the protagonist's expectations, fueled by Arab brotherhood, and the treatment of expat workers who cannot but compare their condition with the privileges granted to European and American expats. Besides the negative depiction of the oil economy's impact on the Saudi society, Said (2004) and Mikhail (1998) highlight the protagonist's alienation, a recurrent trope in migration tales but also in the experience of those intellectuals feeling estranged in their own society (*istighrāb*). While Mikhail sees the meta-textual references to writing as the only way out, Said interviews ʿAbd al-Majīd about this feeling of estrangement:

> Abdel Meguid states in a personal interview on December 1, 2004, that the setting of his novel, the city of Tabuk in Saudi Arabia, stands for an "Eldorado," a city of gold. Like Eliot's "Unreal City," Tabuk is portrayed as a place that has everything and "nothing," a city where human values are replaced by market values, and relationships are sacrificed for concept of material profit and loss. The setting is, therefore, only a domain for presenting the idea of a "paradise lost," a place that promises golden dreams yet reveals itself in a crude nightmarish reality. Abdel Meguid asserts that since the main theme the novel deals with is a universal issue, that is "the alienation of the individual in modern times, then the events can take place anywhere in the world, not necessarily in Saudi Arabia" (personal interview).
>
> (Said, 2004, 2)

As regards the impact of Gulf migration on the Egyptian society, several novels mention its consequences on social practices and family relations. In his vivid portrait of post-Nasserist Egypt, *Dhāt* (Zaat, 1998 [1992]), Ṣunʿ Allāh Ibrāhīm (b. 1937) relates various experiences of migration to the West and the Gulf. Seeing the benefits of those who come back, the protagonist couple dreams of traveling to the Gulf to improve its conditions. However, they seem unaware of the consequences of this economic interdependency, revealed by an ironic game of intertextuality: the newspaper clips expose the financial speculation on the global market involving the Gulf, while the main character Dhāt pays the price in her daily life, marked by an explosion of consumerism and Islamization. Another reference to this migration wave is found in *al-Fāʿil* (A Dog With No Tail, 2008) by Ḥamdī Abū Julayyil (b. 1967). This tale of internal displacement, from a Bedouin village to the city, includes a letter sent to the protagonist by a relative who lives in Bahrain, explaining how to enter the country and find a job there. Moreover, the apartment where the laborers temporarily live is owned by someone who bought it with the money saved in ten years in Saudi Arabia.

To give another example, ʿAlāʾ al-Aswānī (b. 1957) mentions Gulf migration in his latest novel, *Jumhūriyya ka-anna* (The Republic of False Truths, 2018). Even though the story focuses on the 2011 uprisings, the personality of one of the female characters, Asmāʾ, is strongly marked by her father's work migration. She feels that she has grown up without a father, who nevertheless exerts his authority when she reaches the marriageable age. Her personal struggles against wearing the veil, marrying someone she has nothing in common with, and accepting a job in the Gulf reinforce her fight for justice in her own country. In line with the author's construction of the national community as emerged from his previous novels, Asmāʾ leaves her country only when all the red lines have been trespassed, and she finds a refuge at her uncle's place in England.

While Asmāʾ misses her father, *Sījāra sābiʿa* (Cigarette Number Seven, 2012) by Dunyā Kamāl elaborates on the mother's absence. This novel also depicts the youth's participation in Tahrir Square with the intimate tone of a memoir. Central is the protagonist's relationship with her father, elaborated in opposition to the less-frequently mentioned mother, who moved to the Gulf when her daughter was only a child and died when the girl was 14. In a passage about the uprisings, the protagonist views her personal experience as a common trait of the Egyptian youth of her social milieu, a marker of common identity:

> As for me, I tended toward pessimism. When I thought about things rationally, I found myself on the same wavelength as Galal. I could see promising signs. But when I thought about "us" as examples of the people who live in this country, I found us lacking. We weren't able to see anything through. We and most of those around us in the square belonged to a social class that didn't really have to work for anything. I think that if we had done a survey of everyone in the square, we would have found that the majority had parents who had worked in the Gulf in the seventies, during the ugly days of open-door economic policies, only for the sake of returning with a small car, an apartment in the suburbs, and a few gadgets. We, their children, didn't have to work for anything. Our lives were a mediocre compromise. Our demands were a mediocre compromise. We were mediocre at our jobs. We were not at the top of the ladder, like the big shots that my father often included in the bastards category, but neither did we have to struggle to put food on the table like those who might as well be living on a different planet – those whom we discussed with compassion, then forgot as we smoked our imported cigarettes.
>
> (Kamal, 2017, 127–128)

This quotation remarks how Arab migration to the Gulf affected a whole generation of migrants and also those who remained, especially their families and children. Over the decades and the subsequent generations, leaving one's country elicits a sense of disbelief towards the institutions which had already started after the 1967 crisis in the pan-Arab world. Given this background, the next sections examine how *Daqq al-ṭabūl* by al-Bisāṭī contributes to Egyptian contemporary literature of migration to the Gulf by shaping the migrant's identity in the Arab and globalized context. Identity is explored on several levels, such as the national identity of the receiving society, the alienated identity of migrants, and the identity of outcasts who develop cross-national solidarity. The novel's thematic and narrative strategies are examined through close textual analysis, focusing on the multicultural community of outsiders in a transnational space and the impact of displacement on the body. In this account, storytelling emerges as a survival strategy and re-appropriation of the right to speak.

(Im)mobility

The departure from the homeland was experienced by the author in the first place. Al-Bisāṭī was born in 1937 in a Nile Delta village overlooking Lake Manzala, graduated from Cairo University, and worked as a civil servant while pursuing his literary career. Belonging to the sixties generation (Ramadan, 2012), he started publishing short stories in *al-Masāʾ*, *al-Kātib*, *al-Majalla*, and *Jālīrī 68*. A specialist of this genre, he is also known for his novels, some of which were translated into English: *Ṣakhab al-buḥayra* (Clamor of the Lake, 1994) received the Egyptian State Incentive Award, while *Jawʿ* (Hunger, 2007) was shortlisted for IPAF.[4] Despite his long-lasting presence in Cairo, the village has been the setting of most of his writings. Apparently diverting from the author's poetics, *Daqq al-ṭabūl* confirms his exploration of the physical and emotional effects of a certain environment, his interest for social justice and marginal communities rendered with a poetic prose (Allen, 2000; Dawood, 1999). Furthermore, the author spent some time in Saudi Arabia, the UAE, Iraq, and Kuwait (Johnson-Davies, 2010, 73; Lindsey, 2010), but this is not reported as a central experience in his life.

As in most of his short stories, the first-person anonymous narrator of *Daqq al-ṭabūl* is a careful, detached observer of his environment. He is an Egyptian who has been living in the unnamed Emirate for five years, working as a driver for Abū ʿĀmir. He lives in his master's villa with other domestic workers and entails a slightly senior position because of his intimacy with the boss, whom he also escorts in his trips to Paris. These trips, aimed at pure entertainment, highlight the mobility of Emirati citizens and their capacity of adaptation to enjoy a Western lifestyle:

> Abu Amer is a completely different person in Paris. He becomes smooth and dapper: off goes the long, white thawb and on comes the tailored suit, a flashy tie, and a matching handkerchief in the breast pocket of his jacket. He exudes a heavy perfume, and his hair – newly coiffed in a fashionable style – shines slightly.
>
> (El-Bisatie, 2010, 8)

This mobility is confirmed by the main event in the plot when the Emir orders that all citizens should travel to France to support the football national team in the World Cup finals. The government will fully cover the travel and accommodation costs in this sort of sporting mass-pilgrimage. This reversal of the migration trajectory offers an innovative perspective to address "the strangeness of this symbiotic and unequal relationship between foreign labor and wealthy locals" (Lindsey, 2010). Initially, the narrator imagines endless possibilities for the expat workers who might seize power:

> I waited at the airport until the last flock of airplanes took off. Abu Amer and his family had left for France. I drove back to town.
>
> The highway was deserted. As I approached the outskirts of the city a thought occurred to me that made me laugh. The whole country was now in the hands of the foreign workers. If they took over the Emirate, closed the ports, and broadcast an impassioned message to the world demanding recognition for their new regime, on the grounds that everything in the country was built with their toil and sweat, they could well receive some international recognition.
>
> (El-Bisatie, 2010, 15)

Describing this scenario, he recalls a story from a neighboring Emirate whose prince deposed his ruling father when he was abroad for medical treatment. This is the only fleeting political reference in the novel. Nevertheless, as Darrāj (2005) notes in his review,[5] the master's absence does not differ from their presence because the exploitation mechanisms are deeply rooted. This immobility is conveyed by the narrator's description of the transnational community of workers before and after the big sporting event. In both cases he parades the different nationalities, first for their professional qualities and then for their clothes, and describes music and dance performances during the celebrations. He does not suggest a deep interaction between these communities but rather a juxtaposition of anonymous participants in a colorful street parade:

> We foreign workers are a hodgepodge of different nationalities. Most are from the Philippines, probably because of their reputation for being fast serious workers. Perhaps, too, because they are small and compact and so do not take up much room. Somehow this makes their Emirati employers feel more comfortable when dealing with them.
>
> The Indians crammed themselves into one part of the old town. They took over the entire quarter. The other nationalities respected their communal urge and so did not try to move in on them. The Pakistanis took over an adjacent quarter, while the Arabs and other foreigners dispersed themselves over other parts of the city. Despite their historic animosity, the Indians and Pakistanis socialize together frequently and visit the same nightspots in each other's quarters. But, every time tensions mount between India and Pakistan and their respective armies amass along their borders, the exchange of family visits ceases, and not so much as a "hello" passes between the two sides.
>
> (El-Bisatie, 2010, 1–2)

> It was a medley of different nationalities – Pakistanis, Indians, Filipinos, Sudanese, Arabs – most in their native dress, carrying Emirati flags and pictures of the Emirati soccer team and waving and cheering. I was unable to make out the words to many of their songs and chants. The parading revelers kept spaces clear for groups of dancers. A troupe of Sudanese passed by, their white jallabiyas billowing and huge turbans bobbing as they swayed back and forth, clapping to the rhythm of beating drums. The Indians followed, their procession led by a row of men in knee-length tunics, thick mustaches greased and coiled, and jewels glittering in their colorful turbans. They held themselves erect, chests puffed out as they marched with their arms interlocked, as though acting as a dam to stem the gush of the throng.
>
> (El-Bisatie, 2010, 43–44)[6]

The formation of a transnational community is gradual, starting from the private space of the villas until the appropriation of public spaces. Focusing on domestic workers, the novel deals with the most subservient category of employees, who enjoy little freedom of movement due to their employers' close control. Once this control is lifted, the migrants replace the local population firstly in their private spaces by swimming in the pool, having large communal lunches in the garden, and even thinking of sleeping in their beds.[7] The narrator gets to know his co-workers, three Filipinos and five Pakistani maids, and insists that no superiority should be attributed to him as an Arab (El-Bisatie, 2010, 19 and 25). This solidarity leads to reuniting a Pakistani maid with her husband as well as arranging the celebrations in the amusement park and the stadium.

The migrants replace the Emirati citizens also in their support to the football team as if it was their national team. The football team, a national symbol, attracts the hopes of non-nationals that this unique occasion will last as long as possible. This self-interested support involves even religion, a key aspect of the Gulf societies that has an impact on the larger Muslim community. The narrator's irony unmasks the opportunistic use of religion, while presenting it as a gluing factor for migrants: worshippers of all nationalities try to persuade the imam to pray for the defeat of Morocco, a Muslim country, against Portugal since it is the only chance to qualify to the next round (El-Bisatie, 2010, 102–103).

This apparent fixity is reinforced by the representation of space. While the heat and sandstorms convey a gloomy atmosphere in *al-Balda al-ukhrā* by ʿAbd al-Majīd (1990), *Daqq al-ṭabūl* barely mentions the desert and oil.[8] This novel opens with a brief description of the urban changes brought about by the discovery of oil, as if everything happened overnight. In this transformation, the old town acquires multiple meanings for the different sectors of the population: it preserves the cultural heritage for Emirati citizens who postpone its demolition and is a meeting place for live-in servants and a dwelling place for foreign workers. While *al-Balda al-ukhrā* offers detailed descriptions of the working and dwelling places to convey the protagonist's feelings, *Daqq al-ṭabūl* employs a matter-of-fact tone and conciseness:

> They say that after oil was discovered and the building boom began, there was a debate over whether to raze the old town. The major objection was that many people would want to pay the occasional visit to their ancestral homes and the pastures of their youth. Ultimately, it was decided to let the old quarters stand, renovate them in a manner that preserved their historic character and then reconsider tearing them down after a generation or two. Therefore, you can still see some antique lamps hanging on the street corners, crowns of palm trees peering out from above interior courtyards, and the sloping pigeon cotes on the rooftops with those little round windows high up on their walls, no bigger than peepholes.
>
> Foreign workers generally settled in the old town because the rents were cheap. Also, conditions were such that they could live at ease amid their familiar din.
>
> (El-Bisatie, 2010, 3)

Space is also the emblem of social control, as exemplified by the episode of the unattended shop during the first football match, where customers are asked to leave the money for their purchases. A Syrian customer first praises the Emiratis' trust, but then remarks that nobody would dare stealing because hidden cameras are everywhere. The narrator relates this episode with prison administration, which is formally in the hands of the Emiratis but is administered by Indian officers. During the World Cup, the detainees charged with petty crimes are released provided that they report for roll call every morning.[9] However, routine and fear are so strong that these criminals remain in the prison, simply leaving their cells during the day. This unexperienced freedom is an allegory of the slave-like condition of many workers, who nevertheless are grateful to their employers:

> I passed by the police station on my way to the parade. The Indian officer in charge was in his official uniform: dark green with yellow stripes on the epaulets. He was just inside the door, standing at attention, his twirled mustache glistening with grease and his gun hanging in its holster at the side. The prisoners were back behind bars. Their arms reached through the windows waving miniature national flags.
>
> (El-Bisatie, 2010, 122)

Some of al-Bisāṭī's short stories are set in prison, the most famous being *Ḥadīth min al-ṭābiq al-thālith* (A Conversation From the Third Floor, 1998). In this short story and the novel under scrutiny, the author does not insist on crime but rather focuses on the body to express one's feelings. Given the relevance of the body in the author's oeuvre, it is examined as the site of nostalgia and social control in the characters' displacement.

Body and Gender Relations

Sāq al-bāmbū and *al-Balda al-ukhrā* stage the social control over sexuality in the Gulf societies from the internal and external perspective respectively. The former depicts the authority of the old generation over marriage, thus causing a conflict between the young characters' personal aspirations and social constraints. In this respect, Elayyan notes that: "The power of policing sexuality and promiscuity comes in different shapes such as economic sanctions (inheritance law), shaming, and the loss of benefits for those who dare to challenge the social boundaries" (Elayyan, 2016, 90). Shaming is the punishment depicted in a very touching scene of *al-Balda al-ukhrā* in which the protagonist sees for the first time Waḍḥa, a Saudi student accused of promiscuity with a Yemeni boy. The main character compares her dignity with the indifference of the male audience and later falls in love with her.

In *Daqq al-ṭabūl*, control over sexuality in the domestic space is exerted by the house's mistress, who imposes strict working conditions to her maids. For example, Umm ʿĀmir does not allow them to take holidays and visit their families because she always needs them (El-Bisatie, 2010, 23–24), whereas many Emirati families leave for European shores in summer (El-Bisatie, 2010, 11). Another requirement for getting the job is being single. During the Emiratis' absence, the Pakistani Rishim confesses that she had lied about her marriage and finally can meet her husband who recently got a contract in the country. The co-workers arrange for them to meet discreetly, but the husband seems reluctant and refuses to spend the night in their villa. Once again, subversion is limited by the self-imposed control for fear of losing the job, prioritizing the economic interests over one's feelings. The couple finds a compromise, a secret deal expressed through their gestures:

> I turned my attention to Rishim. She hadn't even noticed me. Following the direction of her gaze I spotted her husband sitting among the other men. The two were exchanging wordless messages with their eyes. A secret smile played on her lips as she offered pieces of quail to the men, or ladled out rice mixed with nuts and raisins. As she held out the bottle of sauce to her husband, another man's arm reached out to grab it, but her eyes remained fixed on her husband's. They must have reached some understanding: they'd continue to keep their marriage hidden and only meet in the presence of others. It was too dangerous to advertise this secret.
>
> (El-Bisatie, 2010, 99–100)

The husband's preoccupations are extended to all the male workforce since the fear of losing their job has emasculated them. The narrator explains that he has learned to repress his lust for fear of whistleblowing and expulsion, an over-present punishment also in *al-Balda al-ukhrā*. In the following passage, he relates his self-imposed discipline with idioms referring to parts of the body, fire, and trespassing a threshold:

> I'd heard too many stories to drop my guard: fifty lashes in a public flogging and expulsion, without collecting one's outstanding pay or receiving the end-of-service bonus stipulated in the contract. How many of such cases had there been during my five years here? Seven involving Arab workers. Their assignations had been arranged so cautiously that it was a wonder they could ever have been exposed. The walls must have had ears *[ka-anna hunāka ʿuyūn tarṣud]*. [...] The more I thought about this the greater my conviction grew that eyes were everywhere [*bi-wujūd ʿuyūn*]. The seven cases had a major element in common. They all involved relatively new arrivals; they had been in the Emirate for no more than a few months. Their blood was still warm [*Dammu-hum lā yazāl sākhin*]; they had not yet made the adjustments the rest of us had. Somewhere along the line in my five years here I had shut a door – "the door that lets in the wind," as we say back home [*ka-annanī aghlaqtu bāb taʾtī min-hu al-rīḥ*]. Or maybe the door simply shut by itself. Nothing excites me anymore. Not a beautiful body strutting its hips – and there's no shortage of that here. Not a pair of nicely rounded legs, their smooth glowing skin peaking from beneath a skirt as they swing into a car. I avert my eyes and pick up my pace. I notice nothing.
>
> ... Such were the thoughts that came to mind again and again upon hearing of each of those seven cases, which seemed to occur at three- or four-month intervals. "They're right," I'd think. "The guy who does it with some working girl today could do it with an Emirati woman tomorrow. Once you get used to something it's hard to stop." And so I would say to others, sometimes adding the caution, "The doors of temptation once opened..." [*bāb al-jaḥīm law futiḥa*] along with the advice: "It's easy. All you have to do is resolve to forget, and you'll find you've forgotten. Dead coals don't glow and don't burn those who touch them [*Wa-l-jamarāt al-muṭfaʾa lā wahaj la-hā wa-lā talsaʿ man yalmisu-hā*]."
>
> (El-Bisatie, 2010, 31–33)

The narrator tolerates this privation by dreaming about his wife and recalling the only time he visited her. He postponed going on holiday because he was afraid of impotence, until his boss arranged his vacation, another example of the master's control over every aspect of their worker's life despite his good intentions, in this case. As soon as he arrived home, his virility was restored, compensating all the privations caused by migration. While nostalgia is almost unexpressed in this novel, the narrator misses only his wife and Egyptian food, which might be linked by the concept of appetite. He also experiences nostalgia with one of the five senses when, on the night of the first football match, he falls asleep hearing the sound of finger cymbals that can be found only in rural Egypt, dreams of his wife, but is woken up by the sound of cleaning vehicles.

While this is the narrator's solution, the other transnational workers project their sexual desire on the body of the African, a character who exhibits his virility in a café in the old town in exchange for money. He is the only one to have escaped the curse (*laʿna*),[10] apparently because the drums never stop beating in his head; this episode gives the novel its title. While Lindsey (2010) argues that the curse represents the vitality drained out of the broken-down migrant workers, Lynx-Qualey (2010) suggests that the struggle with impotence does not have the same evocative force as in *Waqāʾiʿ ḥārat al-Zaʿfarānī* (The Zafarani Files, 1976) by Jamāl al-Ghīṭānī (1945–2015). This commodification of the body confirms the narrator's detachment since he is led there by his Filipino colleagues and does not make any commentary after the show. On the other hand, this ritual encourages a certain degree of self-mockery among the Filipinos when talking about sex:

> "The beating of drums does all that? Maybe it's those male potency pills we've been hearing about," said another.
>
> "The curse is more powerful than those pills. Everyone here who's tried them has had no luck. I know, I'm one of them."
>
> "But why did you even bother?"
>
> "Just to see… And I didn't see."
>
> (El-Bisatie, 2010, 71)[11]

While this section has illustrated several forms of self- and socially imposed control on gender relations embodied by male and female migrants, the next section explores physical exploitation and how storytelling is the only way to claim one's rights.

Body and Storytelling

In her interesting exploration of the evolution of exile in modern Arabic literature, Sellman contrasts the modernist view of exile (*mawsim al-hijra*) with globalized forced migration (*mawsim al-tahjīr*). Applying postcolonial literary theory and border studies, she argues that

> these literary narratives [about undocumented crossings] centre on the violence that border-building practices enact on migrants' bodies and often draw on fantasy, different modalities of storytelling, and metaphors of wilderness to stage spaces outside citizenship.
>
> (Sellman, 2018, 752)

Even though *Daqq al-ṭabūl* is not a story of forced migration, the borders of class and gender segregation harm the migrants' bodies; in this literary representation, some migrants regain their right to speak through storytelling.

During the Emiratis' absence, the narrator meets Zāhiyya, an Egyptian maid or nanny (*al-miṣriyya al-dāda*) who lives in a neighboring villa. Two years earlier, she arranged through her co-workers for him to carry a suitcase to her husband and daughter when he was traveling back home, but they have never met in person, nor has he told her something from her family. At the beginning, he is enchanted by her gestures inviting him inside the villa and thinks that she is seducing him. He soon realizes that she wants to talk with someone from the same country, someone she can trust because he has met her family. One visit after the other, he understands the terrible secret she carries: her mistress encouraged her to sleep with the master to stop his other affairs and, when she got pregnant, they pretended that the newborn Sālim was the couple's baby.

Reviving women's storytelling to construct the migrant's subjectivity, this narrative thread highlights the effects of migration on gendered identities. In her study of Ilyās Khūrī's *Sīnālkūl* (2012), Censi (2016) explores the effects of the civil Lebanese war and its related migration on the quest for individual and collective identity embodied by different types of masculinity. Although Gulf migration is distantly related to wars, *Daqq al-ṭabūl* stages the effects of migration on the male bodies as illustrated so far: is impotence a personal choice or a social norm? Is it the price to pay for economic improvement? Conversely, Zāhiyya's story exemplifies the model of masculinity attached to the Gulf society: the patriarchal traditional model (Aghacy, 2009, 19–20),[12] based on strict socio-religious norms and a rigid hierarchy between genres. In this case, it applies to the husband, who affirms his virility by conquering Zāhiyya's body, and the wife, who imposes the oppressive social norms through her power, wealth, and opportunism. In fact, she is so fat (probably an allegory of consumerism) that her husband does not sleep with her, and they cannot have children. This kind of impotence leads her to appropriate her maid's body, especially when she seeks identification with her:[13]

> While we were having coffee she said, "Zahiya, you're part of me now. What goes for me goes for you. What I'd like to do, you can do. So when I ask you about him it's to make sure you're alright, because if you're alright, I'm alright. I can see from the look on your face that you're beginning to take a liking to him. In two or three days he'll come here and tell us that he's locked up the apartment in the suburbs, or sold it. He'll be the old Yasser, again. The Yasser I've always known. So tell me, what did he say to you last night?"
>
> (El-Bisatie, 2010, 96)

The mistress forces Zāhiyya to tell her everything about the sexual encounters and later about pregnancy, so that she can appropriate her stories and reach the ultimate degree of identification. Only during her absence can the subordinate subject regain her voice using the same technique of storytelling. As Lindsey (2010) remarks:

> There are obvious shades of Scheherazade in the way the story is told: the narrator visits, night after night, to hear it unfold. The details are not particularly realistic, but the narrative's intent is clearly allegorical, pointing to the way the servant is consumed and ultimately discarded by her masters. She makes a poignant figure, wandering about their house in their absence like a ghost, incapable even of telling her own story.

As in the *Arabian Nights*, the story unfolds night after night.[14] Every time the narrator visits Zāhiyya, he gets used to her rituals and enters into the meanderings of the house until he is led to the mistress's bedroom. When the maid takes her mistress's place, the social roles are reversed: she gradually moves from talking about Umm Sālim to telling her own story, while the narrator sits in the armchair where she used to sit. Hence, from being an observer, he becomes a listener. As it emerges from this account, the employer thinks that even storytelling can be commodified: Zāhiyya, in fact, was hired to keep the mistress company; she is as a *jalīsa*, as the contract says. Before leaving Egypt, she reads all kinds of stories, and her mistress sometimes asks her to read from the *Arabian Nights* (El-Bisatie, 2010, 75 and 84):

> So in the few months before I left Egypt I read. Goha stories, *A Thousand and One Nights*, tales of the caliphs and of the harems in the palaces. My husband would scour the used book stalls and bring home the types of books I was looking for. And I watched dozens of old Egyptian films, starring Stefan Rushdi and Sirag Mounir and the like, and I tried to pick up the way they moved. Oh, and I got hold of those celebrity magazines in order to bone up on all the gossip about the stars. In short, I accumulated a huge storehouse of stories to keep her entertained. Then from day one, I realized that she'd brought me here so that *she* could talk. And did she ever talk! About everything that happened to her ever since her childhood. Over and over again, about her two childhood boyfriends. She'd talk and I'd listen. That was my job, to listen. But now, after what happened, I'm not sure what my job is anymore.
>
> (El-Bisatie, 2010, 110)

By contrast, from the employee's perspective, storytelling may lead to salvation, as it happens to Shahrazad. However, Zāhiyya watches her son growing up, being kept at a distance, and she is no longer needed. The narrator notes that she looks paler and paler at every visit, and unlike the other domestics, she does not go out to enjoy time-limited freedom because she is entrapped in the house. Finally, the narrator admits that many women have gone through this, but they never talk about it because of their powerlessness: "Of course, I'd be powerless to help if she were in trouble, but at least I could listen" (El-Bisatie, 2010, 108). After their last encounter, he confirms his detachment from the surrounding reality by saying that he is not going to think about anything and follows the crowd in the celebrations until he reaches the villa. This conclusion reminds of the author's mastery at crafting short stories, as Allen remarks:

> Life does not present us with any short stories; they and their endings have to be created. In al-Bisāṭī's case the endings to these artfully detached descriptions of character and incident do not really involve any sense of closure. The narrator rounds off a scene, an incident, or a situation, and then leaves things as they are. The story comes to an end, but life goes on…
>
> (Allen, 2000, 277)

Conclusions

This chapter explores the literary representation of work migration in the Gulf with the purpose of filling the gap between the most representative novels studied so far, *al-Balda al-ukhrā* by the Egyptian Ibrāhīm ʿAbd al-Majīd and *Sāq al-bāmbū* by the Kuwaiti Saʿūd al-Sanʿūsī. In the context of contemporary Egyptian literature, *Daqq al-ṭabūl* by Muḥammad al-Bisāṭī develops this literary theme, focusing on the domestic workers and projecting the migratory experience on the body. This novel, almost a novella, combines reality and fantasy: set in a fictitious, unnamed Emirate, the process of identity discovery starts with the local population's journey to Paris that leaves the migrants in charge of the country. Only a few details are given about their accommodation, working conditions, and interaction with the employers, since the author prefers to convey the general atmosphere through the eyes of a detached, affectless narrator.

The two main narrative threads are the construction of a multicultural community of outsiders and the impact of displacement on the body. At the beginning, this multicultural community is simply a juxtaposition of nationalities recognizable by their clothes, music, and food. They gradually integrate inside the villas, almost as floating islands, and then appropriate public spaces such as the stadium and the amusement park. Nevertheless, they do not free themselves from the social constraints for fear of losing their jobs. This affinity between migrants is reinforced by their common preoccupations about gender relations. When the Pakistani maid Rishim decides to meet her husband, all the domestics help and understand her. When the narrator compensates his repressed desire with his dreams, the male population seems to fight the curse with a collective ritual of virility. Finally, when Zāhiyya is ready to tell her story, she finds someone who can listen to her, even though this does not mean any salvation.

The depiction of domestic work encourages tackling some intimate issues such as sexuality, but this does not mean that the body attains only to the private sphere. On the contrary, the body of the exploited ones keeps record of social norms and economic disparities. This central role of the body, combined with storytelling and irony, allow the author to turn private issues into political ones; this indirect way of exposing the shortcomings of society might be further explored applying the theoretical lens of biopolitics. Further research might investigate female subjectivity in migration literature of the Gulf, the formal techniques and genres combining public and private issues, and the contribution of Asian literatures to the literary representation of this kind of migration.

Notes

1 Because of its soccer-related theme, an excerpt of the novel is available from El-Bisatie and Raab (2016).
2 Saudi Arabia, Kuwait, Bahrain, Qatar, the United Arab Emirates (UAE), and Oman are members of the Gulf Cooperation Council (GCC) established in 1981.
3 From Levantine literature, instead, Elayyan (2016) mentions *Rijāl fī al-shams* (1963) by the Palestinian Ghassān Kanafānī, a classic of resistance literature and a tale of clandestine migration to Kuwait, and *Barārī al-ḥummā* (1985) by the Palestinian-Jordanian Ibrāhīm Naṣr Allāh, a postmodern novel of migration to Saudi Arabia.
4 Al-Bisāṭī was the editor of the book series *Aṣwāt* (Voices), published by the General Organization for Cultural Palaces, and was awarded the Sheikh Al Owais Prize in 2000–2001.
5 For another review of the novel in Arabic, see Khayr (2009). For an interview with the author in Arabic, see al-Bayān (2005).
6 In another passage, the narrator uses a similar pattern to describe three dancing troupes at the stadium (El-Bisatie, 2010, 59).
7 This reminds of Bon Joon-ho's internationally acclaimed film *Parasite* (2019), in which the domestic workers – all belonging to the same family – take the place of their rich employers in the house when they go on holiday. The reversal of roles in this film is abruptly interrupted by the employers' sudden return and is more sarcastic than in the examined novel, which instead portrays a more cautious approach.
8 Oil is mentioned only when a pipeline bursts before the second football match.
9 *Al-Balda al-ukhrā* also tackles the administration of justice, denouncing the disparity between the crime and the punishment as well as the impunity of real criminals.
10 In *al-Balda al-ukhrā*, Tabuk is a cursed city because the Prophet invoked a curse on a tribe that refused to help him: their number would not exceed 20 people and every time a baby was born, a member of the tribe would die (Abdel Meguid, 1997, 42).
11 In another episode, the Filipinos make fun of the Muslim right of having four wives, doubting that the husband has sex with all of them.
12 Censi identifies this model in the representation of one of the three main characters in *Sīnālkūl*.
13 I use the term impotence, instead of infertility, to create a parallelism with the male migrants' impotence.
14 For a study of the appropriation of the *Arabian Nights* in the 20th-century Arabic and global novel, see van Leeuwen (2018).

References

Primary Sources

ʿAbd al-Majīd, I. (1990) *Al-balda al-ukhrā*. Cairo: Riyāḍ al-rayyis.
Abdel Meguid, I. (1997) *The Other Place*. Translated by F. Abdel Wahab. Cairo: AUC Press.
Abū Julayyil, Ḥ. (2008) *Al-fāʿil*. Cairo: Dār Mīrīt.
Abu Golayyel, H. (2009) *A Dog With No Tail*. Translated by R. Moger. Cairo: AUC Press.
Alsanousi, S. (2015) *The Bamboo Stalk*. Translated by J. Wright. Doha: Bloomsbury Qatar Foundation Publishing.
al-Aswānī, ʿA. (2018) *Jumhūriyya ka-anna*. Beirut: Dār al-ādāb.
Al Aswani, A. (2021) *The Republic of False Truths*. Translated by S. R. Fellowes. New York: Knopf.
al-Bisāṭī, M. (2005) *Daqq al-ṭabūl*. Beirut: Dār al-ādāb.
El-Bisatie, M. (1998a) *A Last Glass of Tea and Other Stories*. Translated by D. Johnson-Davies. Lynne Boulder, CO: Rienner Publisher.
El-Bisatie, M. (1998b) *Houses Behind the Trees*. Translated by D. Johnson-Davies. Austin: University of Texas Press.
El-Bisatie, M. (2004) *Clamor of the Lake*. Translated by H. Halim. Cairo: AUC Press.
El-Bisatie, M. (2006) *Over the Bridge*. Translated by N. Roberts. Cairo: AUC Press.
El-Bisatie, M. (2008) *Hunger*. Translated by D. Johnson-Davies. Cairo: AUC Press.
El-Bisatie, M. (2010) *Drumbeat*. Translated by P. Daniel. Cairo: AUC Press.
El-Bisatie, M., and Raab, A. (2016) Literary Selection: Selections From "Drumbeat", by Mohamed el-Bisatie. Introduced by Alon Raab. In A. Raab and I. Khalidi (eds), *Soccer in the Middle East*. London and New York: Routledge, 201–208.
al-Ghīṭānī, J. (1985) [1976] *Waqāʾiʿ ḥārat al-Zaʿfarānī*. Cairo: Maktabat Madbūlī.
al-Ghitani, G. (2009) *The Zafarani Files*. Translated by F. Abdel Wahab. Cairo: AUC Press.
Ibrāhīm, Ṣ. (1998) [1992] *Dhāt*. Cairo: Dār al-mustaqbal al-ʿarabī.
Ibrahim, S. (2001) *Zaat*. Translated by A. Calderbank. Cairo: AUC Press.
Johnson-Davies, D. (ed.) (2010) *The Anchor Book of Modern Arabic Fiction*. New York: Anchor Books.
Kamāl, D. (2012) *Sījāra sābiʿa*. Cairo: Dār Mīrīt.
Kamal, D. (2017) *Cigarette Number Seven*. Translated by N. Youssef. Cairo: Hoopoe.
al-Sanʿūsī, S. (2013) *Sāq al-bāmbū*. Beirut: Arabic Scientific Publishers.

Secondary Sources

Aghacy, S. (2009) *Masculine Identity in the Fiction of the Arab East Since 1967*. New York: Syracuse University Press.
Allen, R. (2000) *A Last Glass of Tea and Other Stories* by Mohamed El-Bisatie and Denys Johnson-Davies: Review. *Journal of Arabic Literature*, 31(3), 275–278.
Babar, Z. (ed.) (2017) *Arab Migrant Communities in the GCC*. Oxford: Oxford University Press.
al-Bayān (2005) Fāntāziyā tuʿarri al-wāqiʿ wa-tafḍaḥ inkisār al-mashāʿir [A Fantasy Uncovering the Truth and Revealing the Disruption of Feelings]. *al-Bayān*, 5 December. Available from www.albayan.ae/five-senses/2005-12-05-1.122931 [accessed 4 March 2021].

Censi, M. (2016) Au croisement de deux appartenances. Corps masculin, déplacement et recherche identitaire dans le roman *Sīnālkūl* d'Ilyās Ḫūrī. *LiCArC Littérature et cultures arabe contemporaines*, 4. Le corps masculin déplacé à l'épreuve de la migration, 171–183.

Darrāj, F. (2005) Muḥammad al-Bisāṭī wa-Daqq al-Ṭabūl ḥikāyat al-sayyid wa-l-ʿabd [al-Bisāṭī's Daqq al-Ṭabūl a Story of Masters and Servants]. *al-Ḥayāh*, 12 June. Available from www.alha yat.com/ arti cle/ 1256978/والعبد-nbsp [accessed 4 March 2021].

Dawood, I. (1999) *A Last Glass of Tea and Other Stories* by Mohamed El-Bisatie and Denys Johnson-Davies: Review. *World Literature Today*, 73(2), 383–384.

Elayyan, H. (2016) Three Arabic Novels of Expatriation in the Arabian Gulf Region: Ibrāhīm Naṣrallāh's *Prairies of Fever*, Ibrāhīm ʿAbdalmagīd's *The Other Place*, and Saʿūd al-Sanʿūsī's *Bamboo Stalk*. *Journal of Arabic and Islamic Studies*, 16, 85–98. Available from https://journals.uio.no/JAIS/article/view/4741 [accessed 4 March 2021].

International Organization for Migration IOM (2004) *Arab Migration in a Globalized World*. Available from https://publications.iom.int/system/files/pdf/arab_migration_globalized_world.pdf [accessed 4 March 2021].

Khalaf, A., AlShehabi, O., and Hanieh, A. (eds) (2015) *Transit States: Labour, Migration and Citizenship in the Gulf*. London: Pluto Press.

Khayr, M. (2009) Ṭabūl Muḥammad al-Bisāṭī [al-Bisāṭī drum]. *al-Akhbār*, 6 Shabbāṭ. Available from www.al- akh bar.com/ Lite ratu re_ A rts/ 143 936/طبول-محمد-الب ساط [accessed 4 March 2021].

Lindsey, U. (2010) Drumbeat: Tales From the Gulf's Back End. *Egypt Independent*, 25 March. Available from https://egyptindependent.com/drumbeat-tales-gulfs-back-end/ [accessed 4 March 2021].

Lynx Qualey, M. (2010) *Drumbeat* by Mohamed al-Bisatie and Peter Daniel: Review. *World Literature Today*, 84(4), 60.

Massad, J. (2007) *Desiring Arabs*. Chicago: University of Chicago Press.

Michalak-Pikulska, B. (2012) *Modern Literature of the United Arab Emirates*. Krakow: Jagiellonian University Press.

Mikhail, M. (1998) Al-balda al-ukhra: A Meta-Text Unveiled. *Arab Studies Quarterly*, 20(4), 75–83.

Ramadan, Y. (2012) The Emergence of the Sixties Generation in Egypt and the Anxiety Over Categorization. *Journal of Arabic Literature*, 43(2/3) Arabic Literature, Criticism and Intellectual Thought From the Nahḍah to the Present, 409–430.

Said, A. (2004) An Arabian Waste Land: Ibrahim Abdel Meguid's *Al-baldah al-ukhra* [The Other Place]. *Al-ʻArabiyya*, 37, 1–20.

Sellman, J. (2018) A Global Postcolonial: Contemporary Arabic Literature of Migration to Europe. *Journal of Postcolonial Writing*, 54(6), 751–765.

Tijani, I. (2009) *Male Domination, Female Revolt: Race, Class, and Gender in Kuwaiti Women's Fiction*. Leiden and Boston: Brill.

Tijani, I. (2014) Contemporary Emirati Literature: Its Historical Development and Forms. *Journal of Arabic and Islamic Studies*, 14,121–136. Available from https://journals.uio.no/JAIS/article/view/4641 [accessed 4 March 2021].

UN DESA. (2017) *Migration Data Portal*. Available from https://migrationdataportal.org/ [accessed 4 March 2021].

van Leeuwen, R. (2018) *The Thousand and One Nights and Twentieth-Century Fiction: Intertextual Readings*. Leiden and Boston: Brill.

4 Writing Arabic in the Land of Migration

Waciny Laredj from *Ḥārisat al-ẓilāl: Dūn Kīshūt fī al-Jazā'ir* to *Shurafāt baḥr al-shamāl*

Jolanda Guardi

Among the Algerian intellectuals and writers who write in Arabic, Wasīnī al-A'raj (Waciny Laredj, b. 1954)[1] stands out as an interesting case study, because although he chose to migrate to France and to use the French language to discuss political and literary issues, he has never ceased to write his novels in Arabic.[2] This marks him as almost the only author who lives in the *manfā* but is fully accepted by Arabic-speaking intellectuals among Algerian writers in exile.[3]

However, Laredj's decision to leave Algeria was not a smooth one, and he continuously returns to this topic in his works. As in *Ḥārisat al-ẓilāl: Dūn Kīshūt fī al-Jazā'ir* (The Shadows' (She)guardian: Don Quixote in Algeria, 1996) and *Shurafāt baḥr al-shamāl* (The North Sea's Balconies: Amsterdam Rains, 2003) – the two novels analysed in this chapter – since 1992 the main subject of Laredj's work has been re-telling Algeria's history, to underline the different cultural contributions that shaped Algerian culture as a polymorphous one (and not as a Muslim culture *sensu stricto*) and how the Algerian identity is embedded in this culture. This identity is forced between Laredj's own necessity and desire to leave Algeria due to the impossibility of "speaking", and his sense of guilt for having abandoned his homeland and the intellectuals who have chosen to stay. Reading the two abovementioned novels will underline this duality.

The Shadows' (She)guardian: Don Quixote in Algeria

Ever since one of his first novels, *Ḥārisat al-ẓilāl: Dūn Kīshūt fī al-Jazā'ir* (The Shadows' (She)guardian: Don Quixote in Algeria, 1996),[4] Laredj has used narrative writing to respond to the following question: how is it possible to overcome the conflict between Arab culture and the West? The answer is also developed in his other novels, such as *Kitāb al-amīr* (The Book of the Emir, 2005), where the main character faces a meeting with the Other and that Other overcomes feelings of aversion to Arab culture, becoming an active part of it. That is to say, a positive rotating of perspective can only be developed when

DOI: 10.4324/9780429027338-5

two cultures meet and express a mutual desire to get to know each other. As Laredj claims, "L'humanité est condamnée au dialogue, qui est le seul moyen pour fuir l'enfer" (Ghosn, 2010, 7).

In this way, migration is the human condition that allows us to get to know each other, and to develop our own culture and enrich that of others. However, migration is also a kind of exile in which Laredj himself lives a constant suffering, though it is a discovery as well: "Je pense que partir c'est certes s'autodétruire un peu mais pour se reconstruire sur d'autres bases" (Yelles, 1997, 4). Laredj immigrated permanently to France in 1994, since he could no longer bear Islamist pressure in Algeria. Several times in meetings and interviews, as well as in personal conversations, he confirmed that he does not consider migration an escape, but a choice that implies continuous responsibility, a sort of open wound, still a necessity so that he can keep writing. In any case, Laredj maintains links with his home country through the Arabic language, which, as he confirms, is his "language of creativity".[5]

Laredj's *The Shadows' (She)guardian* tells the story of Hsìsen, who works at the Algerian Ministry of Cultural Goods and is responsible for cultural relations between Spain and Algeria. One day, he meets journalist Vasquéz Cervantes de Almería, alias Don Quixote, a descendant of Miguel de Cervantes, who, thanks to a cargo transfer reaches Algeria to visit the city in which his famous ancestor lived for a time and where, while he was in prison, he designed the idea of Quixote. The real Quixote and the literary one blend throughout the entire novel, allowing Laredj to speak about the common Mediterranean culture and the deep links that connect Algeria to the history of Al-Andalus. As William P. Childers claims in an article full of meaning,

> Algerian writers' appropriation of Don Quixote belongs to a larger project of reconstructing an alternative national identity to the Islamist extremism that ravaged their country in the 1990s. They look at Cervantes, then, as an example of dialogue across cultures.
>
> (Childers, 2014, 379)[6]

In the novel, Hsìsen has cut his tongue and penis to imply that the fundamentalists prevent not only free speech but also repress desire. For this reason, an intellectual is obliged to leave this "état d'urgence" (see Mokhtari, 2002, 29; Fisher, 2007, 34–77) to be free to speak his own creative language and in whichever language that he writes, and to be free to desire, to be "un être de désir" (Bencheikh, 1988, 38). Therefore, it is not by coincidence that the book, which Laredj confirms to have affected significantly his path, is the *One Thousand and One Nights*, a text he discovered when he was a boy in the mosque library (Ganci, 2010, 1). The framework story is the story of the narrating I, and the structure refers to the rewriting of *One Thousand and One Nights* in the structure of the story inside the story, a topic already addressed by Laredj directly in *Al-laylā al-sābiʿa baʿd al-alf: Raml al-māya* (The 1007th

Night: Raml al-maya, 1993) and alluded to in other of his works.[7] Moreover, throughout the novel, Hsìsen's and Cervantes's language and conversations are tools to confirm their individual existence and their existence as members of a group.

Memory and Writing

Such self-affirmation through writing is at the same time a research subject that occurs through questioning and re-elaborating collective memory. Collective memory is simultaneously the foundation and an expression of group identity, and it represents the past: each group chooses and reorganizes the images of the past with regards to the interests of the present (Namer, 1987). Apart from collective memory, there is also cultural memory or culture of remembrance (*Erinnerungskultur*), a universal phenomenon in which memory constitutes an important part of the identity and cultural construction of a group, be it religious, ethnic, or a specific class. This develops mainly along the time axis that, through planning, constructs social and time horizons. Assman, in *Das kulturelle Gedächtnis* (1997), when dealing with ancient cultures, underlines that in ancient Greek culture, Mnemosine (*Μνημοσύνη:* recollection, memory) is the mother of the nine Muses, among which we find Clio (*Κλειω*), the Muse of history writing, and Calliope (*Καλλιοπη*), known as the Muse of epic poetry but who is also devoted to supervising of rhetoric, philosophy, and science. This relation between conveying history and producing literature establishes the relationship between cultural memory and written production. The outcome of this relationship is collective memory, which is created and strengthened by producing texts, or, in our case, narratives, which in turn act on the emotional aspect through the production of history and myth.[8] In this sense, the narrative text constitutes a part of long-term memory that provides symbolic cultural objectification to those elements that are meant to be preserved, and in that way are given a patina of "objectivity". These elements, thus objectified, are those that further on constitute the canon (Bourdieu, 2005), contributing to the formation of cultural identity: they, in fact, are the reference for the identity of the Self, in a relationship of mutual exchange, and all that does not belong to this symbolic container becomes the Other (Assmann, 1997).

Laredj, who wrote *The Shadows' (She)guardian* shortly before leaving Algeria, transformed the memory into a *nœud de mémoire* (Rothberg, 2010, 3–12; Nora, 1989, 7–24), to connect Algeria's European and Arab cultures. The hub of this memory is identified in the cave of Miguel de Cervantes, where the Spanish author is said to have spent a few days during one of his escape attempts.[9]

The characters' attitude in the novel tells us that Laredj does not conceive of Arab culture and Muslim heritage in opposition to Algerian identity; on the contrary, he supports a harmonious diversity. He believes that the problem lies in the fact that Algerian Islam – peaceful and spiritual – has suffered from the input of foreign ideas, especially after Algeria's independence (1962), when many countries, particularly Egypt, sent their teachers and preachers to support Algeria's Arab identity, thereby introducing the Muslim Brotherhood into the country.[10]

In an interview with *Algérie Littérature/Action* from shortly after he published *The Shadows' (She)guardian*, Laredj explained why he chose Cervantes's descendant as an anti-hero in the novel:

> Je suis attaché à ce grand romancier qui fut Miguel de Cervantès, à son roman universel Don Quichotte et à son discours de dérision que je trouve toujours d'actualité : comprendre avec Cervantès le monde comme ambiguïté c'est avoir à l'affronter, non comme vérité absolue, mais comme vérités relatives qui se contredisent. Je rejoins totalement cette idée de Kundera : à la base de l'écriture, il y a une interrogation et non un parti pris, moral ou autre. Depuis la mort de Dieu, il n'y a plus de vérité absolue, mais une ambiguïté infernale, puisque la vérité divine s'est décomposée en milliers de petites vérités relatives. Le roman est l'expression de cette décomposition permanente. Je pense que le jour où cette décomposition cessera, le roman cessera avec elle. Le roman en tant qu'art est fondamentalement incompatible avec les vérités absolues, si elles existent, ainsi qu'avec toutes les certitudes.
>
> (Yelles, 1997, 1–2)

Therefore, the novel presents a twofold vision: one from the inside – Hsìsen – and one from the outside – the one of Cervantes's descendant. This twofold vision is noticeable in the title itself. The text was published in French with the title *Le ravin de femme sauvage* (The ravine of the wild woman),[11] referring to a legend about an Algerian woman who headed to the woods in the outskirts of Algiers to spend a day with her sons and suddenly lost sight of them, never to find them again. The story goes that the woman, desperate and gone crazy, continued to live in the forest, eating wild plants and fruit. Upon the building of houses and the arrival of new inhabitants to the area, she changed her habits: during the day she remained hidden, but at night she searched for her children to avoid looks and mockery, turning into a shadow until the day her body was discovered in an advanced state of decay.[12] In light of this explanation, the Arabic title of *The Shadows' (She)guardian*, *Ḥārisat al-ẓilāl* is crucial for the explanation of the novel. Indeed, it is the "axis" (Bashīniyya, 2013, 207) of the entire text, because this first part of the title reminds the Algerian reader of the past and its mythological tradition.[13] Meanwhile, the second part of the title, *Dūn Kīshūt fī al-Jazā'ir* (Don Quixote in Algeria), recalls the link between Western and Arab Muslim civilizations – specifically Al-Andalus – establishing at the same time the connection between Miguel de Cervantes and his descendent. *The Shadows' (She)guardian* also refers to the folk "wisdom" that always tells the truth and can be identified through the character Ḥannā, Hsìsen's grandmother, who throughout the novel reconstructs the link between Algeria and Spain. She recalls a shadow culture, that is, a phantom culture, connected with the symbolic imagination and introducing an element of strangeness (a guardian from the shadow?) in everyday life: "a shadows' (she)guardian, lost in the vaults of soulless subsoil" (Laredj, 1999, 218), a guardian, because it expects to find a glimmer of light or, better, enlightenment. This can only come from cultural and mutual acquaintance.

The Shadows' (She)guardian, in fact, speaks of shadows as opposed to light in various passages where the light is represented by the Sun. For example:

> Through Ḥannā I felt the legend of this town, the legend of the shadows' (she)guardian. A woman with no age who waits for centuries, without resting. She never gets old. And she says continuously to all who ask her why she is waiting so painfully while only ruin comes from behind the close horizons: the horizon is closed, but it will change its colour one day. Clouds full of water will release their water on earth. Earth is not a fool, it turns still not in all directions. One day the sun, which hides the earth every night, will show up with majesty and honour. I was confined in the old shadows and I did not choose my condition, nor did I want to spend my remining time in oblivion. I am always waiting for my son Ḥamū, the one who will bring the sun. The sun will let me go out from these shadows to live as all other creatures in the light. It will come back. Just wait a little.
>
> (Laredj, 1999, 170)[14]

Waiting for the sun harkens to the myth of Prometheus, the Titan who gave humanity the gift of fire; this myth is suggested also by the name of the son that the shadows' (she)guardian is waiting to return, Ḥamū.[15] Prometheus, the one who thinks, is also the one who enlightens through knowledge and has often symbolized the struggle of progress and freedom against power. In this way, Laredj overturns the meaning of the legend of the shadows' (she)guardian, offering the reader an analysis of his country through the lens of imagination: the past, in the person of the shadows' (she)guardian, who observes the shadows but also the past itself because, in Arabic, *ẓill* also means "traces", referring to the traces of the past, provoking a series of cultural cross-references to Arab-speaking readers. The son she is waiting for is the one who will bring the sun, that is, the ability to reflect and consequently react against obscurantism (the shadows) in which the country has lived too long. This can only happen by recovering relations with the Mediterranean West. As Laredj himself confirms, we can only insert ourselves in imagination through writing:

> Sometimes we find it in front of us, we take inspiration from our everyday life; other times, on the contrary, we build it. It is, for example, the case of

> the historical imaginary, something on which I worked a lot. I reshaped the Arab-Muslim imaginary my way, a poetic imaginary but at the same time, an aggressive imaginary.
>
> (Ganci, 2010, 3)

Laredj adds that he enjoys deconstructing the imaginary, a memory already deposited and considered untouchable. This provides him an opportunity to expand it and "make it dirty" with another memory, another imaginary, something more beautiful from his point of view.

It is this deconstruction of the (colonial) imaginary that Hsìsen presents to the readers when he, alone, without tongue and without penis (that is, without words and without desires), uses the only means of expression that he still has available: writing, a symbolic call to psychological exile, as Laredj himself names it.[16]

What has been stated above refers to the colonial past and to the way indigenous peoples' knowledge and traditions resist it. The dichotomy between shadows and light and the way the (she)guardian's speeches are constructed in the novel recall the words that Cuauhtemoc – the Aztec ruler – spoke on 12 August 1521 at the end of a battle to drive the Spanish conquistadores out of the Aztec capital of Tenochtitlán. As his last speech, it is therefore considered a legacy statement by indigenous people. Laredj uses the beginning of this speech almost verbatim:

> Our Sun is now hidden from view. The face of our Sun has disappeared, and has left us in complete darkness. But we know it will return again, that it will rise again, and it will begin to illuminate us anew. But while our Sun is away, and remains in the residence of silence, we must swiftly join together and embrace. And in the very centre of our being, we must hide all that our hearts love, and hide all we know that is a great treasure. … This will be until that time when our new Sun rises.
>
> (Tlatoani Cuauhtemoc's Last Speech)

Laredj takes a clear stand in linking his novel to indigenous Latin America civilizations, and in this way he inserts his work into the decolonial turn (Maldonado-Torres, 2018). This means that he refuses the definition of "migrant literature" as a Western construct, to analyse knowledge production in the Arabic language and link Algeria's history to that of all colonized people. In this perspective, the novel not only refers to Algeria's past but also underlines the role played by Western civilization in destroying a common knowledge. In fact, decolonial theory considers the conquest of Al-Andalus as the first destruction project of Christendom, which served as a model for all other conquests in the following centuries (Grasfoguel, 2013, 78–79). The underlying message seems to be that what happened in Algeria in the "black decade" (1990–2000) has roots that go a long way back, and that Western culture has its own responsibility in it, creating solitude and desolation.

The North Sea's Balconies: Amsterdam Rains

Psychological exile, apparent in *The Shadow's (She)guardian*, is even more present in Laredj's *Shurafāt baḥr al-shamāl* (The North Sea's Balconies: Amsterdam Rains, 2003). This novel tells the story of Yāsīn, a painter who leaves Algeria during the black decade to immigrate to North America on a scholarship. Before boarding the plane to his final destination, Yāsīn spends some time in Amsterdam. This time is the one the reader will know of: as a transit place, the Dutch city plays the role of a suspended space (and time) in which the protagonist recalls his time spent in Algeria and his homeland's history.

There lie several similarities between *The North Sea's Balconies* and *The Shadows (She)guardian*, but what changes is the perspective from which Laredj looks at the act of leaving Algeria. If, in the previous novel, exile was a compulsory choice, here, the main subject is the *manfā*, the exile, and its relationship with violence and writing. Throughout the novel we are confronted with Yāsīn's thoughts and his sense of guilt for having abandoned his country exactly in the moment that it needed his presence to react to terrorism. Laredj enacts this personal and fictional dilemma through the dichotomous pairs of self/other, life/death, passion/rejection, prison/freedom, memory/oblivion, and north/south and manages to form a fictional world through an experimental journey of narrative writing. The basic opposition in the novel is the one between homeland and exile, the dichotomy of which is realized by means of narrative techniques such as the dream, evocation, synaesthesia, and soliloquy, with the predominance of memory and the flow of consciousness that slope down this opposition through memory: "I am a prisoner of a memory that opposes death in the moment in which I wish to kill it" (Laredj, 2001, 140).

This memory has been untying for almost half a century, from Algeria's War of Independence (1962) until 1994, the date Laredj left Algeria to settle in France and when he started experiencing the *manfā*.[17] In between these two dates, the reader can detect other significant moments of Algeria's history: 1957, the year when ʿAbbān Ramaḍān disappeared during a trip in the Far East, supposedly at the hands of members of the National Liberation Front (FLN); 1971, the year of the agrarian revolution, a fundamental turning point in Algeria's history; 5 October 1988, the date of the bread riots and the beginning of terrorism in Algeria; and finally 1991, the year of municipal elections in which the Islamists won. This is "the restricted time in which the names have dissolved" (Laredj, 2003, 21), in which "life was lost for us, we have not earned anything from that barbarous times" (Laredj, 2003, 24). In this way, Laredj establishes a parallel between the personal destiny of the self, the narrating I, and the destiny of the homeland through the time that wounded both the individual and collective memory.

Unlike *The Shadows' (She)guardian*, written against the events he tells about, in *The North Sea's Balconies*, Laredj inserts many personal elements into the narrative: the main character Yāsīn, for example, like Laredj originates from a village in western Algeria, leaving it in 1958 to study in Oran and deciding to leave the country in 1994. This parallelism confirms the fact that "there is no space for oblivion. We do not forget when we want to, but rather we forget when the memory wants to forget it"(Laredj, 2003, 24). Yāsīn's flow of consciousness is expressed especially in exposing the situation of the homeland. The story's framework is referenced by the title of the novel as well, where *Shurafāt* (balconies) but also "stages of a theatre" refer to the fact that every chapter puts on an act of a drama in which the readers can assist as from a stand that looks onto the stage of life itself, and at the same time assist the performance of the negative situation of Yāsīn and of the homeland. In contrast, *baḥr al-shamāl*, the North Sea, indicates the local expansion (Nardout-Lafarge, 2013) in which the revival of the graves of memory and the realization of the written piece occur. That way, the space of the *manfā* becomes, once again, a place – literary and not – only at the moment in which by means of memory and reconstruction of the imaginary it acquires meaning for the narrator.

As T. Y. Fu (1977, 17–18) maintains, "Space becomes place as we get to know it better and endow it with value". In this case, memory is expressed through binary oppositions, like I/the other, self/homeland, death/life, passion/rejection, imprisonment/freedom, memory/oblivion, and north/south. The self/homeland opposition, for example, is represented by the character of Fatīna, Yāsīn's first love from when he was still in Algeria. Yāsīn, once in Amsterdam, looks for Fatīna everywhere, in an attempt to domesticate his new space and fill it with meaning. He asks everyone he meets about her and ends up bringing a bouquet of daffodils to the grave of another woman in a cemetery in Amsterdam: Tina the Oranese, whose name phonetically resembles the present/absent Fatīna; this name is also graphically similar to *fitna,* due to the fact that Arabic script writes consonants only (*ftn*). Moreover, in origin – as her name says, Tina is from Oran – the name refers to Yāsīn and even to Laredj. Yāsīn thus seeks Fatīna (i.e. the homeland) in his country of exile; he seeks an identity through the ideal bond with a woman (Tina the Oranese), deceased in exile, because the nostalgia that he feels in experiencing the *manfā* is like funeral music. Laredj underlines the reference to music by naming the novel's chapters as symphony movements or opera "pictures" (e.g. "Requiem for Fatīna's sorrows"; "The wounds of the naked Christ"; "The cantic of the open gospel"), also relating to that Yāsīn is a painter.

If Fatīna represents Yāsīn's love for the city he abandoned, Algiers, the second female character, Zulīkha (a name also present in *The Shadows' (She) guardian*), Yāsīn's sister, represents the bond with the earth. This link is identified in the experience of exile with Narjis (a female name meaning narcissus – and daffodils, a variety of narcissus, are the flowers that Yāsīn brings to the tomb of Tina the Oranese), a television announcer to whom Yāsīn writes five hundred love letters without getting an answer. As Algeria has refused his love, constraining him to leave, so Narjis does not answer his letters, meaning that the foreign land will never be his home, notwithstanding how much longer he will remain there. He meets the Zulīkha-Fatīna character once more when he is in the Netherlands (the "Northern" country, as it is called in the novel), but under another name: Ḥanīn (nostalgia).

Taking into account Narjis's profession – she works with words – and Yāsīn's letters – the amount of which stresses the importance on the written language – one can understand that Narjis-Ḥanīn, in contrast to Zulīkha-Fatīna, represents language, the only tool that enables the writer to overcome *ḥanīn ilā al-bilād* (nostalgia for the homeland) and to maintain a link with his own country (represented by his sister Zulīkha), whom he loved and deeply loves (symbolized by Fatīna). As in *The Shadows' (She)guardian*, Laredj considers language a fundamental tool of expression of the self, to maintain a deep bond with one's own identity.

The destiny of this triple bond, however, is marked by misfortune that manifests in another opposition, that of life/death. Yāsīn's bonds with the three women end in tragedy, in a pessimist vision of love that is resolved in times of solitude, though most of the personalities within *The North Sea's Balconies* are surrounded by tragedy. Suicide is a common destiny of Pushkin, Majakovski, and van Gogh, who are all quoted in the novel; madness was the fate and death of Virginia Woolf – also mentioned in the book – as paralleled in the lives of Fatīna, Zulīkha, and Tina the Oranese. This rotting of love is what makes the narrator say, "It seems to me that love is a mystery that stands on ambiguity, where one is always a loser; the most beautiful thing is that we spend most of our lives repairing failures that originate in this fragility" (Laredj, 2001, 100). If love and the women Yāsīn meets represent the homeland, in this perspective, it is a homeland that generates death, not life. The homeland is a woman without *ʿaql* (reason), because "in this country, the lunatic is the only one who is a natural being" (Laredj, 2001, 19). If so, then Algeria is like a large prison from which the narrating I fled into exile. From there, he has a different perspective: "How great this limited piece of land called Algeria looks from the outside" (Laredj, 2001, 17). Algeria looks great from the outside, but when one lives in it, it becomes as narrow as a prison cell.

To sum, if in *The Shadows' (She)guardian* the author's stance seems more proactive, since despite the novel's described socio-political crisis at the end of the book, the protagonist still has, if not his tongue, his language to express himself, in *The North Sea's Balconies*, the human condition of the *manfā* is perceived as strongly negative. In fact, it becomes a state of being in which one constantly recalls his life in the homeland and rethinks of the beloved people he left beyond, be they alive or dead. In particular, as the novel refers to a human being who leaves his own country to avoid death at the hands of terrorists – a condition that the protagonist shares with Laredj – the act of thinking is linked to a fundamental question: should the intellectual stay and give his life for his country, or leave to share with the Other his existential condition? Laredj leaves it to the reader to find an answer.

Concluding Remarks

Although a writer who has lived in the *manfā*, Waciny Laredj has never been considered a contributor to so-called migration literature. This is probably due to the fact he still writes in Arabic, as is the case with other Arab writers. Indeed, it seems that to be classified as a "migrant writer", one must leave not only one's country but also one's own language. In contrast, Laredj remains deeply tied to Arabic and does not fit the thematic frame of migration literature. The subjects of his novels are linked to leaving Algeria and trying to rebuild their own lives in foreign countries. These characters can of course be inserted into the frame of migration literature, but what Laredj is especially interested in is the rewriting of history. This rewriting is committed to producing meaningful knowledge of a contested past. By this, his narrative ought to be considered a serious, alternative interpretation of the past, offering realistic interpretations, something that scares scholarly interest. Laredj's novels, then, cannot be considered as migration literature, as they address issues of identity not only in the migration country but also in a more general way.

Notes

1 Although Laredj is a well-known author whose works are translated into several languages, critical studies about his literary production in Western languages are very few. About the author, see: Naouel Abdessemed (2014); M. Bashīniyya (2013); R. Benmālik (2003); B. Būshūsha (2004); Lamia Ben Youssef Zayzafoon (2010); W. P. Childers (2014); J. Ghallāb (2013); I. G. Gómez-Benita (2014a, 2014b); Katia Ghosn (2010); Leyla Guenatri (2010); Fatīḥa Kalkhūsh (2007); F. Leggio (1997); Maḥfūẓa Ṣāliḥ and Naṣīra Zūzū (2005); S. Yaqṭīn (1990); Naṣīra Zūzū (2006).

2 Waciny Laredj (Wasīnī al-Aʿraj) was born in Mʾsirda, Tlemcen, in 1954. A highly prolific author, he published novels, poems, essays, chronicles, and graphic novels, among them: *Al-bawāba al-zarqāʾ (Waqāʾiʿ min Awjāʿ rajul)* (1980); *Ṭawq al-yāsamīn (Waqʿ al-aḥdhiya al-khashina)* (1981); *Mā tabqā min sīrat Lakhḍar Ḥamrūsh* (1982); *Nuwwār al-lawz* (1983); *Aḥlām Maryam al-Wadīʿa* (1984); *Ḍamīr al-ghāʾib* (1990); *Al-laylā al-sābiʿa baʿd al-alf: Raml al-mayā* (1993); *Sayydat al-maqām* (1995); *Ḥārisat al-ẓilāl. Dūn Kīshūt fī al-Jazāʾir* (1996); *Dhākirat al-māʾ* (1997); *Marāyā al-ḍarīr* (1998); *Shurafāt baḥr al-shamāl. Amṭār Amstirdām* (2001); *Al-makhṭūṭa al-sharqiyya* (2002); *Maḍīq al-maʿṭūbīn* (2005); *Kitāb al-amīr* (2005); *Krīmātūryūm. Sūnātā li-ashbāḥ al-Quds* (2009); *Unthā al-sarāb* (2010); *Aṣābiʿ Lūlītā* (2012); *Mamlakat al-farāsha* (2015); *Sīrat al-muntahā* (2015a); *2084. Ḥikāyat al-ʿarabī al-akhīr* (2015b); *Nisāʾ Kāzānūfā* (2015).

3 About Laredj's ideas on the Arabic language, see: B. Agour (2009); M. Yelles (1997).

4 W. al-Aʿraj (1996). The novel was published in French with the title *Le ravin de la femme sauvage* (1997).

5 From a personal conversation with the author, Algiers 2015.

6 Algiers keeps memories of Cervantes's experience. The cave in which the Spanish author found refuge during one of his escape's trials lies in Belwizdàd Hills, close

to the mountains, exactly under where today is located the *Maqām al-shahīd* (Monument to the Martyrs [of the revolution]) in front of the Bay of Algiers, on the borders of a neighbourhood that to this day bears his name: Cervantes. Spanish colonials put a marble bust of the writer in front of the cave on 24 June 1894, a copy of which is kept at the National Museum of Madrid. Besides the bust, one can also find a commemorative plate previously placed at the cave's entrance. Another plate was installed in 1905, a gift from the Spanish community, on the occasion of the third centenary of Quixote's publication, at the presence of Mouis Marinas, the counsel of Spain in Algiers.

7 For example, *Sayyidat al-maqām* (1995), on which see van Leeuwen, 2018, 610–619.

8 There is also a normative aspect whose production is assigned to the academic text (the so-called academic memory).

9 On 26 September 1575, Miguel de Cervantes and his brother Rodrigo were on the galley *Sol* at Les Saintes Marines near Marseille. The galley was captured by barbaric corsairs led by Mami Arnaùt. Later sold as a slave to Ali Mami, who he believed was an important personality from the letters found on him, Cervantes attempted escape and was subsequently kept under strict surveillance. His parents sent a certain amount of money in 1577 to pay his ransom, but only his brother was set free. Cervantes tried to escape once more in the same year, but he did not succeed. He nevertheless fascinated Hasan Basha, the son of Khayr al-Dīn Bū Arrūj, who bought Cervantes for one hundred coronas. Towards the end of 1579, Cervantes was ready to escape on a Spanish ship together with other prisoners, but their plan was discovered. In the meanwhile, his family appealed to the king to find help and collect the ransom, but Cervantes had already left Algiers on a galley sailing to Constantinople (19 September 1579). He returned to Spain on 24 October of the same year. During his second escape's trial, in 1579, while in the cave, it is said Cervantes conceived the idea of Quixote, where the Algiers captive is recalled in chapters XXXVIII–XLIII.

10 Several authors share this idea. See, for instance, Zaoui (2013).

11 *Le ravin de la femme sauvage* is the title of one of Renoir's pictures, dated 1881. During his stay in Algeria, Renoir was interested especially in the landscapes of the Algiers neighbourhoods near the area where he lived, on the south side of town. *Le ravin de la femme sauvage* shows a narrow valley that leads to the sea, starting from Boumerdes (Bū Murād Ra'īs), some two kilometres from the artist's residence. It also refers to a woman who "runs a coffee shop in this ravine shortly after the French conquest" (Play-Fair, 1890, 108).

12 I thank Waciny Laredj for having told me this story.

13 *Ẓilāl* means "shadows" but also "traces" and is an explicit reminder of the ancient Arab tradition.

14 All translations from Arabic are my own.

15 From the root ḤMW, to increase in heat (usually referencing sun and fire).

16 Laredj used this expression several times during meetings, congresses, interviews, and personal conversations.

17 This time span is detectable in several *loci* in the novel, where one can find the expression "for seven years…", supposedly since the novel's publication in 2001.

References

(I consciously quote the first names of the female authors, to showcase women's scholarly contributions.)

Al-Aʿraj, W. (1980) *Al-bawāba al-zarqā (Waqāʾiʿ min Awjāʿ rajul).*
———. (1981) *Ṭawq al-yāsamīn (Waqʿ al-aḥdhiya al-khashina).* Bayrūt: Dār al-ādāb.
———. (1982) *Mā tabqā min sīrat Lakhḍar Ḥamrūsh.* Dimashq: Dār al-madā.
———. (1983) *Nuwwār al-lawz.* Bayrūt: Dār al-ādāb.
———. (1984) *Maṣraʿ aḥlām Maryam Al-Wadayʿa.* Bayrūt: Dār al-ādāb.
———. (1990) *Ḍamīr al-ghāʾib.* Dimashq: Dār al-madā.
———. (1993) *Al-layla al-sābiʿa baʿd al-alf: raml al-māya.* Dimashq: Dār al-madā
———. (1995) *Sayydat al-maqām.* Almāniyā: Dār al-Jamal.
———. (1996) *Ḥārisat al-ẓilāl. Dūn Kīshūt fī al-Jazāʾir.* Al-Jazāʾir Marsā.
———. (1997) *Dhākirat al-māʾ.* Almāniyā: Dār al-Jamal.
———. (1999) *Ḥārisat al-ẓilāl: Dūn Kīshūt fī al-Jazāʾir.* Manshurāt al-faḍāʾ al-ḥurr: al-Jazāʾir.
———. (2001) *Shurafāt baḥr al-Shamāl. Amṭār Amstirdām.* Bayrūt: Dār al-ādāb.
———. (2002) *Al-makhṭūṭa al-Sharqiyya* Dimashq: Dār al-madā.
———. (2005) *Kitāb al-amīr.* Bayrūt: Dār al-ādāb.
———. (2009) *Krīmātūryūm. Sūnātā li-ashbāḥ al-Quds.* Bayrūt: Dār al-ādāb.
———. (2010) *Unthā al-sirāb.* Bayrūt: Dār al-ādāb.
———. (2012) *Aṣābiʿ Lūlītā.* Dubay: Dār al-ṣadā.
———. (2013) *Mamlakat al-farāsha.* Bayrūt: Dār al-ādāb.
———. (2015a) *Sīrat al-muntahā.* Dubay: Dār aṣ-ṣadā.
———. (2015b) *2084. Ḥikāyat al-ʿarabī al-akhīr.* Bayrūt: Dār al-ādāb.
———. (2017) *Nisāʾ Kāzānūfā.* Bayrūt: Dār al-ādāb.
———. (2018) *Imraʾa sarīʿat al-ʿaṭab.* Dubay: Midād.

Abdessemed, Naouel (2014) Exil et migration dans le roman algérien d'expression arabe: Le corps des brulures, *La cendre des corps brulés* (Jasad al-ḥarāʾiq, Nithār al-ajsād al-maḥrūqa) et *Les balcons de la mer du Nord* (Shurafāt baḥr al-shamāl) de Waciny Laredj. *Planeta Literatur. Journal of Global Literary Studies*, (1), 149–164.

Agour, B. (2009) Entretien avec Waciny Laredj: "Les langues n'ont pas de problème, les politiques en ont!". *Le Soir d'Algérie.* 11 June, 9.

Assman, J. (1997) *Das kulturelle Gedächtnis. Schrift, Erinnerung und politische Identität in früheren Hochkulturen.* München: C. H. Beck.

Bashīniyya, M. (2013) Al-ʿunwān wa-maʿnā al-naṣṣ al-sardī. Riwāyat "Ḥārisat al-ẓilāl" li-Wāsīnī al-Aʿraj namūdajan. *Majallat kulliyat al-adāb wa al-lughāt, Jāmiʿat Muḥammad Khayḍar Biskra*, (6), 203–228.

Ben Youssef Zayzafoon, Lamia (2010) Anne Frank Goes East: The Algerian Civil War and the Nausea of Postcoloniality in Waciny Laredj's Balconies to the North Sea. *College Literature*, 37(1), 61–80.

Bencheikh, J. E. (1988) *Les Mille et Une Nuit ou la parole prisonnière.* Paris: Gallimard.

Benmālik, R. (2003) Sīmyāʾiyyat al-ʿunwān fī riwāyat *Nuwwār al-lawz* li-l-riwāʾī Wāsīnī al-Aʿraj. In: *Aʿmāl wa-buḥūth al-multaqā al-duwalī al-sādis ʿAbd al-Ḥamīd ibn Hadūga li-l-riwāya.* BBA: Iʿdād mudīriyyat al-thaqāfa. 133–140.

Bourdieu, P. (2005) *Le regole dell'arte.* Milano: Il Saggiatore.

Būshūsha, B. (2004) Jadaliyyat al-waṭan/al-manfā wa-dhākirat al-riḥānāt al-khasira fī riwāyat Shurafāt baḥr al-shamāl. *Majallat al-ʿulūm al-insāniyya, Jāmiʿat Muḥammad Khayḍar Biskra*, (2), 95–110.

Childers, W. P. (2014) Zoraida's Return. *eHumanista/Cervantes,* (2), 379–406.

Fisher, D. D. (2007) *Écrire l'urgence: Assia Djebar et Tahar Djaout*. Paris: L'Harmattan.

Ganci, J. (2010) L'Algeria di Waciny Laredj tra letteratura, identità e memoria. *Osservatorio Iraq Medioriente e Nordafrica*, (5), 1–29. Available from: http://osservatorioiraq.it/punti-di-vista/lalgeria-di-waciny-laredj-letteratura-identit%C3%A0-e. [Accessed 21 February 2016].

Ghallāb, J. (2013) Muqāraba fī "Aṣābiʿ Lūlītā" li-Wāsīnī al-Aʿraj. *Majallat Masārib al-iliktrūniyya*. Available from: http://massareb.com/?p=2614. [Accessed 16 July 2019].

Ghosn, Katia (2010) Waciny Laredj. Un pont entre deux rives. *L'Orient Littérarie*, 54(2–12), 7.

Gómez-Benita, I. G. (2014a) La narrativa argelina actual y el compromiso integrador de Wasini Al-A'rach. *Hesperia, Culturas del Mediterraneo*, 18, 89–104.

———. (2014b) Lengua y ideología en la narrativa argelina actual: la experiencia integradora de Wāsīnī Al-A'raŷ. *Anaquel de Estudios Árabes*, 25, 7–28.

Grasfoguel, R. (2013) The Structure of Knowledge in Westernized Universities: Epistemic Racism/Sexism and the Four Genocides/Epistemicides of the Long 16th Century. *Human Architecture: Journal of the Sociology of Self-Knowledge*, 11(1), 73–90.

Guenatri, Leyla (2010) Contre une décadence programmée: le Don Quichotte à Alger de Waciny Laredj. *Recherches & Travaux [online]*, (76), 41–46. Available from: https://journals.openedition.org/recherchestravaux/402. [Accessed 3 May 2021].

Kalkhūsh, Fatīḥa (2007) Shiʿriyyat al-bunya al-sardiyya fī al-rawāī naḥū tayh Shiʿrī fī-shurafāt baḥr al-Shamāl. *Al-insāniyya*, 28(12), 105–133.

Laredj, W. (1997) *Le ravin de la femme sauvage*. Alger: ENAG.

Leeuven (van), R. (2018) *The Thousand and One Nights and Twentieth-Century Fiction: Intertextual Readings*. Leiden/Boston: Brill.

Leggio, F. (1997) Spazio vitale e spazio mortale in Dhākirat al-māʾ di Wāsīnī Al-Aʿraj. In: Isabella Camera d'Afflitto (ed.), *Le letterature del Maghreb: recupero della tradizione o risposta all'egemonia culturale? Oriente Moderno*, XVI(LXXVII) (2–3), 188–193.

Maldonado-Torres, N. (2018) The Decolonial Turn. In: J. Poblete (ed.). *New Approaches to Latin America Studies: Culture and Power*. New York: Routledge. 111–127.

Mokhtari, R. (2002) *La graphie de l'horreur. Essai sur la littérature algérienne (1990–2000)*. Alger: Chihab Edition.

Namer, G. (1987) *Mémoire et société*. Paris: Klincksieck.

Nardout-Lafarge, Elisabeth (2013) Instabilité du lieu dans la fiction narrative contemporaine. Avant- propos et notes pour un état présent. *Temps zéro*, (6). Available from: http://tempszero.contemporain.info/document974 [Accessed 16 July 2019].

Nora, P. (1989) Between Memory and History: Les lieux de la mémoire. *Representations*, (26) 7–24.

Play-Fair, L. (1890) *Murray's Handbook for Travellers in Algeria and Tunis*. London: no publisher.

Rothberg, M. (2010) Introduction: Between Memory and Memory. From Lieux de mémoire to Noeuds de mémoire. *Yale French Studies*, (118–119), 3–12.

Ṣāliḥ, Maḥfūẓah & Zūzū, Naṣīra (2005) Bunyat al-zaman fī riwāyat *Shurafāt baḥr al-shamāl* li-Wāsīnī al-Aʿraj. *Majallat al-ādāb wa-l-lughāt, Jāmiʿat Wargla*, 4(5) 55–82.

Tlatoani Cuauhtemoc's Last Speech. (1521). Available from: www.aguilaycondor.net/pgs/nuestra/n_a_sec1/n_a_sec1_pg1.html. [Accessed 18 July 2019].

Yaqṭīn, S. (1990) As-sīra wa-l-riwāya: Nuwwār al-lawz li-Wāsīnī al-Aʿraj namūdhajan. *Āfāq. Majallat Ittiḥād al-maghrib. Al-Ribāṭ: Maṭbaʿat al-maʿārif al-jadīda*, 15–22.

Yelles, M. (1997) Waciny Laredj: une écriture algérienne entre Orient et Occident: entretien avec Mourad Yelles. *Algérie Littérature/Action*, 141 –144, 1–9. http://revue-a.fr/extraits/extrait1-141-144-laredj.pdf

Y-Fu, T. (1977) *Space and Place: The Perspective of Experience*. Minneapolis/London: University of Minnesota Press.

Zaoui, A. (2013) Rendez-nous notre Islam algérien! *Liberté*, 25 April. Available from: www.liberte-algerie.com/culture/rendez-nous-notre-islam-algerien-188980/print/1.

Zūzū, Naṣīra (2006) Sīmyāʾ al-shakhṣiyya fī riwāyat "Ḥārisat al-ẓilāl" li-Wāsīnī al-Aʿraj. *Majallat al-ʿulūm al-insāniyya, Jāmiʿat Muḥammad Khayḍar Biskra*, (9), 1–17.

5 Resistant Assimilation and Hometactics as Decolonial Practices

The Stories of Leilah and Ibrahim in *The Orange Trees of Baghdad*

Shima Shahbazi

I am what time, circumstance, history, have made of me, certainly, but I am also, much more than that. So are we all.

(James A. Baldwin)

It is not our differences that divide us. It is our inability to recognize, accept, and celebrate those differences.

(Audre Lorde)

I will plant my hands in the flowerbed
I will sprout, I know, I know, I know
And the sparrows will lay eggs
In the hollows of my inky fingers…

(From "Another Birth" by Forough Farokhzad)

Introduction

Border crossing as experienced by Iraqi transnational writers does have political and social reasons; however, the narratives are woven very differently to those written by other Muslim women of colour writers.[1] The concept of home, the practice of hometactics (Ortega, 2016) and the definition of belonging is approached very differently in Iraqi life writing narratives. In this chapter, I analyse *The Orange Trees of Baghdad* – In Search of My Lost Family (2007), by Leilah Nadir (b. 1971), to shed light on the ways in which "home" has been defined and how assimilation and belonging have been achieved through a practice of hometactics, and decolonial resistance has been performed. As a note before starting the discussion, the characters in this memoir come from three different generations, and they have left Iraq (or have never seen Iraq, as they were born somewhere else) during the Baath regime's governance of Iraq (1958–2003); however, the narrative was written after the 2003 invasion and occupation of Iraq and therefore is an amalgamation of experiences of before and after the war. What is intriguing about *The Orange Trees* is the polyphonic narrative, which not only highlights the lived experience of the author but also brings into perspective both the commonality and diversity

DOI: 10.4324/9780429027338-6

of experiences of oppression arising from the Baath regime and the Western intervention in Iraq. The relation of "belonging" to social location and its intersectional nature is one of the main concerns of this chapter. Another important question to raise is whether a feminist practice of hometactics would lead to the construction of feminist homes.

Critical Underpinnings

In this chapter, I use Latina feminist phenomenology and theories of Gloria Anzaldua, Mariana Ortega, Paula Moya, and Cherrie Moraga to discuss transnational identity and multiplicitous selves.[2] Gloria Anzaldua, in her celebrated book *Borderlands: la frontera*, explores her in-between identity, her experience of living on the border of Mexico and the United States, and her relation to the history of both lands. Her discussion of multiplicity of selves is a kind of corrective to Western phenomenological philosophy. Her ideas surrounding multiple identities have been used by postmodern theorists of identity such as Deleuze and Guattari in their discussions of nomadic identities (Deleuze and Guattari, 1988). Postmodernists[3] generally believe that capitalist modernity has fragmented identities, nationalities, ethnicities, and experiences in general, and this is why Anzaldua's mestiza identity is advocated by these theorists.

Following up these theorists, Mariana Ortega uses Anzaldua's idea of the mestiza's multiplicity of the selves and "la facultad" to make an argument about multiplicitous selves. The question of multiplicity is significant when we are addressing cultural identity, transnational identities, and mixed identities because our lived experience is the result of the intertwining of the world and the self, and our relations to both.[4] Unlike Heidegger, who believes that a self "must be conceived in terms of *being-in-the-world* rather than in terms of being an epistemic substance," Ortega believes that a conscious human being is plural and between the worlds (multiplicitous selves in multiple worlds) (Ortega, 2016, 51). The multiplicitous selves that she introduces in her work are not limited to transnational subjects only. As she argues:

> While the account of multiplicitous selfhood offered here is to be understood as a general account of self – that is, all of us are multiplicitous selves – this work pays particular attention to those multiplicitous selves whose experience is marked by oppression and marginalization due to their social identities, those selves that have not figured prominently in the pages of philosophical discourses. Even though all of us are multiplicitous, some multiplicitous selves – those who are multicultural, queer, border dwellers, and whom Anzaldúa names *los atravesados* – experience more of what she describes as "psychic restlessness" and "intimate terrorism" due to their marginalization and oppression.
>
> (Ortega, 2016, 50–51)

The "intimate terrorism" that Ortega mentions is a term Anzaldua brings forth in her argument surrounding the new mestiza consciousness. It is "the violence and fear of the life of in-betweenness" (Ortega, 2016, 58). The experience of seeing and being in multiple worlds is not an easy experience for the transnational/border crosser subject. Maria Lugones calls the same experience "world travelling," and she believes the world traveller's self has a hermeneutic dimension, since this self that travels worlds is constantly interpreting and reinterpreting these worlds that she occupies and continuously resists the hegemonic logic pervasive in these worlds (Ortega, 2016, 58).

She argues that the multiplicitous self should be celebrated as it is, and the fragmentation and multiplicity make her world travelling and relations easier. When a transnational subject moves worlds, it is not just moving to another world and assimilating; rather, she is moving into another set of relations, and the new world might not have a space for her to be in and experience relationality.

The multiplicitous self that Anzaldua's new mestiza has developed makes her capable of questioning the definitions of home. "Home" and "belonging" questions are almost every new immigrant's daily preoccupation. In the United States, home as "felt knowledge" (Million 2009, 53–76) was epitomized at Ellis Island as an "Isle of Hope" (Behdad, 2005, 2), while also referred to as "Isle of Tears" for those who were never able to make America home. Australia's border protection control policies warn immigrants of certain backgrounds (mostly of Muslim background, of course) that they will not make Australia "home," and the "No Way" logo can be found in most Australian embassy websites as a welcoming start to immigration applications. Ali Behdad very aptly begins his book *A Forgetful Nation* with the image of Ellis Island Museum of Immigration and its "monolithic and patriatic narrative of immigrant heritage [... which] eclipses both the violent history that characterizes the peopling of America and the actualities of the nation's immigration policies" (Behdad, 2005, 2–3). "Historical amnesia towards immigration," Behdad argues, has been essential for the construction of the myth of America as a "nation" (Behdad, 2005, 3) because it obscures reasons such as the "political economy of immigration" and "xenophobia" (Behdad, 2005, 10). The myth of America as a hospitable and xenophilic nation benefits from immigrants and their contribution to "the political project of national identity." Behdad maintains:

> Immigrants are useful to the political project of national identity, through an exclusionary logic that defines them as differential others and also through inclusive means of identification that recuperate them as figures of cultural conformism, exceptionalism, and regeneration. Assimilation as a more subtle denial of difference has been integral to how the United States has imagined itself as an immigrant nation. Since the founding, the notion of cultural and political assimilation has always accompanied

> the myth of immigrant America, as newcomers have been "domesticated" and forced to lose their old national "skins" to become American citizens.
>
> (Behdad, 2005, 12)

Assimilation, then, has been defined as losing one's old skin and growing a new one that accords with the new location. For border crossing multiplicitous selves, a definite place of belonging is an illusion because belonging is not about home anymore but rather "homes" (Behdad, 2005, 195). A sense of full belonging is almost a myth for such identities because homemaking for them is a process that does not take place in one location only but in multiple locations and where they travel. However, the myth of belonging cannot be fully ignored as it is very powerful. Ortega argues:

> It cannot be denied that even for those multiplicitous selves who are border-crossers and world-travellers, the home question is still a question. Perhaps it is even a more painful question precisely because that home seems harder to find or cannot be found given one's multiplicity. Yet, despite the determination of this will to belong that might provide a feeling of security and comfort, we cannot avoid recognizing the limits and pitfalls of such security, namely, the reification of certain identity categories as opposed to others and thus the expulsion of those who do not fit a version of authentic belonging.
>
> (Behdad, 2005, 196)

To come over these feelings of loss and lack of belonging, multiplicitous selves develop "hometactics."[5] Hometactics for Ortega are "practices that we develop as we travel our various worlds and that we can later repeat or maintain" (Ortega, 2016, 206). These practices are strategies of survival, feeling more at ease, of homemaking and making new locations share memories with our previous homes. These practices could be as simple as making the dishes our grandmothers used to make for us when we were kids or using tablecloths and curtains we have brought with us from previous homes, because colour and light actually do matter in our feelings of belonging to a space.[6] In short, as Ortega clearly states,

> the aim of hometactics can be understood as the production of a sense of familiarity in the midst of an environment or world in which one cannot fully belong due to one's multiple positions and instances of thin and thick not being-at-ease.
>
> (Ortega, 2016, 203)

Orange Trees of Baghdad*: A Polyphonic Memoir*

In *Orange Trees of Baghdad*, the concepts of home, assimilation, and belonging are conspicuously different to the other life-writing narratives about Iraq. Leilah, the protagonist, writes about her own experience of home, both Canada and Iraq, at the time of the American invasion of Iraq. But she does not uncover much detail about her own understanding of home; instead, she writes about her father's experience of border crossing and homemaking in the West and the ways in which he assimilated and re-rooted somewhere else. Leilah's narration of the second-hand memories of Ibrahim's (her father) border crossing and homemaking play a great role in clarifying the significance of some of the symbols and cultural references she uses for the reader. Furthermore, her social location, as a second-generation, biracial British-Iraqi, Canadian by citizen, and Christian by birth, affects her vision of home, what it means for her, and what it means for Ibrahim and the rest of the Iraqi identities in her extended family. Using the genre of memoir has enabled Leilah to offer a more complex view of identity by incorporating multiple voices and perspectives, without having to reduce them into a monolithic memoir. If polyphony is maintained throughout lived experience narratives, especially narratives of the marginalized voices, literary forms and genres such as the genre of memoir can function as a means to decolonize epistemologies. Leilah's narrative includes voices of men and women who have lived their lives under the oppressive system before 2003 as well as after the invasion and occupation, and their critical perspective stands as a counter-hegemonic discourse. Memoir as a literary genre can provide the grounds for these voices to decolonize the power of hegemonic discourses and the grand narratives of history that have documented stories from above as "facts" and "common sense."[7]

Leilah starts the story of her father with reference to how little she knows about Ibrahim's relationship to Iraq (Nadir, 2014, 34), as he kept so many of his stories away from them. The background to Ibrahim's story of homemaking in Canada (Nadir, 2014, 34) is that he went to England on an Iraqi government scholarship to pursue his education there as an engineer, and, since he fell in love with a British woman, he decided to stay. As a result, Leilah's grandfather had to pay the scholarship off. Ibrahim never returned to Iraq, although he was supposed to, based on his scholarship conditions. The Baathist regime was ruthless, and he could not make sure that visiting Iraq again would not be equal to punishment. Ibrahim's exile and assimilation story is followed by a description of his personality:

> A successful engineer and businessman, he has a scientific, rational approach to life. He is very reliable, loves math and famously, as his colleagues sometimes tease, "never makes mistakes." He [my father] isn't superstitious, a conspiracy theorist or a reactive thinker; he loves games of strategy like bridge and chess and laughs off mysticism and miracles. Perhaps because he married an Englishwoman, he didn't socialize much with other Iraqis or live out an Arabic life in Canada. He assimilated willingly and easily, and was happy in the West.
>
> (Nadir, 2014, 35)

In this quote, Ibrahim's wilful assimilation is juxtaposed to his rational approach to life. He is described as "not superstitious or a conspiracy theorist or reactive thinker," which recalls stereotypes with which most Arabs, and Middle Eastern identities in general, are identified. Ibrahim is described as a good example of an assimilated migrant who chooses to live outside Iraq, marry an English woman, and move to Canada with her to start a family. Compared to Iranian exilic identities, Ibrahim is never described as homesick for Iraq or for his family. He is said to laugh off mysticism and miracles, which are remarkable cultural references when discussing Middle Eastern religions and cultures. Leilah is not sure if this assimilation is a result of Ibrahim's marriage, or if it stems from his rational mind. Considering the notions of logic and rationality in this context, I would argue against a Eurocentric ground of comparison, which sees rationality and superstition as a binary opposition. This also reminds us of the binary of modern/non-modern societies. I am not saying that Leilah has a Eurocentric view of logic and rationality here; I am trying to demonstrate how juxtaposition of words in this context could produce knowledge that might include epistemic violence. Taking an intersectional perspective, I argue that most of Ibrahim's assimilation in the West is a result of his social location as a middle-class, educated Christian Iraqi who migrates to the UK in that specific era (Baathist regime in power in Iraq).

Like so many of the exilic identities (including Iranians), he isolates himself from the Arabic-speaking community in the UK, and later in Canada, as a practice of hometactics. He does not wish to be identified as an Arab Iraqi, not because he does not want to be considered as a "conspiracy theorist," but because the racial hierarchy that already existed in the West upon his arrival would still other him into that category, even if he were not one. Leilah claims that her father has never experienced racism (Nadir, 2014, 35). This claim partly arises from the fact that Leilah's biracial identity holds privileges that make her unable to see different forms of racism. Racism is not only the blatant disrespecting of someone to their face due to their skin colour or language; a more harmful form of racism is institutional systemic racism, which denies migrants opportunities and forces them into unwilful practices of assimilation, identity negotiations, and forgetting of their past homes. This is why a phenomenological approach to the notion of race and racism is necessary when discussing practices of hometactics and assimilation. The extent to which assimilation takes place is affected by the system and its receptivity to migrants. Ibrahim has been so well assimilated that Leilah cannot see her father's difference to other Canadian citizens; as she mentions, "All [her] life [she]'d never perceived [her] father as an immigrant and so whenever there was a war in Iraq, [she] was startled to be reminded that he came from an enemy land" (Nadir, 2014, 36).

The fact that Leilah never perceived her father as an immigrant is a very important point here. Ibrahim's hometactics and practice of assimilation has been so successful that even his own daughter has not seen the pains of adaptability he has gone through. One reason is that he has never expressed any discomfort while adapting to the new culture, except for a few culture shocks that Leilah has recorded. As Leilah claims, Ibrahim has never experienced discrimination; she writes:

> Some of the Iraqis complained about discrimination, but Ibrahim never experienced it. "I had high self-esteem, so I didn't care if people were rude. Maybe they were reacting to my being Arabic, but I just thought they were being unpleasant. It didn't occur to me that people were discriminating against me because of my race. I thought it was their problem. I never thought it was because of the colour of my skin," he said, shrugging.
>
> (Nadir, 2014, 67)

According to this excerpt, Ibrahim has experienced discrimination; however, his adaptability has been more based on denial than confrontation or acceptance. I argue that this is another form of hometactics: to develop a level of self-esteem and to acknowledge one's own rights of presence and existence in a space. Not all forms of adaptability include confrontation, aggression, victimization, or fantasisation and recreation of past homes. Instead of taking those strategies, Ibrahim develops a high level of agency for his presence. To make discrimination less of a central issue in his migrant life, he avoids terms such as racism and discrimination and replaces them with "rudeness" and "unpleasantness" of behaviour. Using "rudeness" instead of racism does not take any weight out of the heaviness of racism as an experience that most migrants experience; however, as a practice of homemaking, it has made life easier for a migrant like Ibrahim. Ibrahim is married to an English woman and has settled down in the West. Not interpreting rudeness as racism does not mean that he is racially blind, or that, like so many nationalist Iranians, he would bring up the glorious past of the Ottoman Empire or reign of Babylon as a response to racism (framed by the binary of culture/civilization). His act is a practice of hometactics that keeps his productivity and mental health in place. Holding on to one's agency is an act of resistance and a strategic response to others' wilful ignorance, and this is what Ibrahim has been performing in order to keep his family together.[8]

Embodied Homes

Leilah comes to perceive her father as a migrant when the war breaks out and his Iraqiness becomes hyper-visible to her. That is the point when all practices of hometactics, adaptability, resistance, and homemaking in the West are outweighed by the outrage of an imposed war. This is the first time Ibrahim starts talking about his Iraqiness, his homeland, and his view of something that led him to border crossing and exile, which is the Baathist regime:

> "No one hates Saddam Hussein as much as I do, no one would be happier than me to see him gone," he'd [father] replied angrily. "But this war is illegal, immoral! it would be unjustified, it is a pre-emptive war. It would be seen in the Middle East as an unprovoked invasion by the West, against international law, confirming everyone's worst fears about Western imperialism. It would not be acceptable. You can't just decide that you don't like your neighbour and go into his house and murder him. You can't take the law into your own hands. Innocent people will die and then how can the world ever turn to a country ruled by a despot and tell them that such actions are unacceptable? It would be hypocrisy".
>
> (Nadir, 2014, 35)

Home, for a transnational subject who has been in exile for more than 30 years, is a complex concept. Ibrahim, as I discussed before, has had a successful practice of hometactics and performance of adaptability due to his epistemic privilege. He has followed the politics of home from afar and has tried his best not to engage in "illogical" conspiracy theories. But when the invasion of Iraq takes place, and Saddam Hussein is executed with no trial, he breaks his silence, and his adaptability takes a different form of resistance, which, this time, has more of a confrontational nature. He problematizes the invasion of home as a counterproductive act, as an intervention that not only does not reduce despotism in that region but also adds to it and produces more violation of human rights. For so many transnationals like Ibrahim, home is an abstract concept. The homeland in which they have been born and raised fades away as home when they leave and make home in other spaces. But they will always see it as home again when homeland is troubled. Home is not just a spatial concept; as much as it hurts to see the historical heritage in ruin, it hurts even more to see the lives of people turn into ashes, the lives of those people that speak the same language as oneself and know what it means to have the smell of orange tree blossoms everywhere in the city. It is a space, embodied in people and their relations with one another, that makes that very space home.

To put it differently, the concept of home involves bodily memory. One's experience is part of their hermeneutic horizon, which they take with themselves and use to interpret their new experiences. Part of that experience is related to their group identity, and part of it is gender and race-based identity that might not be foregrounded in all contexts but is definitely foregrounded in specific contexts and situations. The hermeneutics of horizons (Alcoff, 1999) allow us to see that our group identities are part of us; however, hermeneutics cannot be used as the only tool because it does not take the body into account. We need to have a phenomenological approach on the side to bring the body and its analysis back into the debate. The degree of visibility is dependent on one's physical manifestation, too; therefore, it is important to take the sphere of the visible into account. To see how the concept of home has both spatial and interpersonal qualities, we need to consider embodiment as an integral part of our hermeneutic horizons.

Ibrahim's early years in England as a 16-year-old boy attending school in Yorkshire were full of homesickness. As Leilah narrates his story, "instead of going 'wild,' he [Ibrahim] went domestic" (Nadir, 2014, 66). He could not survive living with an English family as he missed Iraqi food, which, to him, was the taste of home. His first practice of homemaking was when he started asking his mother and aunties to send him food recipes and he started making his own Iraqi food. Food is one of the most frequent embodiments of home in a transnational life. It is not just the taste of food but the process of making it that evokes the idea of home. Food could be the nostalgic embodiment of homeland and home culture for an exilic identity, or it could be a practice of hometactics for a transnational identity who is developing a level of adaptability to the new space and intends to make life easier in the potential new home. As Ibrahim implies, cooking Iraqi food, playing chess with his friends as people did back home (Nadir, 2014, 66), or writing long letters to his parents were the only strategies he could consume to relieve the anxiety of border crossing. As he explains to his daughter, "people didn't think like that in those days … you just got on with life. There weren't any other options. How would I get home? Plane tickets were very expensive in those days" (Nadir, 2014, 67). Therefore, homemaking and adaptability become a survival strategy, as having a transnational life and crossing the borders back home is not always a viable option at specific times. Ibrahim starts going to pubs with his friends, because according to Leilah's document, "all social activities revolved around a pint or two [of beer]." This practice of hometactics is feasible for Ibrahim, who is Christian by religion; however, we need to remember how difficult socialization would have been and still is for a practicing Muslim who is trying to assimilate.

It would be even harder for a practicing Muslim woman, as the practice of drinking not only has religious and ethnic connotations but is also a gendered practice. A practicing Muslim woman walking to a pub for socialization is hyper-visible. Her hijab, functioning as a politicized flag of her faith, makes her presence function not towards assimilation, but rather towards being othered. Thus, hometactics practices cannot be monolithically applied by all group identities, even if they belong to the same ethnic subgroups (Arab/Persian/Iranian, for instance). They can only be creatively developed in intersections with one's particular social location through the different privileges onto which they can hold. Furthermore, developing a fully assimilated life after border crossing could go beyond the development of a multiplicitous self and instead aim for a unified self that has resolved the conflicts of cultural, social, and religious values and is now ready for a full integration into the new home space. The anxiety of border crossing, or what Anzaldua calls intimate terrorism (Anzaldúa 1987, 20), results from the anxiety of assimilation. The anxiety of moving worlds (border crossing) and living in between worlds (adaptability) does not just arise from moving spaces. As we can see in Ibrahim's case, it is mostly about moving from one set of relations to another, and the new world might not have any space for those sets of relations that one brings from the previous world. Adapting to a new set of relations is also not always a volitional act; it could be motivated by anxieties or post-traumatic responses. Assimilation is a process of receptivity and adaptiveness; however, it is volitional when it takes place through critical thinking as well as strategicness. But even practicing critical thinking while assimilating is a privilege that is dependent on one's social location and does not only come from wilfulness. Not all border-crossers have been able to develop that critical consciousness. This is why, as Karen Barad (Barad 2003, 829) and Paula Moya (Moya 2015, 30) explain, transnational identities need to be explained in relation to "onto-epistem-ology," which is the practices of knowing in being. We do not obtain knowledge by standing outside the world; we know things because "we" are part of the world and the set of relations dominant in that very world.

Tell Me Where Your Home Is

Another practice of hometactics towards adaptability that has been portrayed in *The Orange Trees* is about Ibrahim's learning about English culture from his father before moving to Britain.

> Ibrahim already knew all about British culture from his father the basics of how to dress, how to introduce yourself and make small talk. But there were many terrified students from small Iraqi villages, who were very clever but had never lived in a city before and had no idea how they were going to manage in England. … Couples kissed in the streets which felt almost pornographic to a young Iraqi who wasn't allowed to have a girlfriend or to be alone with a young woman who wasn't a relative. Here, people flaunted their affairs in public.
>
> (Nadir, 2014, 64)

This is another example of moving worlds and noticing a whole new set of relations at work in a new space that is supposed to be the new home.[9] The relations are of a social, cultural, and interpersonal nature and intrinsic to one's existence in the world(s). When Ibrahim has his first encounters in London, he experiences a huge difference in social and cultural practices between Baghdad and London. Adapting to such a new atmosphere requires a great degree of receptivity. Practices such as public expression of emotion or having relationships out of wedlock would be shocking to a newcomer like Ibrahim and his friends; this might be interpreted as "backward" through an end-of-the-twentieth-century Western lens. However, there is another side to this story, too; some practices that would be completely normal and common sense for a young Iraqi man would be shocking to a British man. For instance,

Ibrahim recalls watching a young student smoking half of his cigarette and putting the rest of it back in the box for the next break, and this comes as an absolute shock to him, coming from where people have one single puff of a cigarette and throw it away (Nadir, 2014, 68). These are very simple examples chosen from the memoir to demonstrate the complexities of home-making, hometactics practices, and adaptability for different social identities in different social locations and contexts.

Ibrahim barely talks about Iraq. Even Leilah's mom, Mary, agrees that Ibrahim did not share much about Iraq and his family history, and going back to Iraq after they got married was never a question on the table, perhaps because Ibrahim had not done his compulsory military service and it would have been dangerous to return and be forced to serve (Nadir, 2014, 71). Leilah mentions that when she once tried to press him about why he knew so little about his family history, and mainly his grandfather, who was a translator for the British, Ibrahim responded, "Life was hard then, you know. People had to struggle, people didn't have the luxury to talk about family history or stories about the past, even the middle classes like us. You just got on with life, with surviving" (Nadir, 2014, 43). Ibrahim uses the phrase "get on with life" a few times in his stories. The practice of getting on with life portrays a multi-layered complex social position where, as a middle-class Iraqi man, he does have a life, a position to hold on to, but is not still privileged enough to choose some things, even if he has free will. Choosing a place of living, a country of residence, and making a home there is an act of survival for Ibrahim. He remembers the anxiety of awaiting a visa for admission to Canada when his visa for staying in the UK had expired, and as an Iraqi married to a British woman, he did not want to go back to Iraq and serve in the military. All the choices he had to make (which were mostly driving him farther from the homeland) made him emotionally remote from "his Iraqi home," too. When Leilah asks her mom if she and Ibrahim ever considered going to Iraq and living there, she also responds: "I suppose we didn't think it through to that final conclusion, ... probably we always thought, hoped, that things in the country would improve, that things would change there, that it would be possible to visit" (Nadir, 2014, 72).

The desire for improvement of homeland is a common desire for many transnational and exilic identities. Even the term diaspora suggests an idea of a homeland: diaspora means "the dispersion or spread of any people from their original homeland."[10] Therefore, there is a home from which people have been dispersed, and a possibility of return is implied as a binary opposite to dispersion. For Mary, as a young British woman, Baghdad does not have the same home feeling as it does for Ibrahim or so many other Iraqis. She only bonds with Baghdad because that is the city where her husband was born and raised. When Leilah asks Mary about Ibrahim's accent when they started dating (because, according to Leilah, he no longer had an Arabic accent, which is another sign of assimilation), Mary responds:

> Oh yes he did, a lovely one, … and, he was very exotic. The film Lawrence of Arabia came out around that time, I can't remember when, and we were all very taken with notions of the "east." I remember seeing Omar Sharif in the movie and thinking of your father! The east was very remote, very "other", and we romanticized and idealized it, the way you do as a teenager. Baghdad was this exotic city. When I thought about Baghdad then, it was a place bathed in a golden light connected to the Ottoman Empire. A city with skyline of minarets and domes like Istanbul, but with the Tigris and Euphrates Rivers flowing through it and palm trees everywhere. It was something out of a fairy tale.
>
> (Nadir, 2014, 69–79)

Mary's description of Baghdad is rich in Orientalist perspectives of Baghdad and the Middle East in general. Of course, Mary as a teenager gained that perspective via the media of the time, the movies and pictures representing "the Middle East." Baghdad is represented as a romanticized and idealized land full of gold, domes, and rivers running in between. This is clearly a very Aladdin-like description of the city where Ibrahim was born and to which he does not want to return due to the tumultuous situation, a great part of which has been caused by British coloniality. Ibrahim, looking like an "exotic" Omar Sharif in the West, has had (willingly or unwillingly) to erase his Arabic accent and westernize it so that he fits in his new home. Even if all these assimilation practices are wilful and come from one's full free will and agency, the power of the white-supremacist discourses of integration and assimilation at the time should not be underestimated. Ibrahim and Mary's first experience of migration to Canada is narrated by Leilah. They move to a very small town near Calgary where people are shocked to see such a mixed couple:

> Still, the small town was a shock to Londoners, and they were a shock to the town. The Canadians had known an "A-rab" had been hired and were expecting a traditionally robed Gulf Arab with a red head scarf and his exotically submissive wife. Instead, a green Chevrolet pulled into town and the townspeople watched the new engineer, Ibrahim, with his shaggy black hair, trendy tight T-shirt and jeans, helping out his new bride, Mary, with her long brown hair parted in the middle and flowing down her back, wearing a brightly coloured miniskirt, loud prints on her shirt and platform shoes. This was not the belly-dancing wife that some had expected.
>
> (Nadir, 2014, 84)

Ibrahim does not fit the stereotypes that already exist about Arabs, and Middle Eastern men in general. His "modern" look is not a result of assimilation, though. Ibrahim comes from a secular, modernized Iraq where middle-class men and women are highly educated and are not robed or headscarfed. However, the Western imaginary is still obsessed with the stereotypical *One Thousand and One Nights* men and women. If Mary were not a British woman and she were Iraqi, she would have been expected to be the same submissive woman, fully covered outdoors and belly dancing within the walls of the harem. Through his marriage to a British woman, Ibrahim has achieved some privileges that non-mixed couples might not have had at the time. His conjugal affiliation to whiteness makes him more "one-of-us" rather than "one-of-them" in the Western imaginary. Through this marriage, he has already been filtered as a non-threat and as a liberated Arab Iraqi man. Furthermore, his marriage to an Anglo woman makes his assimilation and achieving a sense of belonging an easier task.

Leilah's biracial identity is also significant. Throughout the memoir, there is more emphasis on her being second generation compared to Ibrahim, and the nature of their nostalgia for Iraq is different. Yet, one big difference with Ibrahim is that she also has access to the cultural and identarian capital of her mother, which is her white Anglo privilege and her "Britishness." Apart from one quote regarding the invasion of Iraq, whereby Leilah considers herself as both the "conqueror and the conquered," the rest of book de-emphasizes Leilah's own "Anglo-ness." This could result from two situations: first, it is because whiteness is blind and once one is born white, in a system that is designed for white people, they do not need to acknowledge their white capital. Second, it could be a practice of hometactics and adaptability, in a condition where whiteness is invasive to her Iraqiness. *Orange Trees of Baghdad* is a second-generation memoir about Iraq, but it is also a biracial memoir that detaches itself from the British sides of the invasion and emphasizes the American side. I am more inclined towards the adaptability hypothesis in this context, because Leilah's nostalgia of a lost Iraq can only be soothed if her invasive British side is forgotten for a while.

As a second-generation biracial, Leilah does not share that kind of experience with Ibrahim. For her, Iraq is her father's home, something she feels in her bones through second-hand memory, and her imaginary is constructed through "what she has heard." However, Leilah's nostalgic imaginary of home is based on not only hearsay but also research and a polyphonic story-sharing among family members and in the photo albums she has inherited. The pictures of home are extremely vivid as she describes them:

> My father's childhood house still stands. The orange trees are still there. I sense the garden only through my family's stories; words and pictures about its smells, the searing heat, the light, the butterflies, the storks, eating the Baghdad delicacy of buffalo cream there. … I imagine Iraq spreading and rippling out in circles with the house and garden in the halo at the centre.
>
> (Nadir, 2014, 16)

As a second generation, Leilah keeps picturing the family house, which she has never seen, lived in, or smelled. Second-generation memory is very complex. The nostalgia of home has not necessarily been passed on from the first generation because, of course, depending on the type of border crossing, many first-generation individuals practice the strongest forms of assimilation; sometimes, even, they do not pass on the mother-tongue language to their children, as they try to fully raise their kids in the new culture and within the cultural values of the new home. On the other hand, some first-generation migrants make an effort to preserve the homeland culture. They only speak their first language at home, teach their children old songs, folkloric dance, and music, and pass on their food recipes. In my ethnographical observation of the second-generation diaspora in Sydney and London, I came across a number of second-generation Iranians and Iraqis, highly educated, socioeconomically middle class (not upper middle class, though), and mostly involved in cultural and educational activities, who mostly identified with the first group of second generations. They were all very passionate about a homeland in which they had not been born, or even lived. Some of them told me that they really wanted to visit their "homeland" (this is the term they used for the country of their background) but had been stopped by their parents, who considered going back a waste of time. They unanimously talked about the confusion that they felt about the concept of home and this nostalgia of a homeland they had never visited. Highly hyperconscious of their accented Persian or Arabic, they still tried to maintain conversations in the mother tongue, telling me how they pictured their homeland. Like Leilah, one of them told me that she feels she has inherited the border-crossing anxiety from her parents. While her parents do not talk about their experience of border crossing, the assimilation process, and the difficulties of making homes at borderlands, she felt the anxiety of homemaking and border crossing in her bones, as if she had experienced it herself. Second-generation diaspora bears the anxiety of displacement and belonging; however, even the very fact that they can question the nature of their anxiety and "care" about a homeland they have never directly experienced places them in a privileged social location. The second generation, like Leilah, does not have to learn a new language in their adult age, or make homes from scratch, because the first generation has already done that for them. However, their "belonging" anxiety, cultural in-betweenness, and second-hand trauma are what turns into an identity challenge and something in life with which they have to "get on."

As I mentioned earlier, so much of Leilah's understanding of home comes from a photo album that has been put together by her Iraqi grandfather. Interestingly, the photo captions are all in English, which confirms Khalil's (Leilah's grandfather) futuristic concerns about the next generations and family heritage. Leilah writes:

> As I look at these pictures, I realize almost of the painstakingly written captions are written in English and there are only a few names in Arabic script. Khalil had even marked small X's directly on the photographs with the names printed out in the margin so that people could be identified. It's as if he had purposely written this for us, his grandchildren, knowing that

> we didn't know Arabic. He didn't make the albums so much for his own children, who knew most of the people and events they contained, but for us, the grandchildren he couldn't know. He knew that all the family history would be lost in a generation if he didn't make the albums. I believe this wasn't an accident – it was his direct intention.
>
> (Nadir, 2014, 104)

Khalil has written and documented the family microhistory in both visual and verbal modes. The fact that he has used English as an archiving language is avant-garde. Khalil has foreseen a future transnational family, a family on the move, as he has lived through the hardest historical moments in Iraq, namely, colonization, dictatorship, the Iran–Iraq war, the Gulf war, and sanctions. One would keep a backup of all family heritage and memories, once they live in constant fear of bombardment and destruction. As Leilah contemplates, Khalil "didn't want us to forget Iraq, our roots. Did he suspect that one day it would be impossible to go back and see the house he built for the family, to collect our possessions, the family heirlooms?" (Nadir 2014, 105). She knows for sure that at the time of her grandfather's death, "Iraq had been cut off from the world for almost a decade. Maybe he knew what that meant, and how easy it would be for that to happen again" (Nadir, 2014, 105). Through these photos and captions as epistemic bodies, Leilah achieves postmemory knowledge. Postmemory, according to Marianne Hirsch, has been defined as "the relationship of the second generation to powerful, often traumatic, experiences that preceded their births but that were nevertheless transmitted to them so deeply as to seem to constitute memories in their own right" (Hirsh, 2008, 103). She sees postmemory as "a structure of inter- and trans-generational transmission of traumatic knowledge and experience. It is a consequence of traumatic recall but (unlike post-traumatic stress disorder) at a generational remove" (Hirsh, 2008, 106). She continues:

> postmemory's connection to the past is thus not actually mediated by recall but by imaginative investment, projection and creation. To grow up with such overwhelming inherited memories, to be dominated by narratives that preceded one's birth or one's consciousness, is to risk having one's own stories and experiences displaced, even evacuated, by those of a previous generation.
>
> (Hirsh, 2008, 107)

Jennifer Bowering Delisle calls Leilah's postmemory "genealogical nostalgia," (Delisle 2013, 384,) which is "the affective drive to uncover, preserve and record our family history and homeland – this notion of feeling a place 'in our bones,' despite never having seen it" (Delisle, 2013, 384). She distinguishes between postmemory and genealogical nostalgia for Leilah; while postmemory is "the inheritance of trauma," genealogical nostalgia is "a yearning to know and understand that trauma"; genealogical nostalgia is "a nostalgia derived not out of direct experience, but out of the very gaps between personal experience and a dominant ancestral past" (Delisle, 2013, 384).

Leilah's understanding of Saddam Hussein, and the brutal regime of the time when her father left Iraq, comes through postmemory. It is not a trauma she has lived through, but it is a trauma of which she has heard different narratives. It seems to her that her father's choice of never going back to Iraq was mostly influenced by this very historical character. When Saddam Hussein is executed on 29 December 2006, Leilah asks her father how he feels about his death, and in response he says "nothing" (Nadir, 2014, 310). Leilah expects more hatred and disgust from her father towards the execution of someone who had killed thousands of people. However, Ibrahim has always known that this day would come, as the fate of dictators is just another repetitive historical story (Nadir, 2014, 311). While Ibrahim has been advised by another Iraqi friend (a Canadian resident) to "just forget Iraq" and "never ever go back" (Nadir, 2014, 311), Leilah has a desire to return and see the trauma of Saddam removed from the lives of people. This is the trauma she has not lived but that she still carries with her through postmemory. She can see her father's discomfort in Canada's cold winters, and she remembers that he has not gotten used to the temperature yet, and that he might never do so. This is how she has inherited the nostalgia of a homeland that exists on the other side of the world but that is still unliveable for so many Iraqis like her father. The fear of going back and seeing the homeland in ruin is what has stopped Ibrahim and so many other Iraqis (even Iranians) from going back. Instead, Leilah imagines going to the homeland:

> For now, all I can do is imagine, in ten or twenty years, with my children perhaps, opening up the old [family house in Baghdad] and going inside. Perhaps the photographs will still be framed on the mantelpiece, my aunts' clothes in the closets, my father's newspaper in a drawer. I walk up on to the roof. I look everywhere, but the house is empty. I go back downstairs and out onto the terrace facing the neglected garden, shriveled and wild. There I am greeted by the ghosts of my grandparents, my great-aunt, my great uncles, all saying at once, "Welcome, welcome. You've come to visit us. Sit down, sit down, we'll drink tea. We knew you'd come one day. We knew you'd be back."
>
> (Nadir, 2014, 312)

This nostalgic description situates homeland in past, present, and future. Leilah's connection to homeland is not just an Arab-Iraqi house with orange trees and mantelpieces; it is the people about whom she has read, heard, and learned to love without having ever met them. Homeland for Leilah is not just a spatial entity, but a set of relations with people she has never met but by whom she knows she would have been loved: people like Khalil, who prepared family albums with captions in English for the future generations that he also knew he would never meet but he would love. Therefore, genealogical nostalgia is not just about homeland as a space; it is for people and affective relations that make people feel like they belong to a space.

The reality of homeland as both space and a set of interpersonal relations hits Leilah when she sees a photograph of Al-Rasheed Street in 2011. She describes the photo as a "shock" (Nadir, 2014, 326) as "everything the eye lights on is broken down, blackened by explosions" (Nadir, 2014, 326). The photos of their family house in Baghdad, which portray home in a state of decay, are the painful reality of homeland and the family house:

> Because of the devastating contrast between these images and my aunts' memories, the photographs are the catalyst for severing the final connection and selling the family home. My aunts looked into the pictures and knew they could never live in the house again, on that street, in that neighbourhood, that they were never going back to Iraq, that the idea was pure fantasy. In ten years, they had lost all their relatives and friends, either to death or emigration. They had once known most of their neighbours, but now only one family remained on the street, everyone else had fled. There was no one to take care of the house and the country was too terrifying to return to. Why would they ever go back?
>
> (Nadir, 2014, 327)

The photographs catalyse fantasy into reality without changing in substance. They portray a present, as shocking as they are, representing a nation's struggles and the impossibility of going back for those who left home years ago. Selling the family house is not just a sort of property management; it is to repress memories of a home that used to bring people together. Stranded houses are very common in Iran and Iraq, especially in middle-class areas of town. People, having once made homes there, have had to leave, and the houses are still there after 40 years in poor shape only because the owners always thought there would come a time when they could return to those houses. Most never return. The old houses, layered with generational memories, are either sold through local lawyers and end up being gentrified, or they are taken over by local government since the inheritors never claim their property. Most people never return because there is no one to return to; as Leilah explains, there is no point in going back home when one has lost all relatives and friends at home, through either death or emigration. What remains of home, or even homes that are sold, are suitcases of documents, albums, birth and death certificates, property documents, and heirlooms. Leilah vividly narrates the sad story of her family's last suitcase:

> The suitcase full of documents that my father had asked Karim to bring when he fled is now housed with distant family members living in Baghdad. One suitcase is all that is left in Iraq of a family whose roots in that landscape, culture and language go back thousands of years, an ancient connection that likely reaches back to the earliest Christians,

> perhaps earlier. A suitcase bereft of even a person to carry it to the next homeland.
>
> (Nadir, 2014, 328)

The suitcase becomes a metonymy of homeland. Leilah's suitcase is all that is left of a homeland she has never directly experienced. Leilah's and her family's only remnants of home cannot even cross the borders. They have to stay in Iraq because Iraq has been constantly struggling with war, invasions, civil conflicts, terrorism, etc., all these years after Ibrahim's emigration. No one has been able to stay in Iraq. Emigration has not been a desirable option for Leilah's aunts and relatives but has been the only way to survive. Amal explains:

> "We want to find out if there is any way she can apply for the family to come to England. They have to get out of Iraq. But she doesn't want to move here and become a refugee. She just wants to stay in Baghdad and for everything to get better." … Reeta leaves the room, taking a few plates with her, but I see she's holding back her own tears. Reeta misses Baghdad already; the idea of leaving forever is tormenting her. … Even though Iraq is in such anarchy, the British government and many other Western countries regard the country as "free" since it has held democratic elections. It is more difficult now to apply as a refugee than it was during the years of Saddam's dictatorship.
>
> (Nadir, 2014, 268–269)

The hometactics that people like Reeta have to practice is very different to the one Ibrahim applied for making a home in Canada years earlier. This excerpt is a conspicuous example depicting why I insist on having a decolonial methodology for reading these lived experience narratives. Many Iraqi women like Reeta have lost their shelter, family members, men of their lives, and children to war, sanction, and unwilful emigration. Reeta is Leilah's second cousin. The first time Leilah meets her Iraqi family members, they all meet in London, halfway from Iraq and halfway to Canada. When they meet, Leilah is wearing her "gold Iraqi-map necklace" which Maha, her blood cousin, has sent her. When Maha sees that for the first time on Leilah's neck, she says "yes, everyone who has lost their country has to wear one of these necklaces. Wear their country around their neck" (Nadir, 2014, 266). The necklace, as a metaphor for a homeland that could be carried around, reminds them of homelessness. They talk about the Palestinians in Toronto wearing Palestine necklaces. It is as if identities with no homelands carry parts and parcels of their home with them. The challenge of homemaking in a new place like London or Vancouver is not just homesickness, adaptability to new relations, language barriers, and culture shocks for young Iraqis like Reeta. The main struggle is how to seek asylum. Leilah narrates the stories of women who were once used as an excuse for liberation and emancipation by the Western imperialist patriarchy; women who lost their family members, homes, and the best years of their lives under war, sanction, and civil conflict, and now, when they have no other alternative but to emigrate and seek asylum in Britain, the British government and many other Western countries, according to Leilah, consider their cases of asylum invalid, because presumably, Iraq has been liberated from its "sole" oppressor Saddam Hussein. Through narrating the lived experience of these women, Leilah is building up a microhistory of the coloniality of power and its lethal effects on men and women's lives. The politics of hometactics has to change when coloniality of power is involved. Before assimilation and integration happens, the reasons why border crossing is *necessary* need to be problematized.

Notes

1 Here, by transnational I mean people who reside in different countries, excluding their homeland or birthplace. I intentionally use the term woman of colour due to its epistemic and political implications as an identity category.

2 Term coined by Marinna Ortega in Ortega (2016).

3 Postmodernist critics such as Derrida and Lyotard talk about the notion of decentred self. The critique of capitalist modernity regarding identity fragmentation turned into a universal lens for looking at identities and, therefore, led to the pathologization of identities and creation of conditions such as borderline personality syndrome. Unlike Latina phenomenologists who celebrate the multiplicity of selves in transnational, biracial, and mestiza identities, Western phenomenology considers it as a condition that needs to be treated as it creates anxieties and loss of a sense of morality. The Eurocentric philosophy is still affected by Western ideas of having a unified self and is against a decentred, fragmented self. Mestiza identity is significant to this thesis because it refers to identities that include multiple selves, including the conqueror and the conquered. This will come up in the discussions of biracial identities in *Orange Trees of Baghdad*.

4 I guess there is still something between the world and the self that makes that relationality work. I cannot name it and am aware that more research needs to be done in this regard, but I do know that it is not a centre as in traditionalist epistemology and it is not a decentred identity as in poststructuralism. It could be a decentred centre that shifts position among our multiple selves.

5 Transnational identities' practice of homemaking has been the object of inquiry for many scholars. As Sandu points out, it is important to see the link between belonging as a feeling and homemaking as a practice and the ways in which the process of uprooting and re-rooting takes place. According to Sandu, "roots are linked to belonging, fixity, positioning a person to a place, while routes allow for a mobile, continuously evolving nature of belonging, reflecting fluid transnational connections and networks. Yet, this mobility does not eliminate constructions of homes based on previous experiences, imagined and desired homes, or as Brah (Brah, 1996) calls it, a 'homing desire'. Moreover, for many transnational migrants, conceptualisations of home are both multiple and ambiguous, often reflecting attachments to more than one place. 'Home' is thus shaped by memories as well as

everyday life, experiences and practices (Blunt and Dowling, 2006). It is the latter aspect that is however less explored, particularly showing how these homemaking practices link migrants to their place of residence." See: Sandu (2013, 498).

6 When I interviewed Sepideh Farsi, an exilic Iranian film-maker based in France, she told me that she prefers Athens as a location for her film settings because the light is very similar to the light of Tehran and it does affect the story line. Hometactics is practiced for not only residence aspects of homemaking but also creative art, because creativity is also affectively inspired by a sense of belonging to a space.

7 Dian Million's Felt Theory sheds light on the epistemic and therapeutic value of storytelling. For further information see Million (2009, 53–76).

8 There's a term Linda Alcoff uses when referring to the idea that we need to keep from negativity as an act of resisting coloniality and racism. It is one thing to critique, and another to engage in negative "pessimism" that disturbs our productivity. See Alcoff (1999, 15–26).

9 Leilah mentions that "for Ibrahim, raised on romantic notions of Britain and the West, it [London] felt like the most horrible place in the world." It is important to see how Ibrahim's imaginary of London was actually different to what he could see in reality. See Nadir (2014, 65).

10 Oxford Dictionary, "Diaspora." https://en.oxforddictionaries.com/definition/diaspora

References

Alcoff, L. M. (1999) Towards a Phenomenology of Racial Embodiment. *Radical Philosophy* 95, 15–26.

Alcoff, L. M. (2006) *Visible Identities: Race, Gender, and the Self*. Oxford: Oxford University Press.

Anzaldúa, G. (1987) *Borderlands: La Frontera*. San Francisco: Aunt Lute.

Barad, K. (2003) Posthumanist Performativity: Toward an Understanding of How Matter Comes to Matter. *Signs: Journal of Women in Culture and Society* 28(3), 801–831.

Behdad, A. (2005) *A Forgetful Nation: On Immigration and Cultural Identity in the United States*. Durham: Duke University Press.

Deleuze, G., and Guattari, F. (1988) *A Thousand Plateaus: Capitalism and Schizophrenia*. London and New York: Bloomsbury Publishing.

Delisle, J. B. (2013) "Iraq in My Bones": Second-Generation Memory in the Age of Global Media. *Biography* 36(2), 376–391.

Hirsch, M. (2008) The Generation of Postmemory. *Poetics Today* 29(1), 103–128.

Million, D. (2009) Felt Theory: An Indigenous Feminist Approach to Affect and History. *Wicazo Sa Review* 24(2), 53–76.

Moya, P. L. (2015) *The Social Imperative: Race, Close Reading, and Contemporary Literary Criticism*. Palo Alto, CA: Stanford University Press.

Nadir, L. (2014) *The Orange Trees of Baghdad*. Mission, BC: Barbarian Press.

Ortega, M. (2016) *In-Between: Latina Feminist Phenomenology, Multiplicity, and the Self*. New York: SUNY Press.

Sandu, A. (2013) "Transnational Homemaking Practices: Identity, Belonging and Informal Learning." *Journal of Contemporary European Studies* 21(4), 496–512.

6 The Negotiation of Identity in Laila Halaby's *Once in a Promised Land* and *West of Jordan*

Sara Arami

Introduction

Born to a Jordanian father and an American mother in Beirut in 1966, Laila Halaby is a member of the new generation of Arab American women writers who choose fiction over poetry, in order to narrate their stories. In her works of fiction, *West of Jordan* and *Once in a Promised Land*,[1] Halaby makes use of various thematic and structural strategies in order to challenge the ossified image of the sexed and racialized female body, contest the orientalist view that fixes Middle Eastern women in the position of passive victims of traditional oriental patriarchy and religious practices, and entail an understanding and a "place" for their nonconformist presences.

The Question of Re-orientalism

Halaby's first work of fiction, *West of Jordan* (2003), is a collection of 37 stories, narrated in the third person by four different female characters, all cousins: Hala, Soraya, and Khadijah, who live in the United States, and Mawal, who lives in Nawara,

> which sits at the top of the West Bank, just west of the Jordan River, east of Jenin and far enough away from both of these places to be a peaceful village that only every so often releases an avalanche of stones and fire.
> (Halaby, 2003, 15)

Once in a Promised Land (2007), set in post-9/11 United States, narrates the story of a Jordanian couple, Jassim and Salwa, as their lives fall apart in the aftermath of the World Trade Center attacks. In this case, the narrative uses an omniscient narrator with changing focalization.

At first sight, Halaby's work might seem to fit into the trend of "re-orientalism", a term that has been coined by Lisa Lau in relation to South Asian fiction and refers to instances of stereotyping in the literary output of the writers she calls "diasporic Orientals" (Lau, 2014, 572). For Lau, these are authors who write "as much *to* the West as *for* the East" (Lau, 2014,

DOI: 10.4324/9780429027338-7

4) and whose self-representation "continues to be filtered through Western lenses, (in very similar style to Orientalism) and to reference the West as 'Centre' in framing the representations and anticipating the audiences" (Lau, 2014, 5). These authors engage in a process of "self-Othering" through which they not only represent themselves as other but also, in the process, relegate the other Orientals they are representing as other (Lau, 2014, 4). Lau is not the first to discuss re-orientalism, and many critics before her, such as Samir Amin (1999), Giovanni Arrighi (1999), Immanuel Wallerstein (1999), have referred to the same concept with different terms, like ethno-orientalism, self-orientalism, internal orientalism, reverse orientalism, neo-orientalism, and so forth.

The question of re-orientalism is highly relevant in discussing Arab American writers, not because, as Lau puts it, they (the authors she refers to as re-orientalist) perceive a demand for "low-quality, exotically flavoured fare" (Lau, 2014, 4), but since they are often caught between opposing allegiances:

> On the one hand, they feel the need to defend their cultures, nations of origin, and religion from hostile media and political attacks in the United States. On the other hand, they are committed to feminist criticism of Arab American culture working to integrate Arab American feminist struggle within the larger US and global women's movements.
>
> (Noman and Asthana, 2015, 496)

Consequently, they write from a precarious position. When they criticize their patriarchal home cultures, they are accused of cultural betrayal. This is an accusation that silences some and has been commented on by several scholars, such as Mohja Kahf (Badran and cooke, 1990, 145). Likewise, they are also accused by Western academia of presenting stereotypical images of their home cultures and thus being complicit in neo-orientalism.

To completely avoid such pitfalls, though, means not to risk writing from the position of Arab American women at all and thus not to make an attempt at shifting the terms of female Muslim American identity from the passive object of patriarchal discourses to the active self-defining subject who contests and reshapes those discourses. Arab American women authors write from a difficult stance, one between two cultures. Thus, any representation of "oriental cultures" in their writings could be viewed as nodal points that might be read as re-orientalizing; however, one should consider that the other choice would be granting a blanket approval, romanticizing, and not criticizing the home cultures at all, a practice that would conflict with the very purpose of their writing. This does not mean, though, that all Arab American women fall into the trap of self-orientalism in their writings. They are aware of the precariousness of their position and attempt to devise strategies to avoid such pitfalls. As Susan Muaddi Darraj, Palestinian American scholar and author, argues:

> "Write or be written." Because the histories we learn in school, the tales we hear in the street, the claims made on our behalf, all somehow miss the point. Or simply get it wrong. We are really not how others write us. At best we are invisible. What we witnessed and were taught was not and is not our heritage.
>
> (Darraj, 2004, xii)

Halaby, like other Arab American women writers, does take the risk of rewriting and thus rebuilding the Arab American female identity from the position of an insider. It is critical to keep in mind, though, that she is writing from a difficult position, one between two cultures, and that such representations of "oriental cultures" in the novel, as with the example quoted above, are those nodal points that could be read as re-orientalizing. The problematic position of the author is thus crystallized in such instances – many others could be found in the novel – where the challenges of the so-called cultural representations are best illustrated.

In *West of Jordan*, the presence of a number of what might be considered as self-orientalizing stereotypical representations, such as fathers who marry their daughters to older men because of money and reputation, husbands who hit their wives and children, and women who seem to have no other occupation than cooking and engaging in petty chatter, might lead the reader to classify Halaby's writing within this category of fiction; however, on a closer look, one would discover the complexities that help to overturn well-accepted gender roles and stereotypes and save the novels from falling into the trap of re-orientalism. These complexities and strategies, which will be focused upon here, seem to signal to the Western readers that if, upon first glance, Middle Eastern women seem to be the passive victims of the patriarchal cultures they live in, it is only because their stories are not known. To put it in a nutshell, then, the novel's project could be identified as filling in the void left by the absence of Arab American women's voices in American society, where their presence has long been rendered invisible, while at the same time rewriting American space in such a way that it would include this presence and as such bring Arab American women into the picture.

Women's Body and National Culture

Halaby focuses on women's sexuality, representing sexual identities that are not only uncontained and unsuppressed but also actively threaten the authority and supremacy of men. To do this, she plays on what Izabella Kimak addresses in her study of South Asian literature, that is to say, the role played by the female body in these cultures:

> Both in the original culture of the writers [...] and in the diaspora, the female body, especially the body of the middle-class woman, functions as the repository of cultural tradition. In South Asia, a chaste middle-class

> female body is believed to personify the chaste nation. … This way of thinking tends to persist in the diaspora, where the female body represents the idealized and essentialized national culture.
>
> (Kimak, 2013, 13–14)

Halaby's novels challenge this symbolic role by focusing upon the sexual identity of her female characters and representing to the readers female sexual desire, various instances of marital infidelity and incest, and questioning women's roles as mothers.

No doubt in the backdrop of Middle Eastern cultures, one of the most important roles given to women is their role as wives. In the context of traditional patriarchy, women's care is transferred from the hands of their fathers to those of their husbands, whom they should obey and to whom they should stay loyal forever. Women's sexuality is considered to be a matter of men's honor, and thus it is strictly surveyed and controlled by them, and any instance of infidelity is severely punished, in some extreme cases by stoning them to death. Bhattacharjee explains:

> A woman is thus expected to forgo her own desires and to sacrifice herself in order to protect both her family and the national cultural values that she epitomizes, as any challenge to the family […] translates […] into a betrayal of national cultural values.
>
> (qtd. in Kimak, 2013, 76)

It is in this context that marital infidelity becomes an act of transgression, one that would seriously undermine not only men's authority but also social order.

In *West of Jordan*, Halaby presents the reader with this context, what could be regarded by some as the self-orientalizing aspect of the book, only to undermine it. The readers learn for example that Hala's mother was forced to come back from the United States, where she had gone to pursue her studies (itself a rare case as her father was very open-minded), in disgrace because of rumors that she had spent the night at some boy's house and was obliged on her return to marry a much older man, 20 years her senior – who accepted to marry her "regardless of the reason for [her] return" (Halaby, 2003, 10) – in order to save her own and her father's reputation. In another story, Khadija's brother tells their father that he saw her kissing a boy at school, in order to take revenge on her for having taken money from him, and their father "came after her with a belt, yelling *slut* and *whore* at her. She didn't go to school for two days" (Halaby, 2003, 31). However, the novel presents the readers with these examples, because there is no other choice than to draw upon the existing discourse in order to be able to turn it on its head. In the case of the above examples, Hala's mother fights for having her daughter pursue her high school and college studies in the United States, asking for it as her final wish when she knew she was dying from cancer and her husband could not refuse it. Later on in the novel, while left alone with her siblings and her father,

Khadija calls 911 to denounce her father, who had started hitting her younger brother and his own father.

In addition to these examples, which in themselves serve to vouch for the inaccuracy of the passive victim stereotype in reference to the female subjectivities represented by the narrative, and in line with the above arguments, the narrative provides the readers with representations of sexual transgression such as marital infidelity. It is generally maintained that diasporic men tend to go back to their home countries in search of wives, because they cannot accept the "liberties" diasporic and Western women believe to be their right. They search for the women who would represent for them "the idealized and essentialized national culture" (Kimak, 2013, 13): women who would function not only at home, but *as* home. This view is expressed in *West of Jordan* through the words of Sitti, Mawal's grandmother, in a subpart framed by Mawal and entitled "America". Sitti describes men from Palestine who go to the United States for work or study and come back after a few years in search of a bride as follows:

> These men were the same way. Unlike my oldest son, your uncle Hamdi, most could compromise and come back to marry and take their brides with them as permanent keepsakes of the village they were leaving behind, if not forever, at least for part of their lives.
>
> (Halaby, 2003, 99)

This view, however, is overturned by Halaby both in *West of Jordan* and in *Once in a Promised Land*. In *West of Jordan*, Soraya tells us the story of Sameer Samaha, who came to the United States from Nawara. Sameer was a hardworking man and saved money in order to be able to "go home and marry" (Halaby, 2003, 86). When he did bring his wife to the United States, on the surface she conformed to all the traditional expectations. She was beautiful and calm and stayed home and cooked meals for him; although one day when Sameer decided to surprise her at home to tell her how much he loved her, he was stabbed to death by a man in front of his house. Soraya's version of the story suggests that Sameer was killed by his wife's lover, who was a witness to the crime, but said she had not seen the killer's face and refused to go back to Nawara after her husband's death, not even for the funeral: "So that is what you get for Working Your Ass Off and then trying to be traditional" (Halaby, 2003, 95), Soraya tells us.

In *Once in a Promised Land*, too, Halaby presents us with a similar story. Jassim Haddad, who has been living in the United States for a while, goes back to Jordan to give a lecture at the university, meets a student, Salwa, who is much younger than him, seduces her with the promise of a better life in America (Salwa is already in an unofficial relationship with another student), and takes her back with him to the United States as his wife. At a difficult moment in their lives and their marriage, both husband and wife get the opportunity to be unfaithful, and it is Salwa who carries this opportunity out and has an extramarital relationship with a younger colleague of hers who finds her exotic. In fact, the story of Salwa and Jassim's marriage is recounted in such a way as to undermine the stereotypical representation of Arab women as might be implied by the above summary of events. These stereotypical representations are dealt with in the novel as views American men hold about Arab women, while at the same time *Once in a Promised Land* attempts to illustrate that Arab women are viewed and treated differently by Arab men. For instance, reflecting on his feelings towards Salwa, Jake (Salwa's co-worker with whom she has an affair) "wondered if all Arab women had this allure (the physical one and the shadow of a man behind them) and if that was why they veiled themselves" (Halaby, 2007, 171), which is in itself ironic since Salwa is not veiled. Towards the end of the novel, when Salwa announces to Jake that she is leaving, she becomes a "Bitch! Goddamn fucking Arab bitch!" (Halaby, 2007, 122). The novel then seems to make an attempt at revealing the stereotypical views pertaining to Arab men and women. The same exact views that have resulted in more publishing opportunities for Arab women writers, especially post-9/11, since judged by the same yardstick as other Arab women, they are perceived as less threatening than men. Evelyn Shakir has summarized the binary view of Arab women as follows:

> According to popular belief, all Arab women can be divided into two categories. Either they are shadowy nonentities, swathed in black from head to foot, or they are belly dancers – seductive, provocative, and privy to exotic secrets of lovemaking.
>
> (Shakir, 1988, 39)

As for Arab men, they are viewed alongside other Middle Easterners as "terrorists and religious fundamentalists" (Karim and Khorrami, 1999, 23). In this sense, *Once in a Promised Land* makes a conscious attempt to deconstruct the orientalist view on Arab men and women, presenting characters to the readers who oppose the already formed ideas they might have.

It would be hard to accuse *Once in a Promised Land* of self-orientalism. Jassim, the male protagonist, does not control his wife in any manner and does not even believe that she should bring him children: "Perhaps he needed to come clean, tell her that he just wanted her to have all the opportunity she wished for so that she would not look back on her life with regret" (Halaby, 2007, 110). On the other hand, Salwa, who is neither "a shadowy non-entity" nor "privy to the exotic secrets of lovemaking" (Shakir, 1988, 39), seems to want children only to fill a void in her life, in the same way as she had wanted to have silk pajamas and the job at the bank, and the next job as a real estate agent.

As mentioned towards the beginning of this chapter, portraying female characters who are not just wives and mothers, but rather Arab women who have abortions and miscarriages, as is the case of Salwa, is a strategy used by some Arab American women writers in their fiction in order to undermine the image of Arab women as passive victims of religious patriarchy viewed and valued exclusively in relation to their roles as mothers and wives. In addition to not having children, Salwa's infidelity helps to further undermine this image. Whereas Jassim is also attracted to another woman who is not his wife, Penny, he does not act upon his desire and does not engage in sexual intercourse. Salwa's sexual relationship with Jake, on the other hand, is described in detail twice throughout the narrative.

The other Arab male character, Hassan, also lacks the characteristics that would link him to any well-known stereotype regarding Arab men. Although in love with Salwa, and engaged to her (in his head, since he does not actually get to ask for Salwa's hand as he is interrupted by her as she spots Jassim), he does not try to stop Salwa from marrying Jassim and leaving with him for the United States. It is Salwa who makes the decision to marry Jassim, and even Salwa's father does not interfere in that decision. When Jassim goes to Salwa's house to ask for her hand:

> "Salwa, habibti, my youngest daughter, would you like to answer this proposal now, or would you like to think about it?" Salwa was sitting back in her chair, watching her father, Jassim thought, with the same expression she might have if she were watching a movie. "I would like to accept".
>
> (Halaby, 2007, 69)

As mentioned summarily above, it is the American men, Jake and another character, Jack Franks, who objectify Salwa, and other women, throughout the novel.

It is worth mentioning that the agency granted to the Arab American female protagonist of the novel and to the same extent taken away from her male counterpart finds its reflection in the book cover. The hardcover and paperback versions of the novel are published with two different covers. The paperback version shows a young Middle Eastern woman (olive skin, dark hair, and dark eyes) in the arms of a seemingly young man. The man, however, has his back to the camera, and so the readers could not see his face. Only his black t-shirt, a gold necklace, part of his neck, ear, and hair are visible to the reader. The girl's face, on the other hand, is visible from the nose upwards, as her mouth and neck are covered by the man's shoulder. Although the woman is not veiled, the image is not an exoticizing one, as is the case with much orientalizing and self-orientalizing fiction, which either present the female characters of the cover veiled or in an exotic manner in order to attract the attention of the Western reader.[2]

The cover woman's gaze is directed towards the camera, inviting the reader to the book, summoning him/her to read her story. The fact that the girl's mouth is covered by the man's shoulder conveys the idea of her being silenced and adds to the mystery of the cover. The woman's agency, however, is illustrated by her intriguing gaze. Plus, the tips of the woman's fingers are also visible to the camera, showing that it is the woman who holds the man in her arms, once again symbolizing her agency with reference to hands as instruments of action. It should also be mentioned that the whole image seems to be viewed from behind a shattered glass, which undermines the implications of the title printed on the cover and signals the disillusionment of the Promised Land to the attentive reader. Care has been taken for the cracks of the glass not to cut through the eyes of the woman on the cover, though, in order for her agency not to be undermined.

As such, the cover succeeds in fulfilling its role in attracting the audience as it manages to create tension and imply unanswered questions, raising the curiosity of potential readers with a rather simple image. The agency of the silenced woman and the shattered glass superposed on the cover's image, which is in turn superposed by the title *Once in a Promised Land*, lure the reader into taking up the novel without taking recourse to stereotypes to please the potential Western reader. Ironically, the unanswered questions created in the minds of the readers echo the unanswered questions they will be left with after finishing the novel. As such, the novel does not keep its promise of providing answers and leaves the readers with a sense of disillusionment in a similar manner as America for the characters of the novel.

The cover of the hardcover version does not figure any woman, as it emphasizes the status of the novel as a post-9/11 narrative, more than a work belonging to the category of women's fiction. Here, it suffices to mention that the man illustrated on the hardcover version is also seen from the back and does not seem to be granted much agency as he is shown floating in water, the shadow of an airplane viewed by his side.

Apart from marital infidelity, the readers of *West of Jordan* are presented with an instance of incest. The incestuous story is entitled "Love Story/ Remembering Story". Soraya who is known throughout the book as the untamed cousin, the rebel, has a sexual relationship with her uncle Haydar. Contrary to all expectations, though, she is not raped or abused. It is she who decides, and desires:

> Some days, weeks, months later during another visit, she risked it all and went to the running man. "In your arms I am beautiful and I can fly," she whispered on his sweaty neck, her words sliding down his chest.
>
> (Halaby, 2003, 176)

The title of the story further helps confirm such a reading. In another story, Soraya revisits the incest and insists:

> My school counselor would say it was Uncle Haydar's fault. If she knew, she would talk about sexual abuse. But she doesn't know and she would be wrong anyhow. I choose what I do. I have always chosen what I do.
>
> (Halaby, 2003, 190)

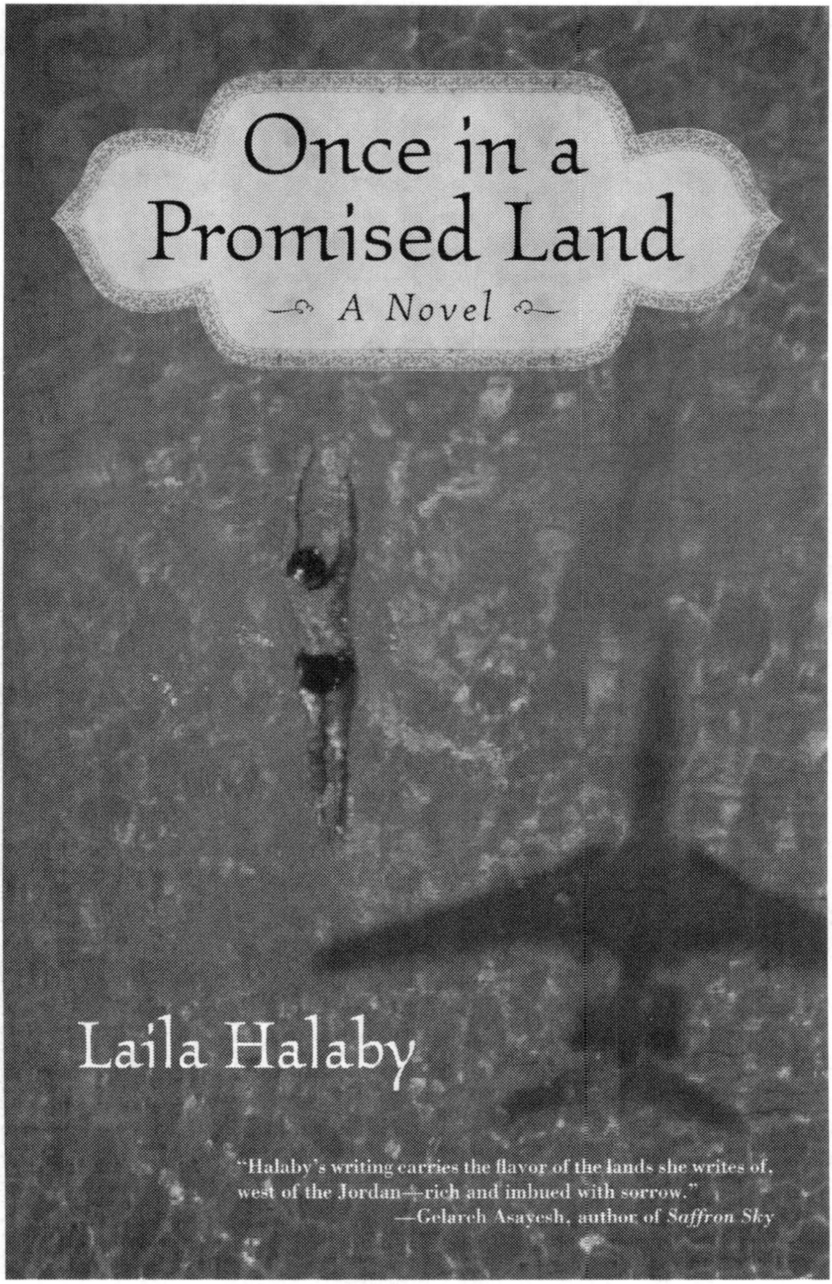

Figure 6.1 The image on the cover of the hardcover version of *Once in a Promised Land* (2007).

Soraya is endowed with agency and chooses to transgress and break not only the codes of female sexual behavior, but also those of society at large. This makes her boundary-crossing much more potent and reverses the passive victim stereotype of Middle Eastern women.

Later on in the narrative, we learn that Haydar is losing his mind: "Clinically speaking he is bipolar, paranoid schizophrenic, but for real life he is crazy. For home he is crazy" (Halaby, 2003, 214), a piece of knowledge that emphasizes Soraya's control and Haydar's lack of control. Furthermore, throughout the novel, Soraya plays on her exotic appeal by using the stereotypes of which she is completely aware to her own advantage in order to get what she wants, and thus subvert the function of those stereotypes:

> "She's Arabian," they say at my high school as I pass by them. "In her country they don't have furniture or dishwashers, only oil." I tell them what they want to hear, which is nasty stories about young men sticking their things into goats and some twelve-year-old girl being carried off on a camel to be the third wife to old Shaykh So-and-So and the five oil wells my father owns.
>
> (Halaby, 2003, 24)

Soraya's awareness of the stereotypes and her invention of stories that would conform to those stereotypes and feeding them to her schoolmates reverts the play of power and puts her in a position of authority.

As hinted at above, another important role assigned to women in traditional societies is their role as bearers of and carers for children: their role as mothers. Here, too, Halaby presents her readers with female characters whose bodies refuse to conform. In *Once in a Promised Land*, Salwa, who skips her pills in order to get pregnant, loses the barely formed baby in a scene described in bloody detail lasting seven pages. Salwa has a miscarriage, while Jassim thinks she is "having a really bad period" (Halaby, 2007, 90). Her body does not accept its role of child bearer.

In *West of Jordan*, too, the role of women as mothers is undermined when Halaby presents us with the story of Um (Umm) Khalid (literally translated as mother of Khalid, her eldest son),[3] narrated by Mawal. Um Khalid has lost her husband, two sons, and her parents in a car accident and is left with an intellectually disabled daughter, Lubna. She always wears a black *roza* (Nawara's traditional dress) without any embroidery and refuses to speak to others, until one day, all of a sudden, she asks to be called Um Lubna instead of Um Khalid, which is a transgressive act in itself in the eyes of a patriarchal society that requires mothers to be called by the name of their eldest son. A mother's identity is thus effaced as her name is replaced by the name of her son, since it is only in giving birth to a son that the woman finds true value. As such, Um Khalid's demand to be called after her daughter becomes an act of subversion.

There is more to this subversive act, though. The daughter that Um Khalid asks to be named after is intellectually disabled: "Why on earth would she want to be called Um Lubna? To be reminded of that horrible creature she brought into this miserable world?" (Halaby, 2003, 64). Um Lubna then asserts the power to define herself instead of letting herself be defined while at the same time undermining society's patriarchal and normative rules by asking to be called after an intellectually disabled girl instead of a dead boy (whose memory it is considered to be her duty to keep alive), and as such her act becomes a doubly transgressive act. Um Lubna also changes her clothes, wearing "outrageous *rozas*" (Halaby, 2003, 66) covered with embroidery.

By the end of the story, readers learn that the changes are because she has found herself a lover, Abu Khuder, whom she had asked one day to come and fix a broken window at her house. Um Lubna transgresses rules that attempt to regulate women's bodies both by wearing clothes that are not considered to be "proper" for a woman who has lost her husband and sons and by willingly and actively searching to satisfy her sexual desires. More importantly, Um Lubna asks her daughter to leave the house in the cold and not to go back until she sees "the man leave" (Halaby, 2003, 72). It is ironic that Um Lubna's maiden name is Safa, meaning "*untroubledness, purity*" (Halaby, 2003, 62), as she privileges the satisfaction of her sexual desires over her duties as mother towards an intellectually disabled child. Safa also leaves the memory of her sons behind her, again symbolically letting go of her role as mother, since, as mentioned earlier, traditionally it is being the mother of sons that determines the value of women, and their identity is supposed to be shaped a great deal by this role.

Moreover, since the setting of this story is Nawara, it would not be unsound to argue that Halaby attempts to question the occidental view of Middle Eastern women, not only in the diaspora but also within the context of the Middle East, and reverse the view that often presents the Middle East and the United States as "polar opposites, the former symbolizing oppression and repression and the latter symbolizing freedom and opportunity" (Kimak, 2013, 14).

In addition to the stories that are given as examples above, all four narrators of *West of Jordan* talk to the readers of their sexual desires. Mawal, who lives in Nawara, tells the readers:

> I want to be mischievous. I want to stare at Miss Maryam's large pointed breasts, to stand this much closer to the vegetable man who winks, to let him touch my hand when he gives me back my change.
>
> (Halaby, 2003, 19)

Although her mother has led her to believe that feelings and thoughts like these will take her straight to hell, Mawal announces that she does not much care. Khadija, the "conservative" (Halaby, 2003, 25) cousin, is caught by her mother looking at porn magazines with a friend, and Soraya confesses to having "men as friends, as well as lovers" (Halaby, 2003, 57).

Hala's transgression, though, is of a different order. It concerns tradition but also, more than that, religion. First she undermines the function of traditional/religious dress, as on her flight back home, wearing a "gray, ankle-length dress" (Halaby, 2003, 5), she is under the impression that "people can peek from all angles". She admits: "I thought the dress would give me confidence – mostly covering me, but pretty – but instead I fold myself, hunch" (Halaby, 2003, 5). Later on, while visiting her uncle at Ibrid, she decides to visit Petra. She climbs the stairs to the top with her cousin, Fawziyya, "though it is not proper for two girls to be racing up steps with foreigners" (Halaby, 2003, 55). Her "improper" behavior does not end there, though. Once at the top of the stairs, on the religious site, she strips naked: "I look around and see no one – so far that it seems we are the only living creatures, except for the lizard and for God [...] I take off my shirt and bra and then my pants as well" (Halaby, 2003, 156), and her cousin follows her. Her uncle has no idea what has been going on up the stairs: "If only he knew what we did at the top of the mountain" (Halaby, 2003, 157).

The female body in this case becomes a subversive tool employed to defy the authority of religion and of men. Ironically, on her trip back to the United States, Hala insists on wearing one her late mother's *rozas* without a belt (which would be the traditional way of wearing the dress), this time defying both home and host conventions and refusing to comply with either. As such, the narrative illustrates an example of the way in which women's bodies are treated as "the ground upon which battles for cultural legitimacy or authenticity are waged" (Kimak, 2013, 14). Soraya's character also uses her body in a subversive manner in order to challenge and undermine the rules imposed on her by the religious and patriarchal orders, the details of which will be discussed further on.

Narrative/Her/Story

Women in Halaby's fiction are storytellers. They are collectors of stories of men and women. It is through them that we learn the histories of other characters, which they mediate through their narratives. This is how these women not only write their own stories but also rewrite history, which has up to now been a male domain. In this case, too, Halaby uses imagery that tightly connects narrative to the female body. In *West of Jordan*, Soraya tells us that Mawal and her mother

> are twins, famous for sitting still and eating up people's stories, gobbling them like *maqluba*.[4] Everyone from our family and from our village goes to them. Like helium in super-stretch balloons that get bigger and bigger and never explode, my aunt and cousin accommodate any hardship. Then

> the people leave, their burdens gone, and my aunt and cousin are a little fatter than before.
>
> (Halaby, 2003, 25)

Thus, stories collected by Mawal and her mother become part and parcel of their body, bringing about corporeal change and as such becoming part of their identity. In this sense, the narrative insists on the paramount role of collecting and recounting/rewriting stories in the process of identity formation.

Soraya herself has another method. She is conscious of the attraction of her body and her exoticness, which adds to her allure in the eyes of men:

> My body is like some of those women. I have a skinny girl's waist with woman hips and large breasts. I know my body is sexy; I can tell by the way men look at me, by the way men have always looked at me... Not to mention that I am exotic.
>
> (Halaby, 2003, 30)

She thus uses her body in order to get men's stories: "I am a new breed. A rebel. My mother and her sisters can spill a story from any woman, but I can make a man talk" (Halaby, 2003, 56). Soraya's body, like Hala's body but in a totally different manner, turns into tool of power, since by collecting men's stories and recounting/rewriting them, she puts herself in the position to define.

Soraya further uses her body in a different manner in her quest for identity and power. She dances "shamelessly where men can see [her] and not just in front of other women and a camera" (Halaby, 2003, 29). Dance for her takes various functions and becomes an act of dissidence. She dances to defy the suppressive rules of patriarchy, to break out of the restrictive chains the home culture tries to impose on her. She dances to make her rage and pain, be it caused by discrimination or rejection, fade away: "shake it all out" (Halaby, 2003, 28–29). She even uses dance to bring about political change: "Once I danced overnight in a black slip with a candle burning in front of a barred window that often had Israeli soldiers on the other side of it" (Halaby, 2003, 28).

Thus, Halaby presents her novel as an instance of history recording by women, while at the same time respecting women's oral tradition, since women in her novel collect stories by speaking with other men and women and then represent those stories in the form of narrative. Furthermore, she turns the meaning of women's silence on its head and gives it a new meaning other than passiveness. If Halaby's women are occasionally silent, it is because "sometimes there are no stories only feelings, only pictures" (Halaby, 2003, 206), or their silence is an act of resistance in itself. For instance, when Um Khalid refuses to speak after her husband, two sons, and parents are killed in the accident, her silence goes against society's norms and expectation: "The elders of Nawara put money aside for her to make sure she and Lubna would never go hungry. Her gratitude? To stop speaking to anyone. Dignified mourning with silent black with no interruptions" (Halaby, 2003, 62).

Yet, in another story, for example, Mawal tells her grandmother, who seems to be affected by Alzheimer's disease, the story of a young boy named Jamal who lived in Jerusalem and threw stones at Israeli soldiers. One day, when the soldiers spot him and start chasing him, he finds himself stuck and asks a woman who is washing clothes for help. The woman strips him naked and starts washing him along with his clothes. When the soldiers arrive and ask the woman if she has seen the boy, "her silence chased them off" (Halaby, 2003, 188). The meaning of silence, then, is also turned on its head as it becomes an empowering tool rather than a sign of passiveness.

Throughout the whole book, Halaby makes use of an extended metaphor, that of the *roza*, "beautiful embroidered dresses" (Halaby, 2003, 15) for which Nawara is famous, to talk about the way stories are connected to form more complex narratives: "So many women come spill their secrets and their joys and their agonies because they know my mother – and I – will keep them safe and do no more than stitch them into the fabric of our *rozas*" (Halaby, 2003, 17). Thus, on the one hand, women are historians who stitch/write stories forming a complex history, and on the other hand, these *rozas* will be worn by women, as dress, an indicator of their identity. Women shape and are shaped by the stories they narrate; history is transcribed on their bodies as "stories are stitched under the skin at birth" (Halaby, 2003, 206), and "Sometimes, during a lifetime, or even half a lifetime, they can grow out of control and cause so much pain that you have to die to spare yourself of the misery" (Halaby, 2003, 206). This explains the function of women's storytelling.

Stories are told in order for women to gain control on them, to stitch them at their will into the fabric of their dresses. This act puts them in a position of authority, and as it saves them from being overwhelmed by their pain, to avoid having to die from the pain, it becomes an act of survival. An instance of how stories could eventually lead to a person's demise is cited with the story of Soraya's uncle Haydar, who, remembering his home and what had happened to his father there, lost his mind little by little.

Presenting storytelling as an act of survival links *West of Jordan* to *Arabian Nights* and as such claims its place within the tradition of Arab writing and by extension world literature. All women focalizers of *West of Jordan* become Scheherazade, their storytelling indispensable. The act of stitching stories into the fabric of the dresses that would later be worn by the women serves another specific function as well, especially within the context of diaspora: to make them always remember and never forget. As we read in the novel: "Stitch in red for life. Stitch in green to remember. Stitch, stitch to never forget" (Halaby, 2003, 103).

In *Once in a Promised Land*, the readers are presented with the figure of Salwa's grandmother as she remembers telling Salwa and her sisters stories. On this specific occasion, Salwa remembers one of her grandmother's stories while she is having a miscarriage. The story, an Arab folktale,[5] plays an important role in the understanding of the whole narrative, and the characters of the novel find their equivalent on some level in the characters of the folktale. As with the case of *West of Jordan*, stories are represented as having an important role in the process of remembering. At the end of the story, the omniscient narrator comments on Salwa's situation: "Too bad that forgetting is so easy, especially for fickle girls in fairy tales" (Halaby, 2007, 98).

Remembering through stories is indispensable for those living in the diaspora; otherwise, Halaby seems to suggest, if they forget their stories and their her/stories,[6] they will become strangers to themselves, losing their identities:

> She [Salwa] searched for herself in this reflection, pleading for familiarity with the thick legs, wide hips, round breasts, simple face, nothing like the bodies and faces shown on American television. She stood up and walked to the mirror so that she and the reflection were face to face, almost touching. They stared at each other, stranger at stranger.
>
> (Halaby, 2007, 211)

And it is indeed the stories recounted by women that allow the characters of Halaby's novels to remember and, by extension, the stories recounted by her and other Arab American women writers that in turn fill the same function in the diaspora.

The American Space and the Question of Identity

Following the previous metaphor, and in a description of Nawara's *rozas*, Mawal explains: "The complicated embroidery on our *rozas* – with both Palestinian and Western stitches and patterns – captures the spirit of Nawara" (Halaby, 2003, 15). This is indeed an appropriate way of describing Nawara, since it reflects the way the homeland and the host land are interconnected. Nawara's stories take place in both Nawara and the United States as they travel back and forth between the two countries, and since "Nawara could have a smaller version of herself in the United States" (Halaby, 2003, 15) thanks to immigration. The homeland and the host land are connected via the bodies that travel between the two lands. America is a permanent presence in Nawara and Nawara and Jordan in the United States as they are transported via memories, photographs, videotapes that are watched and rewatched, and also through objects: gifts that are sent from the United States to family back home and given to those who leave. Um Radwan receives "suitcases filled with comforters, sweaters, deodorant, soaps, aspirin, Kool-Aid, and laxatives" (Halaby, 2003, 16); Mawal gets a "beautiful red bicycle" (Halaby, 2003, 141); and before going back to the United States, Hala receives a gold charm in the shape of Palestine, a gift that marks symbolically the breaking down of the frontiers of home as she carries it with her to the United States. Upon returning from Jordan to her room in her uncle's house in America, Hala covers the white walls with as many pictures from "home" as she can find in her box of photos.

In addition to presenting the readers with the interconnection of the home and the host lands, Halaby further complicates the equation by representing not just double but also triple and multiple belongings. A character like Hala has a Palestinian mother and a Jordanian father and lived in Jordan before moving to the United States, which is also the case of Salwa in *Once in a Promised Land*. In order to emphasize the difference between Arab countries, *West of Jordan* presents us with various explanations and examples. Hala tells us:

> Even though my mother had lived in Jordan since she was nineteen, she was Palestinian and saw my father as something of a foreigner. In distance she was not so far from the home in which she grew up, but in reality, she was in another country – another household – with an entirely different way of thinking.
>
> (Halaby, 2003, 9)

Hala is not the only character in this situation. There is also Hassan in *Once in a Promised Land*, the son of a Palestinian martyr, in love with Salwa. In another story in *West of Jordan*, the readers also learn about Sharif, who tried to get to the Palestinian shore on a dolphin pedal boat with 5- or 6-year-old Hala:

> "Let's swim home," he says with his face still in the sun
>
> "Home? This beach won't reach to Amman. How can we swim there if there is no water?"
>
> [...]
>
> "I mean to Palestine." He turns to look at me.
>
> (Halaby, 2003, 125)

Moreover, Halaby's representation of double or multiple belonging seems to be in line with "Stuart Hall's redefinition of in-betweenness as something not to be experienced in the passive mode, but as something to be embraced as a more empowering theoretical positioning" (Král, 2009, 14). Soraya, the character endowed with the most agency, declares: "I am so sick of everything being *haram* or *halal*, but nothing in between. I am in between" (Halaby, 2003, 117). The main characters in the novel do not reject but rather embrace their multiple belongings and search them out actively, as can be seen in the examples provided earlier.

The porous thresholds of home, be it Palestine, Jordan, or the United States, and its changing character hinted at in the above paragraph are represented by stories that illustrate the constant intrusion of one space into another, resulting in the modification of both. An instance of such intrusion and alteration treated with a touch of humor could be observed in the story entitled "America". "America" is framed by Mawal, and the focalizer of the framed story is Sitti, Mawal's grandmother. The story opens as follows:

> You would think our village is in love with America with all the people who have left, like America is the best relative in the world that everyone has to visit. America is more like a greedy neighbor who takes the best out of you and leaves you feeling empty.
>
> (Halaby, 2003, 96)

This opening immediately undermines the orientalist representation of the two spaces, of Palestine and the United States as binaries. America does not stand in opposition to Palestine, as an enemy would, for example, but rather stands on the same line with it as a relative or a neighbor. Moreover, "America" actually recounts a story that has Nawara as its setting, another sign signaling the non-binary relationship between the two spaces and the intrusion of one into the other. The narrative recounts the story of Karim Sulayman, one of Nawara's young men who leaves for America but comes back home from time to time, first to marry, and then almost every year with his wife carrying "expensive suitcases filled with the finest of America's goods, bedspreads, deodorants, aspirin, and batteries. […] There was always enough to go around too" (Halaby, 2003, 100). Karim then comes back again with a lot of money in order to build a mosque in Nawara. At first, people are ecstatic:

> less for the mosque itself than for the evidence that once our men went to America, it did not mean that they left forever our humble village of Nawara. It was like proof to Israelis that we could not be vanquished: We also had American dollars being channeled in to turn our dirt roads to tar and our rubble to mosques.
>
> (Halaby, 2003, 100)

When the mosque is built, though, the villagers' opinions diversify as the mosque's minaret is equipped with four powerful speakers that wake everyone up at the time of prayer in the morning. Older men seem to appreciate the American technology, but the younger generation have a different opinion: " 'Can you believe the damn call to prayer this morning?' 'God damn Karim Sulayman and his impressive money. May God curse the speakers made in America and dropped by conspiracy in the village of Nawara' " (Halaby, 2003, 101), and the women seem to agree: "The morning was a time of peace, now it is a time of American technology. May God forgive my harsh words' " (Halaby, 2003, 101).

The next day, though, the call to prayer is followed by machine-gun fire. It turns out that the speakers are so loud that their call reaches over the hill and bothers the Israelis. " 'It must stop!' shouted the largest of the settlers in heavily accented Arabic" (Halaby, 2003, 102). As "the settlers" leave people start laughing, to themselves at first and then out loud: "God keep Karim Sulayman and his giant American loudspeakers'" (Halaby, 2003, 103). Two of the speakers are slightly damaged by the gun shots, but the villagers fix them and from then on there are always a few people standing beneath the minaret, watching the speakers. In this story, not only America intrudes into Palestinian space through objects brought as gifts, but American money and by extension America actually modify Palestinian space by providing the money for the construction of houses (Karim builds a luxurious house in Nawara that is referred to as villa by the villagers) and a mosque. These constructions, in the same way as the speakers, are viewed by the villagers as tools of resistance against Israel. As such, the relationship between the United States and Palestine is redefined by the narrative. America becomes complicit with Palestine in its fight against Israel, and thus the two are no longer to be viewed as polar opposites and instead have a more complicated link. At the end of the story, the closing frame once again reminds the readers of the corporeal link between stories and women as Mawal tells the readers: "I tuck this story into my pocket, wishing I could stitch it into my skin, like one of the Bedouin tattoos my grandmother wears" (Halaby, 2003, 103). The narrative then confirms the above-mentioned shift in the definition of America and the function of women's storytelling as an act of history recording: "Are there stories like this in lovely, tempting America? Do my cousins there even know these little histories?" (Halaby, 2003, 103).

The above-mentioned interconnection among spaces is also reflected at a structural level as *West of Jordan* is made of 37 stories for which the setting is Palestine, Jordan, or the United States, with no special order or hierarchy. In the same way, *Once in a Promised Land* is made up of 14 chapters, each divided into many subchapters going back and forth between Amman and Tucson. In this regard, one could claim that the novels are an example of what Susan Stanford Friedman calls "intercultural narratives [...] [narratives that] foreground space and movement through space rather than time" (Friedman, 1998, 137). In the same way, in *West of Jordan* the narration of specific stories is not assigned to certain characters. This means that readers learn about stories of either of the characters from any of the others: stories from Nawara or Jordan could be recounted by characters in the United States and vice versa, embodying what Ketu Katrak refers to as "simultaneity of geography", which is "the possibility of living here in body and elsewhere in mind and imagination" (Katrak, 2006, 201). In this way, the narrative emphasizes the important presence of "America" for the people in Nawara and Amman and the presence of Amman and Nawara in America. A strong symbiotic connection is created that in turn reflects the multiple belonging of the characters (even those who have never traveled outside of their country) and contributes to the complexity of identities represented in Halaby's works.

Notes

1 Both *West of Jordan* and *Once in a Promised Land* are written in English. The language chosen for writing these works of fiction gains significance as the author aims at shifting both the host and the Arab community's view on Arab American women's subjectivities.
2 See for example *Saffron Dreams* (2009) by Shaila Abdullah or *Reading Lolita in Tehran* (2003) by Azar Nafisi or even theoretical work such as *Contemporary Arab American Women Writers: Hyphenated Identities and Border Crossing* (2007) by Amal Talaat Abdelrazek.
3 In Arabic, it is traditional to call a woman – and a man, too – "mother of" and "father of", after the birth of the first child. An example of this could be seen with the character Abu Khuder (father of Khuder) who appears in the story "Flowers From My Roza" in *West of Jordan*.
4 *Maqlūba* is a typical rice dish served throughout the Levant. The ingredients are placed in a pot and flipped upside down when served. That is where the name of the dish comes from, since *maqlūba* literally translates as upside-down.
5 The folktale of "Nus Nsays".
6 The neologism *Her*story was first used by Robin Morgan. The purpose of *Her*story "is to emphasize that women's lives, deeds, and participation in human affairs have been neglected or undervalued in standard histories" (Miller and Swift, 1991, 135).

References

Abdelrazek, A. T. (2007) *Contemporary Arab American Women Writers: Hyphenated Identities and Border Crossings*. Youngstown: Cambria Press.

Abdullah, S. (2009) *Saffron Dreams*. Ann Arbor: Loving Healing Press.

Amin, S. (1999) ReOrientalism? History Conceived as an Eternal Cycle. *Review: A Journal of the Fernand Braudel Center*, 3(22), 291–326.

Anderson, B. (2006) *Imagined Communities*. London: Verso.

Arrighi, G. (1999) ReOrientalism? The World According to Andre Gunder Frank. *Review: A Journal of the Fernand Braudel Center*, 3(22), 327–354.

Badran, M. and cooke, m. (eds) (1990) *Opening the Gates: A Century of Arab Feminist Writing*. Bloomington: Indiana University Press.

Banita, G. (2010) Race, Risk, and Fiction in the War on Terror: Laila Halaby, Gayle Brandeis, and Michael Cunningham. *Literature Interpretation Theory*, 21(4), 242–268.

Fadda-Conrey, C. (2014) *Contemporary Arab-American Literature: Transnational Reconfigurations of Citizenship and Belonging*. New York: New York University Press.

Friedman, S. S. (1998) *Mappings: Feminism and the Cultural Geographies of Encounter*. Princeton: Princeton University Press.

George, R. M. (1996) *The Politics of Home: Postcolonial Relocations and Twentieth-Century Fiction*. Cambridge: Cambridge University Press.

Halaby, L. (2003) *West of Jordan*. Boston: Beacon Press.

Halaby, L. (2007) *Once in a Promised Land*. Boston: Beacon Press.

Horsy, M. E. D. (2017) *Interrogations Into Female Identity in Arab American Literature*. PhD. Paris 4.

Karim, P. M. and Khorrami, M. M. (1999) Introduction. In: P. M. Karim and M. M. Khorrami (eds), *A World Between: Poems, Short Stories and Essays by Iranian-Americans*. New York: George Braziller Inc., 21–27.

Katrak, K. H. (2006) *Politics of the Female Body: Postcolonial Women Writers of the Third World*. New Brunswick: Rutgers University Press.

Kimak, I. (2013) *Bicultural Bodies: A Study of South Asian American Women's Literature*. Frankfurt am Main: Peter Lang GmbH.

Král, F. (2009) *Critical Identities in Contemporary Anglophone Diasporic Literature*. Basingstoke: Palgrave Macmillan.

Lau, L. (2014) *Re-Orientalism and Indian Writing in English*. New York: Palgrave Macmillan.

Miller, C. and Swift, K. (1991) *Words and Women*. New York: Harper Collins.

Montón, E. O. (2017) The Forgotten Victims of 9/11: Cultural Othering in Laila Halaby's *Once in a Promised Land* and Mohsin Hamid's *The Reluctant Fundamentalist*. *Studies in the Literary Imagination*, 50(2), 17–34.

Nafisi, A. (2003) *Reading Lolita in Tehran: A Memoir in Books*. New York: Random House Trade Paperbacks.

Noman, A. A. and Shaily, A. (2015) Woman Voice in the Arab-American Literature. *LangLit*, 1(2), 494–503.

Shakir, E. (1988) Mother's Milk: Women in Arab-American Autobiography. *MELUS*, 15(4), 39–50.

Wallerstein I. (1999) ReOrientalism? Frank Proves the European Miracle. *Review: A Journal of the Fernand Braudel Center*, 3(22), 355–372.

Zbid, N. (2015) Women Literature: Laila Halaby's *West of the Jordan* as a Case in Point in *Knowledge and Politics in Gender and Women's Studies*. Ankara, Turkey, 9–11 October, 738–744. https://moam.info/untitled_5b86f07e097c47235a8b4570.html.

7 "Smotherland" Speaks

Syrian Refugee Identity in the Spaces Between Media and Literature

Roula Salam

Introduction

How does one analyse the refugee in Arab-Syrian fiction, when a substantial body of literature on and by Syrian refugees has yet to materialize, and when some of its authors may not necessarily identify as refugees? How can one explore their narratives when, unlike in the cases of human migration in other studies in this volume, and as Rita Sakr puts it in her analysis of different types of migration tropes in several of Ḥassan Blāsim's short stories, "the public representational frameworks for the asylum-seeker are read as mediating the trope of the infrahuman" (Sakr, 2018, 766)? The "infrahuman" trope here – the Syrian refugee – focusing mainly on survival, rarely enjoys the freedom to travel or the freedom to write. How, then, can identity be expressed by an individual (or group for that matter) that lacks the privilege of speculating on its own emotional health, needs, and self- or group-actualization in the face of mountainous legal and bureaucratic challenges through constant screening? Whereas migrant stories in this volume might build on the construction of a postnational Arab identity, displacement, and the Arab diasporic voice, dealing with stereotypes abroad or the migrant's return home, the literary representations that allow us to glimpse identity narratives of the recent Syrian refugee are just beginning to materialize.

The depiction of the Syrian refugee has been largely usurped by the cacophonic hegemony of media representations since 2011; this chapter questions and complicates the tensions between some of the prevalent media representations of the Syrian refugee and the depictions of Syrian identity by Syrians in Arab-Syrian media, art, and literature, which tend to present us with counter-narratives of forced migration. The refugee's experience of trauma, the struggle to preserve remnants of identity and *turāth* (heritage) in some form of high or low culture, come as a reaction to the experienced violence as well as a response to the dissonance and tensions flaring between the dehumanizing or else glorifying representations brought on by the media. The complex identity narratives that may be traced through the emergent and emerging bodies of pre-revolutionary and revolutionary[1] Syrian war literature

DOI: 10.4324/9780429027338-8

are juxtaposed in this chapter against a discussion of high and low media representations of and by Syrian refugees.

In the first part of the chapter, I explore the semantic and socio-political connotative implications the term "refugee" carries, compared to that of the migrant figure in this work. From this definition, the notion of the subaltern is teased out through analytical discussions of the silences amid the more raucous identity expressions in pre-revolutionary and revolutionary Arab-Syrian culture. The third section explores the phenomenon of dominant media representations that seek to situate and frame the Syrian refugee in specific depictions, many of which have underlying socio-political agendas.

Commencing with a review of pre-revolutionary Arab-Syrian literature to set the ground for a critical analysis of different samples of literature of the revolution, the second part of the chapter discusses the forced migration issue as identity narratives unravel between the then, the now, and the future. While some of the texts may not, at face value, appear to directly address the notion of forced migration, displacement, or refuge, they nevertheless yield a fruitful reading of expressions of place and identity as they begin to teeter on the slippery slope of territoriality, where reclaiming *turāth*, narrating personal trauma, recounting the truth as the writer sees it, and finding a space for self-expression involve a forced migration from earlier tropes and ways of expression into a terrain where the refugee may begin to develop and experiment with their voice.

The culture of silence that has for several decades plagued Syrian writers is carried over from past to present, where decades of cultural censorship followed by the harsh reality of the Syrian civil war[2] and the present reality of a cold war all have imposed certain conditions on recent Arab-Syrian penmanship. While global news sources and popular artistic representations focus on the anonymous figure of the refugee, Syrian authors addressing the crisis tend to focus on the condition of the Syrian in their homeland, or else they depict forced migration very differently from mainstream media in order to recover a sense of the identity that has been lost to the crisis. My discussion of the refugee figure (as opposed to the migrant) suggests that the refugee, by both definition and representation, has been disassociated from most social, cultural, historical, and political ties to their homeland. As such, authorities that tend to usurp the representation of the refugee extend by default to hegemonizing and also subduing socio-political as well as historico-cultural representations. In the narrative silences that ensue, however, there are certain *reactionary* literary trends – what I refer to in the chapter as subaltern narratives – that emerge in revolutionary literature.

Deriving from a translation by Mohja Kahf of a Nizār Qabbānī poem,[3] the concept of "Smotherland" as I use it in the title suggests a tension born of both the newfound assertiveness of the Syrian writer as they attempt to narrate their trauma, and the forces that silence them as they are forced to narrate it through the hegemonic lenses of those wielding power over their representation. Both mass and artistic media tend to position the Syrian refugee within a controlled space where they are objectified, silencing their sociocultural and historical narratives. At the same time, in competition against such dominant media depictions, the stories shared by Syrian authors, I argue, attempt to defiantly reassert their social, cultural, and historical narratives, inadvertently reflecting tensions within which subaltern identities emerge.

The Migrant Versus the Refugee as a Member of the Bottom Societal Strata

The terms used to describe the refugee are linguistically determined to formulate specific policies, treatments, and representations of asylum-seekers, a process that is cyclical and mutually reinforcing. In the realm of media, which largely forms perceptions of Syrian refugees for themselves and others, there exist high-level Orientalist depictions that we find are further reflected in aspects of academic analyses on the topic of these narratives. These depictions often lack historicity and humanity while at the same time may feign objectivity. Even more nuanced studies, which mitigate these factors with high-level scholarly analyses informed by complex discourses, are deeply problematic in their silences on the emplacement of Syrians, their bodies, and the spatial boundaries of both. The result is that artistic or literary narratives by Syrian voices of Syrian identities developing in liminal spaces of the art world or online may be all we have to provide unique insights into fairer self and group portrayals.

Linguistically speaking, the refugee is limited by their label in two ways. Grammatically, the verb form in both English (to take refuge in) and Arabic (*laja'a ilā*) is typically followed by a prepositional phrase indicating who or what the refugee is taking refuge in (a place providing shelter, a person providing support and security, or an authority providing justice, for instance). This presupposes the existence of an object of preposition that also becomes the actor in semantic terms, taking precedence over the subject and imposing a unidirectional relationship between the subject and the object of the preposition. To migrate, on the other hand, is defined as "to move from one place to another, especially in order to find work or better living conditions" (*OED* online). In Arabic, the verb *hajara* in the first form means to leave behind or abandon, where the agent does so usually of their own volition. In its third form, the verb *hājara* means to leave one place for another, where again, as with the English equivalent, the agent is sometimes compelled to leave for their own reasons (*al-Ma'ānī*; my translation). And while *hājara ilā* and *laja'a ilā*, or *migrated to* and *took refuge in*, both presuppose an often-times forced act of departure on the subject's part, the prepositions in each of these verb phrases impose different relationships here. While the migrating subject in the first may still enjoy some freedom regarding the ultimate choice of destination that is not dependent on its object of preposition, the refugee in the second, more often than not, is entirely dependent on the object of preposition, or the person or place they must seek refuge in.

Analogically, these linguistic differences also extend to how international law and host countries treat refugees and migrants. Migration, as Dragostinova explains it, is a "highly structured process built upon patterns, historical contexts, and rational individual decisions" (Dragostinova, 2016, 4), and under immigration law, the migrant is subject to deportation if they do not meet the qualifications of asylum-seeker. The migrant is given time to adapt and express their identity in the new land. The refugee, on the other hand, has much less choice when fleeing areas of conflict. They have to be content with where they are placed, and often with how they are represented. Despite the fact that the refugee is a victim of political strife or economic disaster, the words "invasion," "flooding," and "besieging" are still commonly used by local people to describe refugee movement – especially as it relates to their feelings of fear that the incoming refugees have come to usurp jobs and impose their culture (Dragostinova, 2016, 4). As Connor further explains, the differences between the two mainly have to do with socio-economic factors, where here too refugees often occupy the lower end of the spectrum (Connor, 2010, 379–81). While these differences are not new, they shed light on narrative preferences about migration or movement, shaping media and literary representations alongside socio-political landscapes in mutually reinforcing ways.

To further situate the linguistic issue within a broader political context, we find how the term *crisis* extends itself both semantically and politically, creeping to narratives that have not even materialized. Freedman et al. (2017) explain how in 2011, the term was used by the European Union as a response to describe the steady rise in migration witnessed after the so-called Arab Spring had sprung, particularly from within Syria. The writers contend that the term "[serves] a powerful political and symbolic purpose" in that it connotes an out-of-the-ordinary situation that justifies European powers' intensified security and scrutiny measures and, at the same time, deflects attention from EU leaders' ineptitude in facilitating any effective political solutions. The political spectacle of the term "crisis" seems to have "obscured … the experiences of the refugees themselves" (Freedman et al., 2017, 23–24).[4] In this sense, the refugee is no longer individualized but, rather, is seen as part of a collective problem that requires an immediate solution. In this sense, linguistically, semantically, and politically, the refugee situation remains rather bleak.

Reactions to the Crisis

But in spite of the label – perhaps even because of it – the "crisis" has unfettered the voices of countless Syrian writers, critics, and artists after decades of oppression, as they speak their truths from the heart of the country as well as from exile. Many, such as Zakariyā Tāmir, Khalīl Ṣuwayliḥ, Samar Yazbik, and Nihād Sīrīs were forced into exile, some only recently. Others resolutely chose to return after a temporary absence (such as Khālid Khalīfa), and a few who were in exile (such as Samar Yazbik and Ghādī Francīs) made covert trips into the country to document the events. Several activists and lesser-known artists formed *Comic4 Syria* and stubbornly chose to remain in the country, resorting to the use of social media (Facebook in particular) to convey their art of resistance. Translation itself, as Syrian translator Thā'ir Dīb put it in an interview in 2016, also became a weapon of resistance, where the duty of conveying the horrors and experiences of the foreigner-Syrian to the Western world gained unprecedented urgency. Speculating on this emerging "foreigner-Syrian" concept, we begin exploring the rough terrain this refugee figure must travel in hope of winning back authorial rights to their narrative.

The foreigner-as-other has for a long time been the focus of much postcolonial and poststructural debate. Deconstructing the lenses through which the asylum-seeker is viewed and represented is essential to accessing subaltern narratives, for, as explained by Gramsci, "Subaltern groups are always subject to the activity of ruling groups, even when they rebel and rise up" (Gramsci, 1995, 55). The term subaltern, with all its negative linguistic, social, cultural, and political connotations, stubbornly attaches itself to the concept of the word *refugee* and points a critical finger at a centuries-old Orientalist narrative that tends to objectify the refugee, despite the occasional good intentions. Further emphasizing the need for this deconstructive approach to visual culture, we must ask, alongside Azoulay, questions such as: "Who sees? Who is capable, what, and from where? Who is authorized to look? How is this authorization given or acquired? In whose name does one look?" (Azoulay, 2012, 4). These questions centre around the power of the subject who is behind or in control of the device or tool used to portray the other: the Syrian refugee in the midst of the crisis.

The world watches the events of the crisis as they are narrated through the lens of visual media, yet through these images and exhibits, the world views but a fleeting moment, a snapshot of their journey as a member of "the bottom strata of globalized society," as former U.N. High Commissioner Sadako Ogata put it (cited in Goodnow, Lohman, and Marfleet, 2008, 9). The imperative, then, is to try to view an experience in its historical context – something that Ireland argues has been relegated to the side-lines of subaltern studies for its focus on the *immediacy* of experience. Scholars have too often negated history in their call for "counterhistories" that "have yet to be written" (Ireland, 2004, 11). When historicizing the refugee experience rather than scrambling to create counterhistories, Syrian subaltern narratives can be studied while maintaining something of a socio-historical foothold and, at the same time, opening the possibility not that there is more than one *counter*history to each narrative, but rather that there are multiple, intertwined histories that constitute a narrative of their own. As Wilson (2010) explains, because of its problematic entanglement with "images of powerlessness and vulnerability, as well as issues of risk, harm and threats to the security of the state and the state's cultural identity," the word "refugee" needs reinterpreting through a postcolonial lens (cited in McFayden, 2012, 25). Historicization as explained above is one means to resist the generalizations and Orientalist stereotypes pervasive in the depiction of the refugee.

There is no best approach to tease out the subaltern from beneath the groaning weight of hegemonic discourse and dominant narratives. Recent studies reflecting on this issue depict not only the harsh, persistent reality of the conflict on Syrian ground but also the enormous struggle and frustration academics face in trying to write about the Syrian crisis from a humanitarian perspective while still imposing mostly Western-based theoretical perspectives. For Puumala (2017), for example, the attempt to do away with the hierarchy, to reverse the unidirectionality the very definition of the word refugee presupposes, was impossible. Not because she herself did not make the effort to reverse that unidirectionality in her study, but because the subjects of her study (she refers to them as asylum-seekers in her work) *could not* and *did not want* to ignore it. Perhaps this is the case because on their end, their recognition of the privilege she enjoys inevitably ends up reinforcing it. More often than not, as Puumala's contemplation of her own study suggests, the possibility of such an endeavour and the weighing of what is gained or lost in such an academic exercise often remind one of the delusion of academia in countering the actual horrors on the ground.

With this in mind, despite the inherent value of studies such as Puumala's and McFayden's that help us situate the struggles of relying on various combinations of postcolonial and humanitarian/corporeal discourses to provide a more levelled representation of the refugee, one must keep in mind that these representations do not always adequately address questions of place, space, and limits; such questions are valuable in that they offer insight into the borders where the subaltern voice might dwell in Syrian narratives. As Cacciari explains, our quest for a place in which we can dwell is necessary. Nomads tend to "bring their own place with them – the carpet, in all its symbolic richness" (Cacciari, 2015, 14). However, securing a place to exist demands re-drawing and re-defining the "limits" of that place, which in turn calls for looking differently at the body that inhabits that place (Cacciari, 2015, 14–15). From a European standpoint and in Habermasian[5] fashion, Cacciari's approach to locating a place of belonging revolves around the concept of reimagining it, reinventing it, and thus becoming one of "many."[6] For our purpose, it is not the critic's job to *locate* a space in which to position the subaltern; we must instead *question and deconstruct spatial configurations* within pre-existing visual and textual representations to explore the possibility of a more authentic representation of the Syrian identity, for that which frames the body ultimately defines both the places and the limits of those bodies. The spatial impulse informing postnationalism at the level of identity and belonging, inasmuch as it both complicates but also informs identity discourse, has shaped the writing of numerous Arab authors, and also permeates many of the Arab-Syrian works we encounter in this chapter.

The Silencing Culture of Visual Media

There is no denying that visual images of the crisis led to a global outpouring of grief and outrage, followed quickly by governmental action on the part of European countries and then by North America. At the same time, these images also carry over a sinister history of Orientalism that continues to find its way into these representations. For many critics, as for Puumala, it was the image of Aylan Kurdi that spurred the world to action. Scores of cartoonists and journalists hurried to take advantage of this photo to reframe the toddler in different positions and circumstances in order to push various socio-political agendas. Images of Aylan positioned prostrate on a map of the "New World" on the side of the ocean with barbed wire separating him from land (Alkhateeb, 2015), or Aylan featured on a smart phone with a thumb hitting like/share and a caption reading: "Arab Action" (Yain-Allah, 2015), and many others all suggest a powerful manipulation of representation where the goal is to elicit spurious reactions and responses from the viewer. In one exaggerated response, Chinese artist Weiwei went so far as to photograph himself as the dead Aylan, a representation that has been blasted for being self-serving and over-done. The *Spectator* (January 2016) criticizes Weiwei's photograph as being "crude, thoughtless and egotistical" as well as "[contributing] absolutely nothing to [the refugees]. Instead there is the lingering suspicion that what it mostly contributes to is the flourishing career of Weiwei" (Boreham, 2016, 5).

To help explain how the power of spatial manipulation works here, a study by Wright describes the way in which people respond to media representations of refugees. Wright describes people's reactions to such images as a "moral obligation [that] is something of a triggered response" (Wright, 2002, 54). Each image here is that "of a particular person in a situation of migration in a specific location" (Wright, 2002, 56). However, there also exists on the part of the one capturing these images a certain tendency to "satisfy a preconceived idea"[7] with the presentation of these images (Wright, 2002, 57). In order to capture a facial expression of anguish or a critical snapshot of a refugee in danger or distress, for example, the photographer has to be looking for that specific moment in which to *frame* the refugee.

The use of the camera here further emphasizes the unidirectional relationship between the refugee and the subject (the one in control of the camera) and raises questions of ownership and the "preservation of rigid boundaries," to draw on Azoulay's description of the photograph (Azoulay, 2012, 25). By determining how and in what position the body is to be captured by the lens, the photographer is drawing a "line of contact" (Cacciari, 2015, 16). The clearer this line of contact is defined, "the more it becomes threshold," one that it is impossible for the body to transgress. It is through this threshold, according to Cacciari, that "relations and conflicts are generated," for by "clos[ing] a place off" one does not defend that place "but rather erases it"

(Cacciari, 2015, 16). In this case, victims in the war zone as well as refugees in media images are always living on the edge or the periphery with no access to the centre.

Similarly, the language used to describe such visual depictions has been discussed by scholars such as Hage (2000), Agier (2011), and Bauman (2016). For instance, Hage's white multicultural debate of Australian racist versus multicultural attitudes investigates how both groups (racists and multicultural advocates) "shared in the conviction that they were, in one way or another, masters of national space, and that it was up to them to decide who stayed in and who ought to be kept out of that space" (Hage, 2000, 17). For Hage, the way in which both racists and multiculturalists may be seen as "masters of national space" has to do with how white elitists imagine the space of migrants from other races. For instance, one could use size and number in relation to space to convey a racist attitude, as in perceiving a certain race as ants. Unless they exist in unsettlingly huge colonies inside one's home or within uncomfortable proximity, ants are not really seen as a problem. But when they increase, that is when "practices of violence are directed against them," since it is somehow up to the racist to decide how many are too many (Hage, 2000, 37–38).

Examples abound of such descriptive language used to describe the refugee in media. For instance, the magazine *Spoke*[8] described the Syrian refugees as "Weather-worn people [...] streaming like ants from their homes with all they can carry" (Boreham, 2016, 1). Words such as "streaming," "flooding," or "ants" carry powerful, often negative, connotations. Huggan explains that the "emphasis on spectacle and a commodified appreciation for the cultural other occlude the underlying political mechanisms through which more 'traditional' racial/ethnic hierarchies are preserved." Much of this, Huggan adds, has to do with the "single ambiguity of the term 'multiculturalism' that has allowed its proponents to implement it" (Huggan, 2001, 153). The ambiguity of the term has made it easy for hierarchies to persist, even in seemingly unbiased dialogues. These dichotomies not only position the refugee within such hierarchical frameworks that further relegate them to "the bottom strata of globalized society" (Ogata, cited in Goodnow, Lohman, and Marfleet, 2008, 9), but also oblige them (as Puumala found in her interviews) to accept this passive position. For Hage, they were ants, and for Agier, they were remnants. Of course, there are also the more artistic media ventures that aim at countering this dehumanization but nevertheless play a problematic role.

Take, for example, the work of award-winning Swedish photographer Magnus Wennman and his widely celebrated photo series *Where the Children Sleep* (2016). The series depicts images of sleeping Syrian refugee children (often through forests) as they make their journeys to safer destinations in Europe. It is interesting to note that Wennman partnered with both the UNHCR and Fotografiska, the Swedish Museum of Photography, to raise awareness of refugee children who must spend the night in the wilderness because they have been uprooted by violence. The children are presented in the photos with a caption for each child providing details about their journey. According to Azoulay, this type of representation is problematic, because it suggests that "under conditions of regime-made disaster [...] [t]he central right pertaining to the privileged segment of the population consists in the right to view disaster – to be its spectator" (Azoulay, 2012, 1). However, spectatorship is a privilege, granted only to those who are able to watch from the safety of their homes. Those they observe are destined to remain within the "category of the governed [...], [those] who can have disaster inflicted upon them and who can then be viewed subsisting in their state of disaster" (Azoulay, 2012, 2). A certain scandal attaches itself to images such as these, and while Azoulay discusses artistic photographs in the context of the Israeli aggression on Palestinians, Wennman's photos suggest a scandal in a different context, one that is twofold: there is the scandal of passivity as the world watches without intervening to stop the violence in Syria, and there is that of consent in the face of aggressive interventions, whereby international powers continue to conduct their battles on Syrian soil from the safety of their own.

Another recent example is that of an underwater museum exhibition by artist Jason de Caires Taylor showcasing the fate of many refugees who drowned on their way to Greek or Turkish shores. This "Taylor's Raft of Lampedusa," according to *Al-Arabiya* (February 2016), is located on the ocean bed of the Atlantic a short distance from one of the Spanish Canary Islands. The exhibition opened to the public on 26 February 2016, and consists of statues of refugees erected at a depth of 15 metres under the surface (*Al-Arabiya*, 2016, para. 1–3). This practice of museumification plays a similar role in determining how the refugee is to be spatially depicted. Marfleet points out that the "absence of refugees from public spaces is part of a longstanding problem of their low visibility in society in general" and stresses that [British] museums *need* to "find a significant space for refugees" (Marfleet, 2008, 17–18) in order to include them in historical narratives (Marfleet, 2008, 19). It appears once again that there is a dominant culture whose moral obligation it is to find a space for these refuges, celebrate their narratives, write histories or counterhistories for them, and showcase them in museums through pictures and artefacts that bespeak the harrowing trials they face as they try to reach the shores of those who decide how to represent them.

In response, visual counter-representations by Syrian artists to this hegemonic visual culture burst through like a round of fire against an unseen sniper. Many Syrian photographers chose to counter media representations by depicting their country's narrative through their own lens. There are examples of photos captured by Syrian photographers[9] worthy of being given platform here that document the destruction and aspects of culture the world has forgotten. In *Lens Young* (2014), communities of regular citizens-turned-photographers put themselves at great risk not only to document the strife and destruction on Syrian ground but also, and more importantly, I would add, to portray a strong sense of cultural and social loss. More than that, the representations in these images, though also framed, point to remnants of *normalcy* in a powerful move of resilience and dignity. The tangible evidence of the normal lives that Syrians lost, as well as the casual presentation of their day-to-day cultural practices, are poignant in their simplicity and starkness – these elements are mostly absent in mainstream visual media.

To draw on some examples, "Lovers" (*Lens Young*) features a photo of a young couple sitting together, with the words "love is being together" embossed on its plastic frame. The cheap frame holds great sentimental value, even more so now that it is featured lying on a pile of rubble in an abandoned home (Halasa, Omareen, and Mahfoud, 2014, 121). In another photograph featured in "Graffiti in Homs," the words "We were forced to leave, but we leave our hearts here. [...] We will return" are written on a wall (Halasa, Omareen, and Mahfoud, 2014, 122). Elsewhere, photos of a broken doll on the ground and bloodied laundry hanging on a clothesline are featured. Here, there is a sense of the suddenness of the violence and of the people's conviction that they will come back to reclaim their lives, the seeming normalcy of the images within an abnormal situation, and the resilience of the people.

This resilience is particularly powerful in photographs of graffiti – a well-documented form of resistance or act challenging spatial hegemony. As Cresswell notes, "graffiti [...] challenges the dominant dichotomy between public and private space. It interrupts the familiar boundaries of the public and the private by declaring the public private" and vice versa (Cresswell, 1996, 47). This disruption of familiar boundaries is in direct contrast to the fortification tendencies previously discussed. In addition, graffiti from disaster areas may allow the subjects, applying Azoulay's discourse here, to "recognize the arrogance of the occupier who presumes to control the boundaries of disaster" (Azoulay, 2012, 154). Given the difficulty of narrowing down the perpetrator of violence here, this form of resistance appears to be, at the very least, an expression of self-assertion: I am still here, even if I speak from amid the rubble and the crumbling walls.

Highly provocative among these artefacts are refugee selfies. Studies show how selfies – a more popular means of representation, especially among youth – such as those taken upon reaching the shores of Turkey, or with the Prime Minister upon arrival in Canada, may impact one's own narrative. A recent study by Chouliaraki (2017) looks at the selfie as a means of "symbolic bordering" whereby the refugee may take autonomy over their self-representation. Enabling them to cross digital boundaries even as they cross physical ones, the refugee's circulation of the selfie during their journey can be a double-edged sword, however, whereby the portraits may still be appropriated by Western media. In this regard, Chouliaraki explains that selfies tend to circulate not only horizontally, between more or less equal users of social platforms, but also vertically, from social platforms to mainstream media such as news organizations. The remediation of selfies by these "dominant visual economies" raises important questions about the way in which their value is reinterpreted by the dominant culture and sheds light on the "moral and political spaces" of Western media (Chouliaraki, 2017, 79). In this sense, the ambivalent contextualization of refugees' selfies may fluctuate between "voyeurism" and "disapproval," depending on who is taking them and how they are contextualized. Drawing on Arendt (1988), Chouliaraki argues that because the refugee is "a marginal figure without rights," their selfie "represent[s] nothing but her/his own absolutely unique individuality which, deprived of expression within and action upon a common world, loses all significance" (Chouliaraki, 2017, 92). In other words, once appropriated by the dominant culture, the refugee's selfie transforms from something of personal value to an object of " 'contemplative value' – that which draws attention to the selfie as an object to be focused on, gazed at, and responded to by an undefined body of 'impartial' spectators – the Western body politic" (Chouliaraki, 2017, 83). Here, too, the power of spectatorship determines what significance the refugee selfie may have in narrating a personal story of identity. If we are to agree with Arendt, there seems to be little hope that such minor examples of self-representations could change the dominant narrative of identity representation.

More recently, paintings and graffiti, YouTube videos, Facebook posts, and other examples of popular culture from within Syria and from refugee camps have presented in song, in blog, and in graffiti, in mural, in photography, in poetry, and in other genres poignant snapshots of the silencing of the Syrian refugee. One untitled painting by Sarah Khayat (2021) featured in *Warscapes*, an online magazine serving as a platform for the works of artists, writers, and critics representing war and conflict worldwide, shows a colourful stick figure stuffed with straw with sinister and haunting pictures of a fish, and heart, ravens, a maze, and other suggestive images on a wall in the background. The ragdoll is standing on a field of fire-like straw and her mouth has been stitched shut. Describing Khayat's painting, Riyadh al-Hussein writes the following caption: "Today, we are tired / And maybe tomorrow, too, we'll be tired / My mouth is sealed, and so, I cannot steal you" (al-Hussein, 2021). At the same time, another painting features a naked prisoner with his eyes closed and part of his body depicted as a prison gate. The writing on the painting calls out in bold print for the detainees in Syrian prisons to be returned to their families "before demanding the return of the refugees and displaced" (al-Asmar, 2020).[10]

These examples of popular media and artistic representation help counter representations of the refugee figure by attempting to give the Syrian a voice that reproaches the silencing culture of representation and decries the oppressor(s). Visual art and popular culture in the Syrian world may not carry much clout to counter the narrative imposed by the more dominant culture, but perhaps there is more to be said about literary representation in this regard.

Voices From "Smotherland"

Breaking the Silence and Contextualizing the Literature of the Revolution

In what follows, through the juxtaposition of literary samples against the prevalent culture of visual media, I show how a culture of silence has been broken through a process of reclamation of once unsafe places where authors are now free to speak. The foregrounding of pre-revolutionary literature as the backdrop for a discussion of revolutionary narratives is essential here, inasmuch as it serves to delineate the progression of forced migration in narrative form as it shifts away from earlier forms of the Syrian novel that traditionally, as Ouyang has pointed out, were preoccupied with a "longing for form [that] is national" (Ouyang, 2013, 225). Echoes of uncertainty and fear continue to resonate in these new spaces, allowing subaltern narratives to emerge as well.

The Syria of which Mohja Kahf spoke, once dubbed the kingdom of silence, has now "burst," to use the words of authors Yassin-Kassab and Al-Shami (2016), "into speech – not in one voice but in millions" (Yassin-Kassab and Al-Shami, 2016, viii). Indeed, as al-Turk put it, the silence was never made to last, and it followed that "society must, with its vital force, produce new forms of expression under the register of declarations, public statements and actions" (cited in Yassin-Kassab and Al-Shami, 2016, 16). Similarly, miriam cooke comments on how rapidly the silence was dissipating, as "the politics of fear was transformed into a politics of insult" (cooke, 2016, 63). Beginning with the *muntadayāt* (informal discussion groups) that were first formed by Syrian intellectuals just around the time when Bashar al-Asad came into power, cooke describes how pre-revolutionary writers such as Nihād Sīrīs (*Al-ṣamt wa-l-ṣakhab* [The Silence and the Roar] 2004, trans. 2013) and Khāled Khalīfa (*Lā sakākīn fī matābikh hādhihi al-madīna* [No Knives in the Kitchens of this City] 2013, trans. 2016) used mockery and insult to criticize the continuing incarceration of intellectuals (cooke, 2016, 64). Other artists turned to media that would afford more freedom to engage in rebellious rhetoric, using blogs, cartoons, songs, and graffiti to air their fearless disdain of Bashar (cooke, 2016, 71). Authors and critics such as Yāsīn al-Ḥāj Ṣāleḥ (*Al-khalāṣ am al-kharāb? Sūriyya ʿalā muftaraq ṭuruq* [Deliverance or Destruction? Syria at a Crossroads] 2014, trans. 2014), Samar Yazbik (*Taqāṭuʿ nīrān, min yawmiyyāt al- intifāḍa al-sūrīyya* [A Woman in the Crossfire: Diaries of the Syrian Revolution] 2012, trans. 2012), and Yūsuf Abū Yaḥyā ("*Anā sūrī*" [I Am Syrian] 2013, trans. 2013) (cited in cooke, 2016) expressed their thoughts and experiences powerfully through analyses, novels, memoirs, and poetry.

In terms of culture, both high and low forms existed, and the need to speak intensified as artists "expressed themselves in the streets and online through slogans, cartoons, dances and songs... speaking the truth as they perceived it" (cooke, 2016, 163–74). As Yassin-Kassab and Al-Shami put it,

"Syria's future, like its present, will exist in the space between push and pull" (Yassin-Kassab and Al-Shami, 2016, 182). These spaces in which the writers express their newfound voices exist, but there are also tense, uncertain territories where boundaries are still being tested and defended. This sudden burst of voices and the growing assertiveness of Syrian authorship did not happen overnight; although it manifested more visibly after 2011, changes began taking place at least ten years prior to that.

Of course, this burst brought forth emerging trends, particularly in fiction, that were precursors for more recent literature, and thus figure greatly in this discussion on forced migration and identity representation. While Syrian sociocultural and historical identity have always been a focus for many authors, the emergence of strongly pronounced political views was especially apparent in this new mix. To discuss an important example here, Fawwāz Ḥaddād's *Al-mutarjim al-khā'in* ([The Unfaithful Translator] 2008, trans. 2009) criticizes the rampant corruption of Syrian intelligentsia by depicting the story of a translator who intentionally (mis)translates the defeatist ending of a Sudanese author's Arabic novel so that it ends on a more patriotic, optimistic note. Known for standing up for justice in his writing, Ḥaddād is able to create a space for subaltern narratives that are significant simply because of their presence and is thereby creating new possibilities of countering nationalistic narratives in both content and form that imposed themselves, along with cultural and political censorship, on literary production at the time.

Ḥaddād's narrator is rewriting history in this fiction (as the title suggests, the translation is "unfaithful"), but in so doing, he is also introducing the possibility of having different versions of history intertwine. In his confrontation with a critic who questions him on this horrendous breach of ethics, the protagonist Ḥamīd falters at the start of the confrontation, uttering the words *lākinna-nī* ("But I") (Ḥaddād, 2008, 89), indicating, as it were, a state of trepidation, a moment of hesitant silence and uncertainty in the face of the intimidating authority before him. Rushing to his defence, the authorial voice jumps in to tell the critic Ḥallūm (whose name, incidentally, is also that of a squeaky white cheese popular in the Levant):

> How can I translate a story from any language, time, or place without being influenced by the age and the place I am living in? [...] I don't simply translate a book from another time and place; I also translate what connects it to the present time and place. They are all intertwined.
> (Ḥaddād, 2008, 89, my translation)

The subaltern voice occupies that uneasy place in the moment of hesitation between "But I" and the narratorial voice that follows, lingering for a moment before the narrator finds his tongue and explains why he has transgressed. In this important example, the narrator's need to connect past history(ies) with present realities, to create a place where it is possible – indeed, crucial – to migrate, even in fiction, marks a critical turning point in this narrative.

The possibility of wayfaring to another reality, of envisioning it through fiction and thus being able to use it to create and migrate to new spaces, opens up a whole new dimension in Arab-Syrian fiction where the quest for and the actualization of identity may be achieved by, as Ouyang (drawing on Borges) would put it, a re-narration of the past as a form of engagement with it through intertextuality, whereby tradition is absorbed, disappears, and is then revived to occupy the centre of the author's reality (Ouyang, 2013, 65). In the above example, it is a forced migration from authority, a form of rebellion against a rigid nationalist approach to history, the start of taking ownership of textual representation and identity depiction. In the examples that follow, this trend is more visible.

Novels of the Revolution[11]

For the most part, the more recent novels of the revolution deal with the universality of the human experience during the Syrian war, on the one hand, and with very specific and minute socio-political and cultural details, on the other. It is an attempt not only to convey to the world the immediate and urgent experience of war and suffering, but also a frantic effort to preserve one's individual identity, at risk of being annihilated in body by the war and in self by the dominant culture's appropriation. As we saw earlier through media representations, the hegemony of representation over the Syrian refugee through visual culture places them at risk of being acknowledged only as refugees, dependent, invisible to some extent unless present in large numbers. The role of literature in this regard is very important as it attempts to reassert some aspects of this lost identity. The theme of forced migration, in some instances more obvious than in others, takes on both real and imagined forms.

On the one hand, authors writing about the revolution tend to be, with good reason, more aggressive in their overall critique. Unlike in earlier pre-revolutionary novels where the antagonist was usually the oppressive regime, the oppressor in many of these more recent works tends to be anything and everything that inflicts violence upon the Syrian. Many of these works, particularly the ones written in exile (by Mahā Ḥasan and Samar Yazbik, for instance), include taboo themes of sex, adultery, and highly graphic and disturbing content. Transgression, alongside translation, becomes a major form of resistance, and space is artfully adapted by Syrian voices to suit that purpose. Indeed, in many of these novels, space and place themselves *are* the main characters, as several titles suggest. Drawing on theorists such as Bakhtin (1981), Kolb (2008), and Latour (2005), in the ensuing discussion I will situate Nabīl Mulḥim's novel *Bānsyūn Maryam* (Maryam's Boarding House, 2012), ʿAbd Allāh Maksūr's *Ayyām Bābā ʿAmrū* (Baba Amro Days, 2012), and its sequel, *ʿĀʾid ilā Ḥalab* (Returning to Aleppo, 2013) within the context of the argument on identity representation, forced migration, and the analysis of subaltern narratives through spatial depiction.[12]

In the aforementioned novels, the authors are not themselves migrants, nor are the characters populating their novels. How does one then discuss the notion of (forced) migration and identity here as the foreground for emerging refugee identity narratives? Here, I argue that migration may be mapped against a different topography, one that I introduced earlier – that of a postnational imagined landscape. Drawing on Davenport, Ouyang (2013) explores the Arabic novel's shift from the traditional to the modern by adapting the former's argument on how the "imagination [is] mapped by our notions of space and time" to create a metaphoric fabric grounded in historic-geographic realities but transformed into a Bakhtinian "chronotope" or a specific "time-space conception" (Ouyang, 2013, 143). Through this new lens, the reader is able to re-conceptualize new vistas of the world, its modes, and the actions taking place therein within the fabric of imagination in this postnational approach in the Arabic novel where "geography and history exert influence on the workings of imagination, [and where] imagination in turn reshapes space and time and restructures their relationship" (Ouyang, 2013, 144). In this regard, in the following examples, our perception of migration must be stretched in such a way so as to restructure "how we take stock, think, and articulate our views of the world, as well as how individuals, communities and events are related to this world" (Ouyang, 2013, 144). For the Arabic Syrian novel, the nation-state as episteme has traditionally often served to shape earlier texts and inform the social, political, and historical discourses present within. A redeployment of the "spatial impulse and mobility inherent in classical geographical literature," Ouyang explains, has made the "presence of the reshaped past in the present paradoxically gestur[ing] towards a hopeful future" (Ouyang, 2013, 146). The little-explored aspect of textual (as well as sometimes physical) forced migration allows, as Sakr (2018) also explains in her discussion of Blāsim's short stories, for a richer imagination of Syrian literature of the revolution that can "expand the horizons of our understanding of a different kind of displacement from the Arab world, specifically relating to post-conflict clandestine movement" (Sakr, 2018, 767). While Sakr's article focuses on trans-European forced migration, other depictions of migration and identity representation abound in the following examples. These depictions are in and of themselves forms of resistance against the totalitarianism of representation alluded to earlier. At the same time, tracing the subaltern throughout these identity narratives also helps uncover the underlying tensions as the forced migrant figure explores these newfound territories.

To begin with Maksūr, both of his novels contain the title of two Syrian towns or cities. Baba Amro is a town just southwest of the district of Homs, and Aleppo is the second major city in Syria after Damascus. Realism permeates the novels as the narrator, a reporter wishing to record the events in the Syrian town, travels from Baba Amro to Aleppo and through the war-torn neighbourhoods, shanties, and winding alleys to record events and testimony of people who mostly were known by their nicknames. In between the narratives of the characters whom the narrator encounters, there are intertwined and extended networks of other narratives, with people and places mingling in mysterious ways. Inside Aleppo (in *Returning to Aleppo*), place takes on a significant presence when, within the Sayf al-Dawla neighbourhood, a school is transformed into a prison/training centre where young people are recruited to become terrorists. The walls of the school themselves are reconfigured as spaces where supposedly religious teachings are written on a bullet-riddled concrete canvas. The narrator criticizes every faction as well as the regime itself; there are no more heroes in this war, except for the regular citizen who, despite the bombing and shooting, continues to resist by playing games of *ṭāwleh* (the colloquial name for the game of backgammon).

In Mulḥim's novel, events take place within and outside a boarding house in Damascus run by a laconic Syrian woman called Maryam. Here too, as in Maksūr's novels, the title and central character in the book is a place. The boarding place houses people from all walks of life, and again, there are a number of intricate subplots, where networks of characters and narratives are mapped throughout the novel. It may be said that the lodge itself is a microcosmic cross-section of a nation in which different actors exist uneasily in close proximity to each other, where power struggles are enacted and tensions arise quickly, while on the outside, corruption, violence, lewdness, lust, sectarianism, and class discrimination run rampant. Interestingly, in both *Returning to Aleppo* and *Maryam's Boarding House*, games of risk and gamble are alluded to, and the authorial voices make use of various opportunities in the novels to present social criticism through these symbols. Towards the end of Mulḥim's novel, for instance, the waiter tells Jalāl:

> Son, gambling is not only in card games […] it is also in politics and women and everything […] for example, I'm gambling right now as I sit here with you, who is to convince me, for example, that you are not a murderer or a thief?!
>
> (Mulḥim, 2012, 131, my translation)

Maryam is very cautious of whom she allows to enter her boarding house, and the end of the novel sees her closing her doors to any new residents. Both authors tend to shock with their vivid depictions of sexual and moral transgression as well as their graphic representation of violence and death. Identity is stripped to the core, revealing human nature at its basest in light of the war ravaging the country.

There are intermingling networks of narratives that manifest in these novels that may be classified according to Latour's ANT theory (2005) as actor-network associations between social and political actors, where the actor is "the moving target of a vast array of entities swarming toward it," and it is necessary for us to retrieve the multiplicity of the "actor-network" by locating all actors and entities involved (Latour, 2005, 46–47). Groups are constantly being formed and reformed, and our goal is to locate the traces left behind in the wake of these formations (Latour, 2005, 34). Therefore, understanding the dynamics of actors moving across the country or in and out of the boarding house allows us to grasp less obvious social and political identities through associations made and networks formed in the novel, for they are those that are *ever-changing* and very difficult to capture and frame. According to Latour, the social and political are *movements*, not fixed entities; they are associations between actors that are only made visible when actors are reshuffled together (Latour, 2005, 64–65), not unlike on a chess board or in a game of cards!

Movement from one place to another here becomes an act of defiance and risk, unpredictable, speaking only for itself, refusing to be captured or framed. The imagined spaces within which these movements occur become important nexuses of forced migration, where characters confront their own truth only when and as they are confronting the truths of others in these forced associations, where multiple histories intermingle, clash, and collide to produce violent narratives of trauma. Similarly, in discussing forced migration trajectories in Blāsim's work, Sakr alludes to certain ecological spaces (e.g. the forest in her analysis of Blāsim) as being both real and imagined: a nexus or border accentuating the experience of trauma as "the imaginative locus of a complex exploration of the biopolitical and ecological implications of material and discursive violence welded against clandestine migrant bodies" (Sakr, 2018, 767). Herein, I argue, also lurks the subaltern voice. We glimpse it when, for instance, Maksūr, in the example I have provided, describes how the so-called school in Sayf al-dawla combines Egyptians, Iraqis, Jordanians, Palestinians, Tunisians, and other nationalities of jihadists ready to become martyrs no matter where they are sent. The narrator (and the reader) may express contempt and horror for such people; at the same time, however, upon listening to the horror stories of Syrian actors in the story who were subjected to extreme torture, the narrator himself is not much surprised about how someone could decide to become a jihadist. This response hints at untold stories of torture inflicted and associations made, not as with a static character in a story, but as part of a complex network consisting of fluid, mobile identities. Latour's network captures "energy," "movement," and "specificity" (Latour, 2005, 131), and because the social and political are so difficult to locate except "at the fleeting moment when new associations are sticking the collective together" (Latour, 2005, 159), these spaces of tension are where subaltern narratives emerge. These, too, are the spaces where both character and reader must migrate to be exposed to new truths, new realities, and intertwined histories.

Although Mulḥim's and Maksūr's novels are situated within Syria, there is also the sense that microcosms within the novel have been created whereby both characters and readers are forcefully transported or, more aptly, *absented* from the country. In reference to Sellman (2014), who explores and plays on the multiple meanings of the Arabic word *ghāba*, meaning forest as a noun but also sounding like the Arabic verb for absented or disappeared, Sakr discusses the forest trope as "becom[ing] the most conceptually dense geographical anchor for the exploration of the perilous dynamics of forced and clandestine migration as well as their related geopolitical and representational parameters" (Sakr, 2018, 769). And while Mulḥim's and Maksūr's novels do not have forests, they do feature boarding houses, schools, and winding alleys, all of which become microcosms or geographical anchors that capture fleeting movements, forced encounters, sinister spaces in which identity and trauma are confronted, associations are examined, and histories merge together.

Memoirs, Poems, and Narratives of Incarceration

Other non-fiction genres provide further examples of how aspects of socio-cultural and historical identity are portrayed in representations of forced migration to counter master narratives we encountered in the first section. I use examples of close readings here drawn from Samar Yazbik's *Bawwābāt arḍ al-ʿadam* ([The Crossing: My Journey to the Shattered Heart of Syria, 2015], trans. 2015), which is a memoir, and excerpts of poetry and prison narratives from the anthology *Sūriyā tataḥaddath* (Syria Speaks, 2014, trans. 2014). In the first example (a memoir), there is a forced migration back to the homeland; in the second (a short poem), there is a forced cultural–linguistic transgression; and in the third (a prison narrative), there is a corporeal forced migration. In all three narratives, identities and world views are expressed very differently but share the similar goal of reclaiming the Syrian story.

In Samar Yazbik's memoir, the writer's feminist views come across strongly and are presented in various examples of spatial representation in her work. Yazbik gives an account of her threefold covert journey into Syria across the Turkish border in order to record the harrowing accounts of the experiences of people across the country. What is noticeable in *The Crossing* is Yazbik's transgression of many borders as a *woman*. Her translated memoir opens as follows:

> The barbed wire lacerated my back. I was trembling uncontrollably. After long hours spent waiting for nightfall, to avoid attracting the attention of Turkish soldiers, I finally raised my head and gazed up at the distant sky, darkening to black. Under the wire fence marking the line of the border a tiny burrow had been dug out, just enough for one person. My feet sank into the soil and the barbs mauled my back as I crawled across the line of separation between the two countries.
>
> (trans. Gowanlock and Kemp, 2015, 3)

As this is a time of war, most of these public spaces are exclusive to men. miriam cooke (1996) writes that "the front and home front" (traditionally gendered spaces) impose restrictions on women who "occup[ied] spaces that had little if any direct access to the spaces of power that the men in general occupied" (cooke, 1996, 14). Not only is Yazbik able to access a male-dominated warzone on her side of the border, but in doing so, she attempts to construct a counter-narrative to some of the more patriarchal hegemonic depictions of the Syrian refugee, where variations of Biblical prototypes such as the "migrant mother," "Mary and Joseph," "Madonna and Child," and "Exodus" (see Wright, 2002, 57) may occasionally characterize some present-day representations.

Yazbik's emphasis of the physicality of the opening scene also resonates in two ways. At one level, the barbed wire itself at the start of the memoir gives a physicality to the borders that she must cross, and through the graphic representation of the crossing, Yazbik may be attempting to disprove with her boldness and her authorship the marginality that is imposed on some female Arab writers. On this topic, Jackson (2011) notes that "the notion of a border giving physical presence to a state of marginality is recurrent in both women's and postcolonial writing" and that "spatial segregation" is often determined by "gender, ethnicity, social class and other categories of identity" (Jackson, 2011, 57). In this regard, to what extent does Yazbik's crossing of the barbed wire involve the "remaking of spaces" (Jackson, 2011, 57) if she herself is a member of the elite? To use Jackson's argument here, as she crosses these barriers, Yazbik may be to some extent challenging "the distinction between the public and the private" (Jackson, 2011, 58) as she accompanies men to the front lines where the fighting is most intense and sits with them during their meetings and councils. She may also be challenging political powers as she attempts to dispel the Western obsession with ISIS that often translates into negative portrayals of the refugee. At another, less obvious level, though, there is the inescapable irony: Yazbik is crossing simply *because she can*.

What gives the text an added distinction is how Yazbik challenges media representations of the Syrian narrative head-on. If we are to think of her in terms of the refugee definition discussed in the first section of the chapter, we find she defies the very definition by going against its unidirectionality. She also disrupts the aesthetic efforts such as those made by Wennman to capture the romanticized image of the refugee by attaching political significance to her narrative. She avoids the limits imposed upon her by the camera through looking "up at the distant sky, darkening to black" (Yazbik, 2015, 3) even as she is crawling under the wire. As Casey (2015) puts it, escape from the density of the world "lies close at hand. All I need to do is look up – straight up. When I do, a generous canopy of air and light open above me" (Casey, 2015, 27). The sky has an embracing, welcoming, and liberating presence in this sense, allowing the wanderer to freely roam, even in a space that has borders. Indeed, Casey might as well have been talking about Yazbik.

Other narratives of expression may be traced in the blogs and social media of ʿAbbūd Saʿīd (2014). In *Afham shakhṣ bi-l-Faysbūk* ("The Smartest Guy on Facebook"), Saʿīd, a "working-class poet," posts this poem in Arabic:

> "You think you're Baudelaire?" she says to me.
> I ask: Who's Baudelaire, a poet?" / fuck / history created them, these people /
> Homs is more important than Troy.

And Abdel Baset al-Sarout[13] is braver than Guevara.
And I am more important than Baudelaire."
She laughs. She thinks I'm joking.
(trans. Sabeel, 2014, 279)

For Saʿīd, as a young Syrian, his heroes and places are far more important than those celebrated in the Western cultural canon. His question of "Who's Baudelaire?" followed by "history created them, these people" stands as a criticism against a hegemonic culture that imposes its dominant version of cultural history. Saʿīd's poem conveys a powerful sense of national and cultural pride and a rejection of sympathy. There is a process of deconstruction where one culture is taken out of its context and contested against another culture to challenge it. In this sense, the writer is waging his own war on Facebook turf, using social media to forcefully transgress, question, and destabilize hegemonic cultures and re-establish his own. The practice of using the Facebook platform to publish posts, pictures, poetry, videos, and other media forms has also become a popular method of expression; while this poem may not so obviously conform to the traditional narrative of forced migration, it does attempt to transgress over into the turf of the other culture to restore a tiny segment of the writer's own *turāth*.

While attempts such as the above to salvage the remnants of Syrian history and culture may function in themselves as counter-narratives against museumification and cultural hegemony, these are feats that, I argue, also depict spaces of tension. Saʿīd's poem, defiant as it is, resonates with bravado but may conceal an underlying sense of insecurity. In the space between using his own language and attempting to criticize some aspects of the hegemonic culture, there is a slight nuance of hesitation. As Julia Kristeva writes (1991), a polyglot, or one who speaks more than one language, is "like a handicapped child – cherished and useless." Thus caught "between two languages, your realm is silence, [as] by dint of saying things in various ways, one just as trite as the other … one ends up no longer saying them" (Kristeva, 1991, 15). While Saʿīd writes in Arabic, many of the cultural references in his poem are Western. Also, as a writer who was unable to complete his high school education, Saʿīd represents the opposite end of society as compared to Yazbik. His writing is more representative of the underprivileged portion of Syrian society, whereas Yazbik represents the elite. Perhaps Saʿīd has not read Baudelaire and is not familiar with Greek history, but it is important to take into account that his narrative also represent different aspects of Syrian sociocultural identity, and that here are some of the spaces that remain fraught with tension where the writer is attempting to cross linguistic and cultural boundaries to make a strong statement.

The final representation in Syrian literature of the revolution that I wish to discuss here is also the grimmest, for it focuses primarily on images of incarceration, death, and decay of the human body. The genre I use in this last discussion is that of the prison memoir, for which I turn to Syrian author and journalist Dārā ʿAbd Allāh (born in 1990, a member of the Kurdish minority) in his memoir *Al-waḥda tudallilu ḍaḥāyā-hā* (Loneliness Pampers Its Victims, 2014, trans. 2014). The gruesome but real depictions of imprisonment and gore as described by ʿAbd Allāh strongly allude to what Julia Kristeva (1981; trans. 1982) describes as the abject. My reason for using Kristeva's definition of the abject here is because at this stage in the Syrian narrative there is the sense that rock-bottom has been reached, and the only space left to migrate to is that of the human body. Kristeva's illustration of the abject provides the final frontier of forced migration. The reader may not like what he reads, but in being forced to read it, he will face his own greatest fear: the horror that is his own body.

For Kristeva, the abject appears as a "threat that seems to emanate from an exorbitant outside or inside" and is beyond any conception of what is "possible," tolerable," or even "thinkable." It is not, however, something that can be clearly defined as an object, nor is it something that its subject can escape. Indeed, one cannot seemingly "detach" oneself from the abject because its only recognizable quality is "that of being opposed to the 'I'" (Kristeva, 1982, 1). The abject defies definition as it draws the subject to that "place where meaning collapses." The abject subjects the "I" to unimaginable suffering, but the "I" has no choice but to put up with it, for loathsome as it is, the abject is simultaneously "Not me" but is also a "something" that exists on the borders of my existence, a reality that, if confronted, would destroy the subject (Kristeva, 1982, 2). The space here is the human body, and the spectator is both the owner of that body and soul as well as their author. Kristeva's abject resides in the revulsion we feel when we encounter something rotten that may cause us to vomit. That "cesspool and death," stripped of all masks and finery, "*show* me what I [must] permanently thrust aside in order to live" (Kristeva, 1982, 3). These are the things human beings cannot tolerate about death, because they exist "at the border of [one's] condition as a living being," and to survive one must remove one's self from that border (Kristeva, 1982, 3–4).

ʿAbdullāh's depiction of a dying man in prison aptly illustrates Kristeva's notion of the cadaver as abject. The narrator in his memoir is imprisoned in the al-Khaṭīb Branch in Damascus where the size of the cell/grave is such that "its length never allows you to fully lie down, and its width never allows you to sleep in a foetal position" (Halasa et al., 2014, 145). The claustrophobic space and vile conditions of the cell at the *mukhābarāt*[14] prisons allow one neither rest nor healing from any wound. When Abū Samīr, a fighter with the Free Syrian Army, is moved to al-Khaṭīb, he is suffering from a deep bayonet wound. Abū Samīr is greatly loved and respected and thus "welcomed with fervour" by the other prisoners (Halasa et al., 2014, 147–48); however, when his wound begins to fester, the narrator changes his tone while his prison-mates change their impression of him.

The description of the wound festering and the slow, painful death of Abū Samīr is not meant to evoke compassion. Death is presented here in its ugliest form as we are confronted with our greatest fear and loathing. The narrator describes the scene as follows:

> One of the most pungent, intolerable smells in nature is that of a decomposing body. How odd it is that human beings are the source of everything beautiful, and at the same time everything that is ugly? The stench of this man's rotting wound permeated the cell. It was a pungent, sharp smell that seemed to pierce the brain. The whiteness of the bone in his leg was hard to distinguish from the large number of maggots, the larvae that eat the corpses of the dead. What eats the dead was already alive in his body. An inner struggle raged in everyone's heart: the impossible ugly smell on one side, and noble empathy on the other, a conflict between ordinary daily feelings and the absolute purity of heroism.
>
> (Halasa et al., 2014, 147)

At this point, many of the other inmates begin vomiting due to the stench, and as the gangrene spreads to his blood, Abū Samīr's body begins to swell up and "a white odorless fluid" oozes from his body. At that stage, the narrator writes, "compassion was almost nonexistent," and the unbearable stench "revealed every hidden, nasty selfishness in us and every simple primal fear, as though it made glass of our bodies." The narrator reveals that his "capacity for hatred was redirected into the collective rejection of [Abū Samīr]" and discovers that the only way he could dispel the stench was by displacing it with the stench of his own body. Thus, he begins "placing [his] hand in the space between [his] groin and thigh and sniffing the accumulated fetid smell of the remains of semen." Once the narrator discovers in himself that same horrid rotting smell, he finds that he "has enough rotting [of his own] that would make Abū Samīr smell beautiful." The narrator observes that: "your own putrid smell is closer to your heart than that of others" (Halasa et al., 2014, 148).

This gruesome account is necessary to discuss for three reasons. For one, it forces the reader to cross that "border that has encroached upon the barriers of everything" (Kristeva, 1982, 4). From another, psychoanalytical point of view, it is *necessary* to experience this abjection; it is an experience that culminates in us forfeiting our own selves, because at some level the abject is our "recognition of the *want* on which any being, language, or desire is founded" (Kristeva, 1982, 5). In the context of her discussion of the foreigner, Kristeva (1991) argues that living with the foreigner is not simply a matter of not "being able to accept the other, but of *being in his place*, and this means to imagine and make oneself other for oneself" (Kristeva, 1991, 13). It is a form of empathy so extreme that it entails crossing all possible thresholds of horror and abjection within us to become that which we loathe the most. It is an empathy, as the above scene suggests, that necessitates the decentralization of experience if we are to understand the experience of the Syrian inmate. The feelings of revulsion we feel at the description of the rotting prisoner are matched only by our disgust for ourselves; the only way to accept and embrace the other is when we recognize that we are not witnessing someone else's decomposition, but that of our own. Finally, the narrow space of the cell is fitting in that it allows for this focused contemplation of the self and the other. The prisoners are not allowed to run away from the stench, and neither are we as readers. The forced migration here has us cross all thresholds and emerge either as more empathetic if we are able to recognize that the abject is within us, or more loathsome of the other if we cannot endure that confrontation.

A similar discourse has been applied in a different way by Rabinowitz (2010) in the context of Palestinian refugees, where he argues that, while something may appear as horrid and disgusting, it may also be good for us. Like the Palestinian refugee, the Syrian has no autonomy because their fate is "regularly sealed by regional and global powers, leaving [them] with limited control over [their] destiny and a desperate quest to break the shackles of dependence" (Rabinowitz, 2010, 510). The body-as-nexus becomes here the land of forced migration; the prison becomes, to use Sakr's description of Blasim's nightmare realist wilderness setting that refugees must cross traversing Europe, a "radical non-place-time" (Rabinowitz, 2010, 770). While Blāsim's short stories deal mainly with clandestine crossings of Iraqi asylum-seekers, the invisibility of the clandestine refugee as discussed by Sakr is not so different from the Syrian prisoner; they both suffer in silence and are depicted as "literally bare bodies" (Rabinowitz, 2010, 776) and as "human animals" (Rabinowitz, 2010, 778). In both cases, these texts confront us "with a heightened and sustained sense of a crisis representation urging the need to create imaginative responses" (Rabinowitz, 2010, 778), which is what compels us to think about forced migration in a very different way than mainstream media depicts.

Conclusion

The Syrian narratives as presented in this chapter extend beyond stories of refugees trying to reach safe havens, or the images of pitiful death and misery, the insinuations of swarming threats and infestations circulating in the media. Why must there be a "Refugee Council's Refugee Week [...] in which the wider community is invited to celebrate refugee experiences" in South Yorkshire, or a "Museum of Immigration and Diversity" in East London[15] (Goodnow and Marfleet, 2008, 24) to showcase refugee narratives? The representative practices of hegemonic cultures, as I have suggested, often decontextualize the refugee narrative and thus obscure their history, culture, and identity. In order for the refugee to reassert themselves, they must reclaim a space in which they are able to do so.

In this chapter, I have argued in the first section how global media representations at both popular and artistic levels may situate the Syrian refugee within a hegemonic cultural space; the framed portrayal of the Syrian refugee in many of these examples usually serves ulterior socio-political motives intended to elicit specific responses from global audiences. Even the more nuanced humanitarian/artistic attempts tend to de-historicize and decontextualize the subject in their portrayal. It follows that the fair and authentic representation of the Syrian as forced migrant is at stake due to the prevalence of such a loud visual culture. In the second section, I explained how Syrian authorship has evolved from its culture of silence to break through with louder, more assertive voices resonating across a plethora of different genres. Syrian writers have attempted to re-establish a sense of Syrian identity after it had been quashed for decades by authoritarian regimes, censorship, and trauma. However, in discussing the emerging socio-cultural, political, and historical identity narratives that emerged in this chapter, it was also important to hearken to the subaltern narratives embedded within the louder identity narratives through an ethical reading of the texts. Using a variety of critical approaches that combine elements of spatial discourse, poststructural, and postcolonial critical theories, we teased out the subaltern narratives and highlighted the importance of reading through the lens of a postnational imagination to better understand the themes of forced migration in the texts. Discerning and discussing these more subdued narratives alongside the dominant ones allowed us to better trace the development of Syrian authorship and the ways in which certain forces may impact the representation of identity in the text.

Hoping to do justice to different voices emerging from the revolution, the works I have selected for this chapter encompassed writers of different age groups, different genders, different religions and ethnicities, and different social and political backgrounds. However, what they have in common is a desire to be heard, a desire to express their own experience of war trauma as well as the richness of Syrian culture.

Notes

1 Here, "pre-revolutionary" and "revolutionary" are used with some reservation. As Kadalah argues, we would err were we to assume that the anti-regime revolutionary wave of literature began only with the onset of the 2011 revolution; there is a substantial corpus of literature criticizing the Assad father-son politics well before then (hailing back to the 1982 Hama massacre). However, as explained in this chapter, the body of literature published before 2011 adopted, for the most part, an allegorical approach or else took a more subdued position in their revolutionary stance, forced as it was by the heavy-handed censorship of the cultural arena at the time. The works published after 2011 were far more vocal but still relied on and developed from the foundations established by the pre-revolutionary literature that preceded them (Kadalah, 2016, 2).

2 The biased documentation by government-controlled national media of the massacres, uprisings, and demonstrations instilled Syrian writers with a sense of urgency to describe, whether through visual art, social media platforms, or myriad genres of fiction and nonfiction, "the massive social and political transformation that Syria was experiencing for the first time in more than forty years" (Kadalah,

2016, 3). What began in writing with the first wave of uprising in Daraa was in the form of graffiti at the hands of a group of youth and continues in writing at the hands of impassioned Syrian authors, bloggers, artists, and social media gurus.

3 The title of the poem is "Top Secret Report from the Country of Smotherland"

4 The cited work focuses primarily on "gendered experiences" emerging from the crisis.

5 Habermas's "postnational constellation" argument (drawn from the title of his essay collection by that name in 2001) explores the concept of a postnational identity within a globalized world and the ways in which political and cultural identities may be expressed.

6 From an interview by *Barcelona Metropolis* with Cacciari in the summer of 2010.

7 Wright suggests that some of the images of refugees conform to prototypes of Biblical origins (Wright, 2002, 57), a topic which I take up in another study.

8 The Newspaper of Conestoga College's Journalism Program

9 See for more examples the work of *Lens Young*, communities of regular citizens turned photographers who put themselves at great risk not only to document what was happening in Syria, but also to portray its culture and to convey a strong sense of the nature of the losses that families experienced.

10 The two examples are from creativememory.org

11 A Note on Translation and Publication: Most of the literary texts I have chosen for close reading in the following section have been translated into English (as well as other languages), and it is important here to discuss some pertinent matters of publication and translation that may influence the reading of these texts as well as my interpretation. Many of the texts on the revolution were translated in the same year they were published, particularly the texts of authors in exile. In the case of Yazbik's memoir and the anthology on Syrian literature I use, both books gained immense popularity in their *translated* versions, raising the important question of what may have been lost or compromised through these transactions. For some of these works, it appears that the target audience is a western one, and this alone complicates our reading of these works. Are the authors addressing *only* a western audience? What is the intended message, and to what extent is it packaged in the work? For instance, Yazbik's memoir has increased her popularity, and nowadays she is considered as one of the "Bad Girls of the Arab World," which is the title of a collection of works by Arab women published in 2017. This anthology of women writers (edited by Nadā Yaʿqūb and Rūla Qawwās), according to *Middle Eastern Studies*, "focuses explicitly on Arab women's often-fraught engagement with the boundaries that shape their lives in the twenty-first century" (from the University of Texas webpage). These factors do not necessarily detract from the value of the writing; indeed, this could provide an opportunity for the writers to express themselves in ways that may not have been possible had the works been addressing a mostly Arab readership. At the same time, however, the sensationalism and popularity surrounding some of these texts must not go unnoticed.

12 Nabīl Mulḥim was born in 1953, while 'Abd Allāh Maksūr was born in 1983.

13 A beloved Syrian football star who played a major role in numerous demonstrations in the country.

14 Arabic for (the Regime's) secret intelligence.

15 Marfleet lauds the efforts made at establishing museums and institutions dedicated to representing refugees, but sees that much more must still be done (Marfleet, 2008, 24).

References

'Abd Allāh, D. (2014) *Al-waḥda tudallilu ḍaḥāyā-hā*. L. Zyiad (trans.). In: M. Halasa, Z. Omareen, and N. Mahfoud (eds) *Syria Speaks: Art and Culture from the Frontline*. London, UK: Saqi, 145–48.

Agier, M. (2011) *Managing the Undesirables*. D. Fernbach (trans.). Cambridge: Polity.

Al-Ali, N. (2012) Gendering the Arab spring. *Middle East Journal of Culture and Communications*, 5(3), 26–31. https://doi.org/10.1163/18739865-00503017.

Al-Arabiya English. (2016) Underwater museum spotlights Syrian refugee crisis. *Al-Arabiya English*. Available from https://english.alarabiya.net/variety/2016/02/15/Underwater-museum-spotlights-Syrian-refugee-crisis. [accessed 20 March 2017].

Al-Asmar, A. (2020) Give us back the detainees and disappeared. In: *Creative Memory of the Syrian Revolution*. Available from https://creativememory.org/en/archives/?fwp_keywords=refugees-en [accessed 20 May 2021].

al-Hussein, R. (2021) Untitled. In: *Creative Memory of the Syrian Revolution*. Available from https://creativememory.org/en/archives/?fwp_searchwp_archives=al-hussein&fwp_categories=paintings&fwp_keywords=refugees-en [accessed 21 September 2021].

Alkhateeb, R. (2015) Aylan Kurdi. *Takepart*. Available from www.takepart.com/article/2015/09/03/artists-around-world-illustrate-why-syrian-toddler-death-matters/ [accessed 20 May 2021].

Arendt, H. (1976) *The Origins of Totalitarianism*. New York: Harvest Books.

Azoulay, A. (2001) *Death's Showcase: The Power of Image in Contemporary Democracy*. R. Danieli (trans.) Massachusetts: MIT Press.

Azoulay, A. (2012) *Civil Imagination: A Political Ontology of Photography*. London: Verso.

Bakhtin, M. (1981) *The Dialogic Imagination: Four Essays*. C. Emerson and Holquist (trans.). Austin: University of Texas Press.

Bauman, Z. (2016) *Strangers at Our Door*. Cambridge, England: Polity.

Bhabha, H. (1994) *The Location of Culture*. London: Routledge.

Boreham, P. (2016) Syrian refugees finding new home in Canada. *Spoke*. Available from https://spokeonline.com/2016/02/syrian-refugees-finding-new-home-in-canada/ [accessed 20 February 2016].

Cacciari, M. (2015) Place and Limit. In: J. Malpas (ed.) *The Intelligence of Place: Topographies and Poetics*. London: Bloomsbury Academic, 13–22.

Casey, E. (2015) Place and Edge. In: J. Malpas (ed.) *The Intelligence of Place: Topographies and Poetics*. London: Bloomsbury Academic, 23–38.

Chouliaraki, L. (2017) Symbolic bordering: the self-representation of migrants and refugees in digital news. *The International Journal of Media and Culture*, 15(2), 78–94. https://doi.org/10.1080/15405702.2017.1281415.

Connor, P. (2010) Explaining the refugee gap: economic outcomes of refugees versus other immigrants. *Journal of Refugee Studies*, 23(3), 377–397. https://doi.org/10.1093/jrs/feq025

cooke, m. (1996) *Women and the War Story*. Los Angeles: University of California Press.

cooke, m. (2007) *Dissident Syria: Making Oppositional Arts Official*. Durham: Duke University Press.

cooke, m. (2016) *Dancing in Damascus: Creativity, Resilience, and the Syrian Revolution*. New York: Routledge.

Cresswell, T. (1996) *In Place/Out of Place: Geography, Ideology, and Transgression*. Minneapolis, MN: University of Minneapolis Press.

Dīb, T. (2016) Interviewed by R. Mustapha. *Status*. Available from www.statushour.com/en/Interview/227 [accessed 29 April 2017]. (Arabic).

Dragostinova, T. (2016) Refugees or immigrants? The migration crisis in Europe in historical perspective. *Origins: Current Events in Historical Perspective*, 9(4) 1–16. Available from http://origins.osu.edu/article/refugees-or-immigrants-migration-crisis-europe-historical-perspective [accessed 3 August 2022]

Freedman, J., Kivilcim, Z., and Ozgur N. (eds) (2017) *A Gendered Approach to the Syrian Crisis*. Abingdon, Oxon: Routledge.

Goodnow, K., Lohman, J., and Marfleet, P. (2008) *Museums, the Media and Refugees: Stories of Crisis, Control and Compassion*. London: Museum of London and Berghahn Books.

Gramsci, A., and Boothman, D. (1995) *Further Selections From the Prison Notebooks*. Minneapolis: University of Minnesota Press.

Ḥaddād, F. (2008) *Al-mutarjim al-khāʾin*. Beirut: Dār Riyāḍ al-rayyis.

Hage, G. (2000) *White Nation: Fantasies of White Supremacy in a Multicultural Society*. New York: Routledge.

Halasa, M., Omareen, Z., and Mahfoud N. (eds) (2014) *Syria Speaks: Art and Culture from the Frontline*. London: Saqi, 118–129.

Huggan, G. (2001) *The Postcolonial Exotic: Marketing the Margins*. London: Routledge.

Ireland, C. (2004) *The Subaltern Appeal to Experience: Self Identity, Late Modernity, and the Politics of Immediacy*. Montreal: McGill-Queen's University Press.

Jackson, E. (2011) Gender and space in postcolonial fiction: South Asian novelists reimagining women's spatial boundaries. In: A. Teverson and S. Upstone (eds) *Postcolonial Spaces: The Politics of Place in Contemporary Culture*. UK: Palgrave Macmillan, 57–66.

Kadalah, M. (2016) The representation of the Syrian revolution in literature. *Warscapes*. Available from www.warscapes.com/literature/representation-syrian-revolution-literature [accessed 20 March 2021].

Khayat, S. Untitled. In: *Creative Memory of the Syrian Revolution*. Available from https://creativememory.org/en/archives/?fwp_categories=paintings&fwp_keywords=refugees-en [accessed 20 May 2021].

Kolb, D. (2008) *Sprawling Places*. Georgia: University of Georgia Press.

Kristeva, J. (1982) *Powers of Horror: An Essay on Abjection*. L. Roudiez (trans.). New York: Columbia University Press.

Kristeva, J. (1991) *Strangers to Ourselves*. New York: Columbia University Press.

Latour, B. (2005) *Reassembling the Social: An Introduction to Actor-Network-Theory*. Oxford: Oxford University Press.

Maksūr, ʿA. (2012) *Ayyām Bābā ʿAmrū*. Amman: Dār Faḍāʾāt.

Maksūr, ʿA. (2013) *ʿĀʾid ilā Ḥalab*. Amman: Dār Faḍāʾāt.

McFayden, G. (2012) The contemporary refugee: persecution, semantics, and universality. *eSharp*, Special Issue, 9–35. Available from www.gla.ac.uk/esharp [accessed 29 April 2017].

Mulḥim, N. (2012) *Bānsyūn Maryam*. Beirut: Atlas.

Ndlovu-Gatsheni J., Mhlanga S., and Mhlanga B. (2013) Borders, identities, the "Northern problem" and ethno-futures in postcolonial Africa. In: J. Ndlovu-Gatsheni, S. Mhlanga, and B. Mhlanga (eds) *Bondage of Boundaries and Identity*

Politics in Postcolonial Africa: The "Northern Problem" and Ethno-Futures. South Africa: Africa Institute of South Africa, 1–22.

Ouyang, W. (2013) *Politics of Nostalgia in the Arabic Novel: Nation-State, Modernity and Tradition*. Edinburgh University Press. https://doi.org/10.1515/9780748655700

Puumala, E. (2017) *Asylum Seekers, Sovereignty, and the Senses of the International: A Politico-Corporeal Struggle*. London: Routledge.

Rabinowitz, D. (2010) The right to refuse: abject theory and the return of Palestinian refugees. *Critical Inquiry*, 36(3), 494–516. https://doi.org/10.1086/653409

Saeed, A. (2014) The smartest guy on Facebook. Y. Sabeel et al. (trans.). In: M. Halasa, Z. Omareen, and N. Mahfoud (eds.) *Syria Speaks: Art and Culture From the Frontline*. London: Saqi, 279–83.

Sakr, R. (2018) The more-than-human refugee journey: Hassan Blāsim's short stories. *Journal of Postcolonial Writing*, 54(6) 766–780. https://doi.org/10.1080/17449855.2018.1551269

Sellman, J. (2014) The forests of exile. *Portal 9 Stories and Critical Writing About the City*, (Fall) 37–51. https://doi.org/10.1080/17449855.2018.1555207

Spivak, G. (1990) *The Postcolonial Critic: Interviews, Strategies, Dialogues*. New York: Routledge.

Tāmir, Z. Al-Mihmāz [The Spur]. Available from www.facebook.com/%D8%A7%D9%84%D9%85%D9%87%D9%85%D8%A7%D8%B2-222667394486441/ [accessed 20 March 2016].

UNHCR. (2017) Syria regional refugee response. Available from http://data.unhcr.org/syrian refugees/regional.php [accessed 20 May 2017].

Wennman, M. (2016) Where the children sleep. *UNHCR*. Available from https://www.unhcr.org/news/stories/2016/6/5702c1594/where-the-children-sleep.html [accessed September 2016].

Wright, T. (2002) Moving images: the media representation of refugees. *Visual Studies*, 17(1), 53–66. https://doi.org/10.1080/1472586022000005053

Yain-Allah, A. (2015) Arab Action. *Twitter*. Available from Twitter @Aimantoon. [accessed September 2016].

Yaqub, N. G. et al. (2017) Bad girls of the Arab world. First edition. Texas: University of Texas Press. https://doi.org/10.7560/31335

Yassin-Kassab, R., and al-Shami, L. (2016) *Burning Country: Syrians in Revolution and War*. London: Pluto Press.

Yazbik, S. (2015) *Bawwābāt arḍ al-ʿadam*. Beirut: Dār al-ādāb.

Yazbik, S. (2015) *The Crossing: My Journey to the Shattered Heart of Syria*. N. Gowanlock and R. Kemp (trans.). London: Random House.

8 The Global Migration Context and the Contemporary Iraqi Novel

Ikram Masmoudi

Introduction

Migration has developed from a romantic/modernist trope in twentieth-century Arabic novels for exploring identity, alterity, and negotiated ideas of cultural modernity in the postcolonial context to a gritty representation of the global context. In this chapter, I explore narratives of Iraqi migration experiences, as reflected in three novels by Iraqi authors: Shākir al-Anbārī's *Anā wa-Nāmiq Spencer* (Namiq Spencer and I, 2014), Janān Jāsim Ḥallāwī's *Hawāʾ qalīl* (Scant Air, 2009), and ʿAlī Badr's *ʿĀzif al-ghuyūm* (The Musician of the Clouds, 2016).[1] For these authors, migration serves as a metaphor for the perpetuation of war, border violence, trauma, and alienation.

Earlier Arabic migration novels, such as al-Ṭayyib Ṣāliḥ's iconic *Mawsim al-hijra ilā al-shamāl* (Season of Migration to the North, 1966), still fascinate Arab writers; and we can trace some intertextual connections between it and newer writings on Arab migration. Nevertheless, I argue that the current migration experiences depicted in the novels under examination are also shaped by the present grim global context, characterized at home by not only new wars, perennial violence, and traumas of war but also racism, xenophobia, and rejection in Europe. I demonstrate the shift from the postcolonial to the global in four areas: depiction of the country of origin, personal relationship patterns, defamiliarization, and the return.

Al-Anbārī's *Namiq*: A Point of Departure

In Shākir al-Anbārī's 2014 novel *Namiq Spencer and I*, the unnamed narrator, a man in his fifties, returns from Copenhagen to his home country, Iraq. The place is consumed by the sectarian civil war, and he is on a mission to document and report the violence in Baghdad for a gazette published in Arabic in Copenhagen. Soon after his arrival, he hears an explosion, coming from Tayaran Square, rocking the city. He thinks to himself that for the first time he will be able to read the effects of such a horrific event on people's faces.

Waiting to meet his friend, a female reporter who helps him in his documentary project, he sits at a nearby coffee house called Café-Sudan where

DOI: 10.4324/9780429027338-9

Sudanese, Somalis, and other Africans usually sit. Next to the café, a Sudanese man with a stand for watch repair captures his attention. The narrator considers that this man must be thousands of miles away from his hometown and that probably he is thinking of his native village, situated perhaps on the outskirts of the city of Khartoum. He envisions himself in this man, who reminds him of the alien, exiled person he was when he lived in Copenhagen, London, Berlin, and other world capitals for many years.

Thinking about the alien Sudanese living and working in Baghdad immediately reminds him of the iconic novel by Sudanese author al-Ṭayyib Ṣāliḥ, *Season of Migration to the North*. He muses that this is "the novel that I always wanted to write" (Al-Anbārī, 2014, 159). He continues:

> What we lived during the last few decades could be material for tens of novels like *Season of Migration to the North*. For sure the anxiety, the sadness, feeling lost in a different environment, working jobs below one's credentials, and one's desires… This applies to everyone sitting here in this café. They are not very different from the people we find in Norrebro in Copenhagen. The ethnic mix is certainly more noticeable there. There are not only blacks, but people from all continents, all of them finding refuge in Denmark. They left their cities – their villages, friends, languages, and traditions; and they came looking for safety or perhaps for a better chance at life. Isn't ethnic blending the characteristic of our times?
>
> (Al-Anbārī, 2014, 159)

In this reflection, the author draws a parallel between the Sudanese living in Baghdad and the many migrants living in Copenhagen. The Sudanese living in Baghdad and the people in the neighborhood of Norrebro are not very different: they are animated and motivated by the same desire for mobility and the urge to seek safety and a better life. Prior to the 2003 war, Baghdad was for the Sudanese what Copenhagen is to the more ethnically diverse crowd one can find these days in the Danish capital. Al-Anbārī draws a parallel between these two migratory contexts. On the one hand, the postcolonial context includes the migration experiences of Arabs to Europe during the second part of the twentieth century, as depicted for example in Ṣāliḥ's novel referenced here. On the other hand, today's more global migratory movements provide the context for the narrator's (and the author's) migrations, having just returned home from a long exile in Europe. The narrator, clearly a lover of literature, seems to be thinking about writing a novel on migration. He suggests that despite the two different contexts, he could have found in essence the same kinds of materials, and the same experiences for inspiration, in order to write "a dozen novels" like *Season of Migration to the North*. He holds up al-Ṭayyib Ṣāliḥ's novel as a model, perhaps even the quintessential migration novel.

By invoking al-Ṭayyib Ṣāliḥ's novel, the narrator, this new returnee to Iraq, sounds quite nostalgic about the postcolonial era of the mid-twentieth century and its intellectual and literary context. But is he making good and well-informed comparisons? Is it possible to think about the recent experiences of Arab migration to Europe today in the same terms as the earlier migration of the latter half of the twentieth century? Or are we in fact facing a new wave of writing Arab migration experiences that is quite different from the one encompassed in Ṣāliḥ's novel? After all, the times and the contexts have changed quite a bit. And is al-Anbārī in his novel *Namiq Spencer and I* trying to write a novel like *Season of Migration to the North*? If so, what parallels can we draw between *Season* and *Namiq Spencer and I*?

Shifting Focus in Arabic Novels of Migration

Recent scholarship on contemporary Arabic literature of migration to Europe suggests, in the aesthetics and politics of writing about mobility, a shift from the earlier concerns and experiences found in novels of the mid-twentieth century. Mass mobility, clandestine migration, increased border control, and management of borders are all new concerns relating to globalization. Together they have changed the way Arab experiences of migration are reflected in the novel. The emergence of what is called in Maghrebian literature *Harraga* novels and clandestine Mediterranean crossings are good examples of the new narrative focusing on borders and borderlands and the violence enacted on new migrants.[2] The short stories of Ḥasan Blāsim represent another example of undocumented migration and border subversion.

In her recent article on contemporary Arabic literature of migration to Europe, Johanna Sellman states that contemporary Arabic migration novels have shifted focus from a postcolonial discourse that centered on political exiles, intellectuals, and students traveling for study abroad to a larger narrative exploring the perspectives of forced migrants, refugees, and asylum seekers, all figures and subjectivities that are the result of new contexts shaped by border managing and global inequalities. Drawing on border studies, she observes that, "The new aesthetics and politics of contemporary Arabic literature of migration are being created in the context of mobility and precarious migration and in a climate of heightened anxiety about state sovereignty, which animates border and wall regimes" (Sellman, 2018, 753). She argues for extending the scope of the postcolonial to include the experiences and concerns of recent Arabic novels of migration, concluding that the "Arabic migration novel is both postcolonial and global/planetary" (Sellman, 2018, 762). Building on this claim, we need to consider how new colonial wars, occupation, and war traumas weigh heavily on the new migratory movements and migrant subjectivities, as reflected in recently published Iraqi fiction of migration.

From Nahḍa Discourse to Iraqi Portrayals of Migration in a Global Context

Firmly rooted in the postcolonial context and Arab renaissance (Nahḍa) discourse, within the east–west debate that characterized the earlier part of the twentieth century, al-Ṭayyib Ṣāliḥ's novel *Season of Migration to the North* (1966) formulates "a dual critique of the discourses of colonialism and the *Nahda*" (Hassan, 2003, 89). Its two main characters, Musṭafā Sa'īd and the narrator, are both Sudanese and studied in England. They had different experiences abroad, but on their return, they both developed a critical view of local culture and of themselves. The novel redefined the east–west relationship in terms of conflict, in contrast to the romantic terms of previous migration novels, such as Yaḥyā Ḥaqqī's *Qindīl Umm Hāshim.*

New literary experiments venture into reimagining migration and depictions of migrants' subjectivities in the light of the new challenges of an age marked by mass migration triggered mostly by wars and violence. And it is no surprise that Iraqi writers are taking the lead in refashioning and writing the Arabic novel of migration. Iraqi migrants are now portrayed as either refugees or clandestine migrants to Europe in a time defined not only by increased global displacement, but also in a context characterized by upheaval, neo-colonial wars, and exacerbated violence. Iraqi novels address questions of border crossing, encounters with foreign societies, issues of return to Iraq, and deportation, all within the larger context of the late years of Saddam Hussein's regime, the collapse of the Iraqi state, the American occupation, and the violence that engulfed Iraq for years thereafter. These migration narratives continue the traditional framework of earlier postcolonial migration novels, which portrayed traveling students and intellectuals in the twentieth century. Yet, they also build on it by adding new characters, such as the refugee, the forced and clandestine migrant, the deported traveler, etc. These new characters lack the romanticism, intellectual charisma, and shine of the twentieth-century migrant archetype. The new migrants, as we will see in the recently published novels by Iraqi writers living in Europe, are people who have had close encounters with danger and death in Iraq. They escaped wars and coercion; they carry with them trauma and a history of violence and suffering. But they also face threats and dangers in their places of arrival, in contexts rife with racism and isolation.

In this chapter, I compare and discuss three Iraqi novels of migration to northern Europe published after the year 2003, articulating the subjectivities of Iraqi migrants. Despite the contextual differences framing the new narratives of migration published after 2003, we can trace a continuity among them and an affiliation with earlier models of migration novels, such as the one claimed by the narrator of *Namiq Spencer and I.* This affiliation and fascination, as we will see, are most palpable in the persistence of certain patterns such as the cultural encounter, albeit in a modified format, as well as the idea of return and political commitment. The novels also focus on the limits of the question of return and the impossibility of change in a context where violence keeps proliferating. The assessment of the return to the homeland is accompanied by the critique of a false idealization of Europe in a context rife with rejection and increasing global mobility restrictions. Like *Season of Migration to the North*, the new migration novels formulate a double critique of western violence as well as Iraqi society, encompassing both the postcolonial violence of the dictatorship that pushed dissidents to flee and migrate and the global climate of new wars and cultural deterioration in Iraq that leads to a false idealization of Europe.

I analyze three novels portraying Iraqi migrants in northern European countries. Al-Anbārī, Ḥallāwī, and Badr are all expatriates of Iraq, living respectively in Denmark, Sweden, and Belgium. All three are well published but not equally known to audiences outside of readers of Arabic. In these novels, traumatized and alienated Iraqi migrants try to navigate tortuous paths of migration, layers of migratory history consisting of journeys within journeys, and unsettled and unsuccessful returns to the homeland, contrasting sharply with the more hopeful optimism of earlier migration and return patterns found in twentieth-century migration novels.

Namiq Spencer and I (henceforth *Namiq*) and *Scant Air* depict migrants from Iraq who were either deserters of the Iran–Iraq War or former political dissidents, and either Communists or Kurds who opposed the Baath party politics and its wars. This falls under the category of forced migration, as defined by the International Organization for Migration: "a migratory movement which, although the drivers can be diverse, involves force, compulsion, or coercion including threats to life and livelihood, whether arising from natural or man-made causes" (2019). Many migrants of the 1980s escaped Iraq and found refuge first in neighboring countries (Iran and Syria) and later in Scandinavia (Denmark and Sweden), which were not yet common destinations for Iraqis. As for the main character in *The Musician of the Clouds* (henceforth *The Musician*), he represents the recent migration wave by a younger generation of migrants crossing borders into Europe illegally in a global context marked by new wars (Iraq, Afghanistan, Syria, etc.), the rise of extremism, and increased security regulating migrants' mobility. When they return home, these migrants are shocked to see their country in the throes of yet more lethal violence.

Continuing Violence at Home

> The Iran–Iraq War pushed us to this country like a crazy storm.
>
> (Al-Anbārī, 2014, 20)

> I was coming from Baghdad, having rejected the war, the Baath party, and the life we were living, searching like Namiq for the city of the dream.
>
> (Al-Anbārī, 2014, 240)

During the Iran–Iraq War (1980–1988), many Iraqi soldiers sought to escape the war. Desertion was punishable by death under Saddam's regime. These deserters were later represented in the fiction that emerged after 2003 to re-examine the war record. Whether portrayed in the novel or in real life, Iraqi desertion stories usually meet at the mountains of Kurdistan with the deserters joining the Kurdish rebels. From there, some make it to Iran, only to end up in Iranian detention centers.[3] The roads and mountain paths away from Saddam's longest war attracted many Iraqis who preferred their freedom, with the high risks this entailed, rather than serving in the unpopular war that devoured many of their peers. The narrator of *Namiq*, a recent university graduate specializing in literature, was guided by smugglers. They took him to the location of the Kurdish rebels in the mountains, where he took refuge "as someone who was against the war, oppression, and discrimination" (Al-Anbārī, 2014, 234):

> There was a war, as well as an ongoing conflict between the Iraqi government and the Kurds. Death was roaming freely between the fronts, in the streets and inside the prisons. I deserted the front, with a fake ID, into the Kurdish mountains. It was a successful escape from the claws of death.
>
> (Al-Anbārī, 2014, 234)

The narrator was not alone in dreaming of desertion and escape. Such dreams were nourished and shared by many of his generation, in particular his closest friend, Namiq, a Kurd who never joined the front and dreamed of leaving the country. Stories about the mountains, the rebels, and desertion to Kuwait and Syria fueled these young men and encouraged them to think about their own escape.

The friendship between the narrator and Namiq was strong, in a time when the war and the Baath party "erased trust from the hearts of the Iraqi people" (Al-Anbārī, 2014, 236), as the narrator put it. Namiq disappeared, leaving his friend wondering about his whereabouts until he found him already among the rebels in the mountains. In a time of war and coercion, it is not easy to arrange an escape. The narrator highlights how the mystery and secrecy engulfing his adventure was encapsulated in one word:

> "arranged." "I arranged my escape from Baghdad toward the Kurdistan Mountains." When I say "I arranged," it's a shorthand. Who I arranged with, where and how I met that person, how he trusted me and why, all of these questions hide behind the expression, "I arranged."
>
> (Al-Anbārī, 2014, 236)

The narrator's new life among the rebels in the mountains, with his best friend, was not quite what they were looking for. It was only a first step on the road that took them to Iran and Camp Karj, 40 kilometers from Tehran:

> It was a camp precisely for those Iraqis who deserted the wars or fled from prisons, seeking an opportunity to see a world other than the miserable East. Camp Karj was manufactured from human dreams, all aiming for paradise, i.e. Europe, the myth that lived with us in that gloomy stone building: the Europe of blond girls, wine, languages, and splendid gardens.
> (Al-Anbārī, 2014, 249)

It was in this Iranian camp that Namiq and the narrator met another fellow deserter, Nader Radio, so nicknamed because he always held a small radio to his ears to listen to the news of the war back home. Namiq was nicknamed Namiq Spencer after he grew a beard and started looking like the actor Bud Spencer. The trio became inseparable, but life in this borderland was full of fears, doubts, and dreams to cross into another country. News of the many Iraqis who managed to leave fueled the imagination of the deserters. Their next stop was Damascus, where they worked fruit-picking jobs in the orchards of the Ghouta area, among other jobs. They felt compelled to keep moving. Their Syrian friend urged them on: "Continue the journey, go toward the cities of snow and women and don't look back: Copenhagen has started receiving Iraqi refugees" (Al-Anbārī, 2014, 271). While this first wave of forced migrants/deserters was triggered by the context of the oppression of the postcolonial state, it nevertheless replaced "a postcolonial conception of spaces of international migration" (Agier, 2016, 46). These migrants headed to European countries, which were not yet a common destination for Iraqi migrants. They were not traveling toward the domination of a country that had previously colonized their home country. This shift in the conception of mobility away from the postcolonial connection with a former colonial nation to broader possibilities reflects itself in the geographies of Iraqi novels of migration to Europe. It brings necessary changes in the representation of the relationship of Arabs in Europe to European cultures.

All three, the narrator and his two friends Namiq and Nader, belong to "a generation devoured by wars and migration," as Namiq put it (Al-Anbārī, 2014, 57). Even thousands of miles away from Baghdad, the narrator is still haunted by the fear of the Iraqi authorities. He suffers from nightmares in which he sees himself walking down Palestine Street in Baghdad when militia men arrest him and ask for his ID. He awakes disoriented and drowning in his own sweat and in his fear of Baghdad's police. "For dozens of years, I lived in terror from the police, the army, and the militia. That is what made me run away" (Al-Anbārī, 2014, 54).

Yet, the news of gratuitous killing, kidnapping, and death in Baghdad follows the narrator into his exile in Copenhagen. This occurs not only in the form of the traumatic reenactments of his fear of being caught by the Iraqi authorities, but via the Internet. He receives an email informing him of the killing of his brother and nephew by a car bomb: "the bad news of Baghdad stopped surprising me [...] the series of violence still follows and finds me from across the seas, the cities and the mountains" (Al-Anbārī, 2014, 57). He remembers with sadness his brother who, unlike him, spent the best of his youth on the frontlines fighting in the Iran War. The narrator recalls, not without guilt, how he was enjoying his time in the bars of Copenhagen and having a good time with blonde women while his brother Kamel was living through one of the darkest pages of what he calls the "archive of violence," which started in the 1980s with the Iran–Iraq War to extend over more than a decade, to the fall of the Baath regime in 2003.

This same history of persecution and coercion lies behind the forced migration of Youness in *Scant Air*. Youness is an Iraqi from Basra who arrives in Ljusne, a small village of the Soderhamn province in Sweden. A former communist and political activist who escapes persecution in Iraq, he is placed in this remote and cold area of the world map by the United Nations' High Commissioner for Refugees (UNHCR). In his orientation session, Youness and other Iraqi refugees are briefed about basic facts about the place. The immigration agent casually warns against cold, gray weather: "The weather is cold, but you will get used to it. It's not hell, just cold, gray weather" (Ḥallāwī, 2009, 15). The agent also warns the freshly arrived refugees that "racism is everywhere," acknowledging it as if it were as much a part of the human geography of the place as the cold weather (Ḥallāwī, 2009, 15). However, she downplays her observation by reminding the Iraqi refugees of their own racist history back home: "You Iraqis, didn't you persecute each other?" (Ḥallāwī, 2009, 15).

This reminder resonates with the way other Iraqi refugees still treat each other many miles away from the homeland. At his first language orientation session, Youness sees many other Iraqis in attendance: Chaldeans, Shiis, Turkomans, Kurds, and Sunnis. All are present, as though in a systematic representation of the ethnic and religious fabric of Iraqi society. Youness also observes how the Kurds insult their other Iraqi fellow refugees and give them the cold shoulder; they still hold onto old grudges, going back to the days of Saddam Hussein's war against the Kurds. It is the same traumatizing history of persecution that nags Youness, too. Though thousands of miles away from Iraq, he is still haunted in his nightmares, chased by the Baghdad police:

> "They are looking for you in our neighborhood."
> "Did they get here?"
> "Yes, you have to flee from the back door."
> [...]
> He ran away with all his might; the police were behind him. He was terrified and continued running. He stopped at a checkpoint; the soldiers pointed their guns at him. They stopped him and asked for his ID. He jumped; his mouth was dry and his forehead cold with sweat; he was shaking from fear. He calmed down; then he recognized his room. He regained his breath, feeling relieved that he was in his house in Ljusne.
> (Ḥallāwī, 2009, 91–92)

Fast forwarding to the context of post-2003 violence, neo-colonial global war, and the war on terror, *The Musician of the Clouds* dramatizes the most recent wave of migration to Europe. In the wake of the U.S. occupation and the sectarian violence that ensued, cultural and social life in Baghdad is subject to the rule of the "mob" and the Islamist militia. A visible clash between two sets of values unfolds in Iraqi society. The Islamist militia of his neighborhood breaks the cello of Baghdad musician Nabil (Nabīl), harassing and humiliating him. This experience conveys to him the depth of the cultural clash in Iraq and the necessity of leaving the country:

> He realized that in this country there are two cultures opposing each other ferociously: the culture of arts, which was on the decline since Saddam's wars, and a rising popular culture based on violence and bloodshed, which was trying to take the place of the state that had just collapsed.
>
> (Badr, 2016, 40)

The smashing of his cello by the Islamists convinces Nabil that there is no room for him as a musician in Iraq. As he once said to his professor:

> It's not an easy thing to play classical music in the Middle East. Not only is it difficult, but it is at once tragic and comic; it's as if you brought a polar animal and transferred it to a place where temperature is beyond forty degrees Celsius in the summer.
>
> (Badr, 2016, 17)

In the face of this dilemma, Nabil's plan is to flee to "a life overseas." This is the expression he likes to use, rather than words such as "migration," "refugee," or "exile." As an intellectual who has lost hope in his country and a musician who feels that he has no place in Baghdad's dark cultural landscape, Nabil conceives of going to Europe in vague and shallow poetic terms. As he sets out on the crossing journey, he recalls the following verses of a poet whose name he does not remember: "We will go over there; we will go to a utopian city, overseas / There, where the artist lives as if he were playing music on the clouds" (Badr, 2016, 36).

The extent of the cultural setback caused by the 2003 war and its devastation is reflected in Nabil's blind idealization of and fascination for Europe. *The Musician of the Clouds* paints a dark tableau of the situation in Iraq. This lofty intellectual-musician had already become disconnected from Iraqi society before immigrating. His flawed perceptions led him to become an alienated immigrant once in Brussels. Nabil's fascination with the West and his loathing of his home country's culture can be read as vaguely reminiscent of Ismail, the protagonist of *The Lamp of Umm Hashim.* Despite the difference in time separating the two texts, just as Ismail was appalled by the conditions in his hometown of Cairo, upon his return from England, so Nabil is also appalled by the situation in Baghdad, even before arriving in Europe.

Ismail, an eye doctor, smashes a revered saint's lamp. It is a symbol of cultural tradition, but also of backwardness, as his cousin lost her eyesight due to the use of the lamp's oil to treat her trachoma. Ismail's destruction of the lamp angers the people in his neighborhood, but later, a concoction synthesizing science and religion returns Fāṭima's eyesight and a semblance of cultural balance. In the case of Nabil, the religious extremist mob that attacks him and smashes his cello sees the instrument as something forbidden and a symbol of western culture and music:

> "We don't want to hear this ugly instrument."
>
> "It's my job."
>
> "A despicable forbidden job; have you not heard the Imam in the mosque?"
>
> "Leave me alone with God. He knows best if music is forbidden. Mind your own business."
>
> "But you are disturbing us and we don't want to be subjected and forced to listen to something forbidden."
>
> (Badr, 2016, 21)

On his crossing journey, Nabil makes sure to recall all the negative images that invoke for him the deterioration, the filth, and the hypocrisy that characterize his culture, to ensure that he will not waver in his decision to depart. However, his idealization of Europe and life there blind him to realities such as racism and xenophobia. *The Musician of the Clouds* presents two ideas of migration to Europe: one flawed, idealistic, and bourgeois (Nabil's idea) and the other a down-to-earth rendering of the current situation and the real circumstances of clandestine, illegal crossing, which reflects the increasing policing and illegal ways to circumvent it. In this regard, Nabil's fancy ideas and his poetic dreams clash sharply with the materiality of the conditions of his trip. He travels like the many migrants who cross illegally to Europe, smuggled by suspicious smugglers in dangerous conditions. His journey reflects this contradiction between his lofty ideas and the reality on the ground, which only exacerbates his illusions and his later disappointments.

When he decided to depart for Europe, he chose the easiest way even though it was the most expensive. He didn't want to cross in a plastic boat from Ezmir in Turkey to Greece, where the boat might capsize and he would become food for fish. He was horrified just by thinking about it. One of his relatives advised him to travel along a track that would take him from the Turkish border, delivering him directly to Brussels, without dealing with borders or police, and without a boat capsizing or any other dramas. "A VIP refugee!" This is how his relative described him (Badr, 2016, 41).

Nabil's journey was framed by doubts and fears, amid the many rumors and stories circulating about dishonest smugglers, scams, and deceptions. As he sat next to the driver, he wondered:

> What if there was no journey to Europe? What if this was just deception and fraud? […] It was possible that the car he boarded could just travel over and over through the same city without taking him anywhere. It would turn and turn all night long. He had heard many stories about smugglers' tricks and deception.
>
> (Badr, 2016, 43–44)

When Nabil embarks on a clandestine journey from Baghdad to Europe, fleeing a culture dominated by the rise of extremism and fundamentalism, he never expects to find the mirror image of part of the environment he left in Baghdad in a European capital. After a very long journey hidden inside a wooden box in a truck crossing through Europe, Nabil is told by the driver that he has reached his destination: Brussels. The driver drops him off in "a dirty plaza that looked like any plaza in a third world country" (Badr, 2016, 49). In disbelief, Nabil thinks the driver is playing games and trying to fool him. But the driver pulls him by the hand as Nabil pulls out his suitcase, taking him to an apartment in an old building:

> "Are we in Brussels?" Nabil asked disapprovingly.
> "Yes, this is Brussels, are you drunk or what?"
> "No, but it is dirtier than Baghdad!"
> "This is an area where Muslims – Moroccans and Turks – live."
> "Ah, I see!"
>
> (Badr, 2016, 50)

Everything in the neighborhood, the building, and the apartment keep Nabil in disbelief and denial that he has arrived in Belgium, and that he is in Brussels, its capital. He keeps asking himself, "Is this real? Am I in Belgium? … Am I in Brussels? … Where are we?" (Badr, 2016, 51). He blames the smuggler, who must have fooled him and left him in a neighborhood of Istanbul or Izmir or maybe in Iran. His fears and doubts culminate when he hears someone praying with a loud voice, like the voice of his grandfather, and when he notices that the TV has all kinds of channels except for porn channels, his favorite.

The grand ideas on art and harmony that he nurtures set him on a delusional path about acclimating to Belgian society and culture. He thinks he fits well into his new society and culture; he belongs there. He sees himself as more deserving of being integrated into this western setting than the many Islamists or Muslims who live in Brussels and do not deserve its freedom and its culture. He believes they are persecuting him again. As a result, Nabil lives in a bubble consisting of his Belgian girlfriend, provoking neighbors with her screams of sexual enjoyment at night. During the day, he spends time in the bars and cafés of Brussels, paying for rounds of beer and trying to impress young students with his foggy ideas about harmony theory. Fearful of the extremists that the new global context of migration brought to Europe and whom he despises, he is deluded about Europe and the kind of freedom and life he thought he could enjoy there in order to fit perfectly into this western society and its lifestyle. Nabil recovers his sanity and lucidity only after being beaten one day by a group of political conservatives, at one of their demonstrations against immigrants. The novel is a satire about the confusion of this musician and his fantasies about musical harmony and utopia, as well as his delusional ideas of integration into a new society. The shock of xenophobic rejection awakens him from his illusions.

Nabil's migration is emblematic of the withdrawal of the intellectual-artist in the face of the rise of a culture of extremism that alienates him from his environment. His migration is part of a global wave of forced migration of people fleeing for their safety and their lives. The context in which the clandestine migration of Nabil takes places and the persecution and humiliation he suffers in Baghdad, as well as the risks he takes by trusting a chain of smugglers, do not distinguish his journey as unique from others. This contrasts sharply with the way this musician perceives himself as an artist above the crowd, and in particular the fundamentalists and Islamist extremists of Baghdad who reject music and western culture. Nabil also sees himself as superior to the diaspora of other groups of migrants, including some of the fundamentalists he fled from, and who ironically end up being his new neighbors in Brussels. However, he must negotiate new terms for mutual existence and mutual understanding in a global era of migration.

Shifting Personal Relationship Patterns

Whether in the context of postcolonial violence of the nation-state that forced Namiq and his friends, as well as Youness, to migrate to Scandinavia, or in the context of the new global war ushered in by the occupation of Iraq, which pushes Nabil to find refuge in Brussels, reference to the global replaces postcolonial conceptions of mobility and migration. This confirms recent findings in migration studies, as well as literary studies. In his book *Borderlands: Towards an Anthropology of the Cosmopolitan Condition*, Michel Agier states that:

> Reference to the planet in its global dimension is increasingly replacing a postcolonial conception of spaces of international migration (when migrants from the south headed for their former metropolises), and migrants no longer see the country of reception as the only country for their establishment.
>
> (Agier, 2016, 46)

In this assertion, the transition from the postcolonial to the global is not only geographical but also cultural and political, relying on an understanding of the postcolonial "as an experience of continuing domination exerted by a former colonial nation and a conception of the global where domination is more diffuse with less clearly chartered migration patterns" (Sellman, 2018, 754).

In the postcolonial Arabic novel of migration, the theme of the cross-cultural encounter is usually at the center of novels such as *The Lamp of Umm Hashim*, *al-Ḥayy al-Lātīnī* (The Latin Quarter, 1953) by Suhayl Idrīs, and *Season of Migration to the North*. This encounter, approached through the east–west binary, was couched in romantic terms in the earlier novels and in lethal, violent terms in *Season*, in which Ṣāliḥ deconstructs the east–west discourse and attacks colonial representations of Arabs and Africans. Yet, whether framed in patterns of desire or hostility, these personal relationships are always inscribed in structures of power and domination. In the new context of mobility, away from the domination of a former colonial nation, the relationship patterns and cultural encounter terms are reimagined and reconfigured in ways that diffuse the tension/domination in the personal relationships.

Not to overplay the presence of cross-cultural personal relationships, it is important to remember the constant difficulty immigrants have in building new friendships. As the narrator of *Namiq Spencer* explains, for Iraqi men it is challenging to develop relationships with Danish women due to the widespread idea that these men come from an environment of violence and killing. Such ideas undermine their chances of building social connections. The narrator is well aware of this misperception. He tries to look his best when he meets his ex-wife Mary and his daughters after returning from Iraq to Copenhagen to see them:

> I don't want to look bad in front of Mary and the girls, and I don't wish to look like a person coming from Iraq, continuing the idea that we are a hotbed for killing, crime, and suicide bombing. For this was the shared stereotype about us in Denmark, especially among women. This is why it was hard for Iraqi men to make serious relationships with Danish women, as Nader told me. They only find addicts and unstable women. … Things were different from when we first arrived in this country: back then we used to pique their curiosity with our black hair, light darkness, and strong emotions that we always show women from the very first encounter.
>
> (Al-Anbārī, 2014, 101)

It was in the context of his work in a language school that the narrator of *Namiq Spencer* first met Mary, a Brazilian woman from Sao Paolo. He was a custodian in a language school for foreigners, where he also attended some classes. The school brought him into contact with multitudes of migrants: "Students from all over the world, from Iraq, Iran, Lebanon, Chile, Somalia, and from eastern Europe as well, men and women, all came to learn Danish in this school" (Al-Anbārī, 2014, 42). Working in this school and interacting with these migrants speaking different languages broadens the narrator's perspective. He comes to revise many of his received ideas and opinions: "Our language was no longer the most beautiful language, and our country no longer the most beautiful country, our religion no longer the only religion in this wide world, and our ideas were not necessarily always right" (Al-Anbārī, 2014, 42–43).

The friendship with Mary quickly developed into a personal relationship conceived by the narrator as a mere fling. The physical description he gives of Mary compares her to an Iraqi woman:

> a petite, dark-skinned woman; she had an attractive brown body with a firm, nice butt. … She had the features of an Arab woman … As Nader said, she would be beautiful if not for her coarse black hair that made her look like an Iraqi woman from Basra.
>
> (Al-Anbārī, 2014, 46)

As the narrator describes his courtship of Mary and her culture, we can easily find traces of reversed orientalizing language and an exotic tone recalling the seductive atmosphere of Muṣṭafā Sa'īd's room in *Season of Migration to the North*:

> Mary's first project was to start teaching me Portuguese. I showed interest, as this helped me lure her to my room within a month after meeting her. She showed me how to dance samba in my room and she introduced me to the songs of the carnivals of Sao Paolo. … Sometimes she performed samba for me with music from tapes she had brought with her. Mary would start swaying slowly. Then she would pull me to the dance ring, which was comprised of the space between my bed and an old dresser. We danced as the small waves of the North Sea loomed in the distance, like a field made of iron.
>
> (Al-Anbārī, 2014, 47)

After he marries Mary in Denmark, he travels with her to San Paolo. There he learns more about her culture and "the magic of Latin America": carnivals, Samba, the Amazon Forest, the favela and its poverty, and the world of coffee and cocoa. In Brazil, he discovers a new continent, "neither European nor Asian." It was "the world of Jorge Amado, mulattos, dancing samba in the carnivals of San Paolo and Rio de Janeiro, in the land of magic" (Al-Anbārī, 2014, 62). There, with the eye of the experienced migrant, he gets a firsthand account of not only the rich cultural and ethnic mix of Brazil but also the flagrant economic and social disparities of the global system.

Instead of the self-orientalizing pattern of personal relationships with European women as found in *Season*, in *Namiq*, Al-Anbārī represents this Iraqi migrant on an equal footing with the woman he meets and marries, thus displacing the east–west cultural encounter and the pattern of power dynamics of the postcolonial narrative, as found in *The Lamp of Umm Hashim* and in *The Latin Quarter*. With the protagonist marrying a Brazilian woman in Copenhagen, and living with her in Brazil as well, the narrative reflects the social and cultural impact that globalization has brought to patterns of personal relationships within the migration novel. Moreover, it breaks free from the old tradition of the eastern man falling for the western woman and her culture, both perceived as superior. The narrative of *Namiq* creates a third space or third-party cultural sphere. Replacing the north–south relationship pattern with a south–south pattern is emblematic of the change from a post-colonial perspective to a global one. This new scheme liberates the contemporary Arabic migration novel from the love/hate relationship with western culture, and the violence that implies, and from the weight of the romance with the western woman and the fascination with western European culture and its associations. This also applies to the narrator's two friends, Nader and Namiq, who marry women from Poland and Algeria.

The depiction of the migrant's relationship with European women and culture is also at the center of *The Musician of the Clouds*. However, it takes the form of a satire of the intellectual's idealization of western culture and the traditional fascination with western women. Through the character of Nabil, the alienated Iraqi musician, Badr offers a caricature of the Arab intellectual, with his illusions and preconceived ideas, as well as his fantasies of western culture and western women. For this musician-dreamer, who lives in a bubble of ideals and finds refuge in Europe, music harmony functions as a barometer for gauging the integration of people into a given society. Nabil is guided by his understanding of music theory, as defined by al-Fārābī, in which:

> music is produced from different sounds, harmoniously arranged. Harmony is achieved from the consonance and the congruity between the different sounds, lest the differences in tones and sounds become dissonant and negate the basic concept of music.
>
> (Badr, 2016, 63–64)

Nabil comes to Europe thinking that he will find a harmonious society. He expects to experience a sense of belonging in Brussels, as someone trained in the classical music tradition. For him, the presence of other migrants in Belgium is like a dissonance in the musical scale that represents Belgian culture. In the same way, as a classicist and a cellist, he had been the dissonant cultural note in Iraq after the extremists and fundamentalists tightened their grip on society. When he meets Fanny at a party in a bar in Brussels, he falls in love at once, physically, sensually, and sexually:

> He was conquered from the first sight. Like any eastern man, he didn't think rationally at the sight of a half-naked body in front of him. She was from a Cartesian culture, even if she had never read a line from Descartes. She quickly turned the matter over in her head and saw in him a handsome brown man and a talented musician.
>
> (Badr, 2016, 65)

From their first encounter, Nabil is overconfident in his ability to understand and communicate effectively with Fanny, beyond their cultural differences. By virtue of being a musician and a cello player, he thinks of himself as someone who fits in western society: "What he is looking for in Europe is the foundation of internal harmony, or perhaps the idea of the structure that finds its precise meaning in classical music. This will eventually lead us to the utopian city" (Badr, 2016, 65). He explains to her his lofty ideas on music, harmony theory, and the ideal society, employing the image of an orchestra. Westerners are stringed instruments (the most important), Latinos are reed instruments, Orientals (including Arabs, Persians, Turks, and Kurds) are brass instruments; lower in this hierarchy are Africans, percussion instruments, and Asians, cymbals.

Nabil constantly compares this Belgian woman to a degraded image he draws of Arab women: in his mind, she was their opposite in her sensuality, care-free, exhibiting naturally "her peaceful bare nakedness." "She was beautiful, thin, and fragile like a Japanese painting with stunning colors. She was the opposite of Arab women who are dark skinned, with shabby thighs and breasts as a result of eating too much hummus" (Badr, 2016, 66–67). Nabil is fascinated by Fanny's authentic relationship with her body and how she enjoys sexual pleasure without restrictions. Her cries of enjoyment during intercourse resonate throughout the entire building where he lives in an area of the Turkish immigrant community, angering other residents. Not only does he hold Fanny as a model in her natural and sensual relationship to her body, but Nabil contrasts her with a traditional eastern relationship to the body and sex: "Nabil never saw this peaceful nakedness even in his most erotic dreams. … Sex here was unlike in the Orient: it didn't grow in obscurity, but in the light of day, mixed with voices, movement, smells, and music" (Badr, 2016, 70).

When Nabil's Turkish neighbor expresses displeasure with the noises, which cause embarrassment for his family, Nabil lets Fanny take charge of the situation. She does so with arrogance and condescension:

> This man is asking you not to let out loud sounds of pleasure during sex because he's got teenage veiled daughters, and he doesn't want them to know anything about that. … Fanny got angry and yelled, "What?! I am in my country and I do as I please. Let whoever is unhappy take their daughters back to their own country where they can hear only the call for prayers. Here, I do what I want."
>
> (Badr, 2016, 72)

In an act of defiance and further provocation, she opens all the windows of Nabil's apartment at night to make sure her cries of enjoyment are heard. The Turkish neighbor takes his revenge on Nabil, breaking his nose and his newly purchased cello.

Nabil's infatuation with Fanny continues his dreamy ideas about life in the utopian city, justice, and the theory of harmony. He had dreamed of reaching the utopian city where all elements would live together in harmony, without dissonance. Yet, day after day the reality on the ground shows him that he is mistaken; the utopian city is a chimera existing only in the head of a confused musician. He discovers that the utopian city cannot be achieved, as he had believed, not even in Europe. Hordes of "dissonant voices" had already found their place in Europe before he even arrived. In addition, the Europeans are divided between those who are openly racist and those who simply expect him to show gratitude and be happy with what he is offered. In this condition, all that he has is Fanny. She is his only solace.

However, Nabil's feelings for Fanny evolve. As he explores more bars and cafés, he meets new people. Eager to impress young women and students from the suburbs and rural areas with his confused ideas about harmony and the utopian city, he offers rounds of beer and other drinks and cracks jokes at the expense of other immigrants. He recounts the episode of his Turkish neighbor and his virgin daughters. Ridiculous scenes of Nabil's drinking in the bars, with Fanny's money (without her permission) verge on the comical. He ends up totally drunk, on the floor and crawling between the tables, with nobody helping him.

Nabil's flawed and artificial relationship with Fanny reflects his superficial relationship with Belgian society and culture. He realizes that as a refugee and an immigrant, he cannot criticize the society; he is expected to express only gratitude toward for being saved from a miserable life in Iraq. One day, sitting in a coffee shop, he listens to a song about a girl's desire to migrate and leave Europe. Surprised, he wonders where these Europeans want to go; he thinks the depressed looks of some are totally unjustified.

> It was quite strange that even the Belgians wanted to leave and find refuge somewhere. [...] Nabil knew all too well that Fanny didn't want to hear what he thought about Belgium. She never asked him what he thought of the comedians who made fun of the country, or what he thought about the pessimists who viewed Belgium as sinking in a political quagmire. [...] He felt that in this country, he was allowed to talk about only two things: the tragedy of his country and the happiness that he gained in Belgium.
>
> (Badr, 2016, 91)

As a refugee in Belgium, Nabil is expected to be happy and express gratitude for a country and a society that welcomed him. Hearing his gratitude as an immigrant is the only thing that unites Belgians and makes them proud of their own country, which they may otherwise criticize endlessly, but not him – he is not allowed to do that.

Defamiliarization

> Soderhamn looks like a city without human beings. ... Cities of the north tend to be spacious, with very few people, like extensive decor made of silence, isolation, and old age.
>
> (Ḥallāwī, 2009, 132)

Unlike familiar patterns of migrants' personal relationships and social belonging, migration novels now offer a new paradigm, framing migrants' experiences through their connection to nature and borderlands. Authors stage migration experiences in Nordic countries "using metaphors of nature and the wilderness to imagine alternate forms of hospitality in spaces that are outside citizenship" (Sellman, 2018, 760). In *Scant Air*, Youness (Yūnus) is a "Basrawi", "a man of the steppe, who lived all his life in the outdoors with the dust covering his hair and the sun burning his skin" (Ḥallāwī, 2009, 21). He dreads the indoors, which confronts him with his loneliness, his nightmares, and the PTSD of one who escaped for his life. He dislikes being confined indoors because of the cold, but his feelings toward the natural environment and the unfamiliar landscape are mixed and confused.

At times, Youness feels enchanted and in tune with the beautiful wintery scenery of the north. But at other times the snowy wilderness only adds to his alienation and desolation. On weekends, when he goes out to bars, he takes a path through the forest. He feels connected with the secretive forest. He compares the image of the village at night to a deserted planet. He finds the magical atmosphere of the snowy landscape fascinating. The tall pine and poplar trees add to the unreality of the situation. The surrounding silence makes him feel "as if something imminent might happen. He wouldn't be surprised if a dwarf greeted him from one of the windows, or if a witch riding a sleigh pulled by reindeers winked at him" (Ḥallāwī, 2009, 26). His imagination is sparked by the surrounding wilderness, but the emptiness and darkness of the forest at night revive his feelings of loneliness. Likewise, the local village seems closed in on itself, surrounded by white snow and plunged into the silent darkness. The polar cold of Scandinavia, the wilderness of its forests, and the empty or uncultivated areas of the natural environment with its snowy white landscapes and trees of ice make these migrants feel outside the community, accentuating their social isolation and loneliness.

The unfamiliar is reflected in both the natural landscape and the social landscape. Trying to rationalize the xenophobia and the unfriendly gazes, Youness concludes that he must be invisible to blue-eyed people because all his life he has only been perceived through the gaze of dark-eyed people. Gazes full of hatred and contempt attack him when he goes out to smoke a cigarette in front of the public library, or when he rides the bus. For the people who spit on the ground when they see him, he tries to find excuses until he understands that this is a sign of hatred directed at him. Perplexed by the rejection, he finally focuses on the idea of counteracting the evil of hatred with love and compassion. He decides to wear a hat decorated with a yellow cross on a blue background, a symbol of the Swedish flag, to ward off hatred. His co-worker mistakes Youness for a drug dealer and asks him if he can sell him some marijuana. Everywhere he is perceived as a curiosity and an anomaly as he keeps talking to himself. "Women look at you as if you were a loose monkey in the streets; behind closed doors, neighbors are upset with the alien immigrant" (Ḥallāwī, 2009, 93). The woman he meets at a bar alleges that she lost her gold ring the morning after their one-night stand. In the laundry room of his apartment building, an elderly neighbor offers to hire him to help her do errands at home. One day he receives an anonymous phone call with a voice asking him to go back to his country. All of these dejecting and degrading incidents dig deep into his wounded soul, eroding his confidence, and destroying his humanity and his self-esteem.

The only time that Youness feels in harmony with his fellow Swedes is Friday and Saturday evenings, the drinking nights. On the weekends, he is impressed by their behavior. They become intoxicated, indulging in sensual pleasure and expressing their humanity, as though taking their revenge after a tough week of work.

> Every Friday evening Youness gets very excited to enjoy beer. Its golden color, its foam on his lips, and its taste make him happy and remind him of drinking parties he used to have with his friends back in the bars of the East.
>
> (Ḥallāwī, 2009, 130)

Before going out to the bars at 10 pm, Youness starts his drinking ritual at home, listening to traditional Iraqi music by Salima Murad and Nadhum al-Ghazali. Absorbed by the melodies as if they spoke to him alone,

> he forgets everything around him. His memory takes him back to that faraway country with its hot days, its steppes, palm trees, rivers, and people. He starts singing as part of his melancholic participation in the ritual of the town, but his own party belongs to a bygone age and a faraway universe.
>
> (Ḥallāwī, 2009, 130)

The xenophobic environment where Youness lives and the loneliness and rejection he feels leave him gasping for breath. Navigating the hardships and the administrative obstacles to find jobs suffocates him. At night, he is prey to either anxiety and horrible insomnia when the sun doesn't set properly during the long summer days, or he is seized by recurring nightmares, visited by the ghosts of the past and the fears of the present. When he sees a doctor, in the hope of receiving medical leave from work, he honestly describes his condition as follows: "I suffer from night suffocation. I wake up gasping for breath; it lasts a few seconds, with no or little air. Then I recover my breath, feeling paralyzed with horror" (Ḥallāwī, 2009, 185). *Scant Air* clearly departs from traditional themes of cultural encounter and belonging, highlighting instead how defamiliarization has become a central trope of recent novels depicting migration to Nordic countries.

Failed Returns

The migrant's return to the country of origin is an important narrative component in the Arabic novel of migration. Sometimes it is the starting point in the narration, with the technique of the flashback used to recover the experience in exile, presenting an opportunity for critical self-introspection and reflection on the overall experience. This structure is still favored in the recent Iraqi novels explored here.

In a variation on this theme, *Namiq Spencer and I* opens, not with the narrator's return to Iraq, but with his second arrival in his Danish exile, which he leaves yet again a few months later to return to Baghdad with a project and a new commitment. However, this return to his homeland proves disappointing. At the end of the novel, he readies himself for another departure after his stay in Baghdad has ended in absolute failure. Both his project to document violence and his love affair with Sura, a woman reporter from Baghdad, have fallen apart.

Unlike the narrator of *Season*, this broken man of the borderland, now in his fifties, feels like "a feather in a storm, a feather under the sunlight, a feather in a sad sunset" (Al-Anbārī, 2014, 139). After many travels, from south to north (Iraq–Copenhagen), but also from north to south (Copenhagen–Brazil), he feels lost between multiple places and cultures; he does not belong anywhere. "Sometimes I feel as if I were living in absolute singlehood, as if I were a human being with zero connection: no relatives, no friends, no wife, no lover, just a single person confined to its own thin skin" (Al-Anbārī, 2014, 142). He sees himself as an eternal traveler, crossing continents and cities, constantly haunted by his homeland and its woes. What motivates the narrator to go back to Iraq is the need to understand violence. The rise in violence and passion crimes among immigrants in Copenhagen piques his interest. He starts covering these topics for an Arabic newspaper of the Arab community in Copenhagen, headed by one of his Syrian friends.

The project starts with the idea of documenting local violence within immigrant communities in Denmark and analyzing the motivations behind the crimes they commit. In one case, a young man kills his Danish girlfriend because he saw her with another man. He stabs her more than 100 times, raising fears of terrorism and religious extremism. Some rightwing newspaper reporters conclude, "there is an archive of violence behind each foreigner, and in particular behind each person from the East, and more precisely behind every Muslim" (Al-Anbārī, 2014, 135). In light of the violence sweeping the broader Middle East, the old question of "progress" versus "backwardness" seems to be approached differently. The narrator asks the question, replacing progress with peacefulness and backwardness with the equivalent of violence:

> The essence of the question is why did they progress where we failed? Why are we so violent while they are so peaceful? What is the reason behind this? This is the archive of violence that interests me: the spiritual

> archeology of violence. It all begins there. This archive has not yet been opened. Nobody knows for sure what its infinite pages contain, as if everybody is scared from approaching it.
>
> (Al-Anbārī, 2014, 164)

The project to document violence locally turns into a bigger idea: to investigate the archive of violence in Baghdad in order to get to "the root of the problem." The assumptions and speculations about violence among Middle Easterners and Iraqis are numerous and contradictory:

> My friend Namiq believes that violence is part of us, part of our genes; it goes back all the way to our ancestors, the Sumerians. It cannot be explained by the living conditions and other causes outside the personality of the human being. He takes as example the killings mentioned by historians, from the beginning of the Sumerian alphabet to the explosions targeting markets, schools, and hospitals following 2003. It is a point of view. [...] I used to think that violence was motivated by external causes and could not be inherited.
>
> (Al-Anbārī, 2014, 145)

Thirty years after his desertion, this man, who is still traumatized and tortured by nightmare scenarios, has learned to fear death no more. He hurries back to Baghdad via Damascus, carrying the same suitcase he had when he had come to Copenhagen. The idea of documenting violence in Baghdad has captured his mind.

> "The archive of violence," he muses, "is a term I really like." The city is rife with violence: it feeds on violence, takes explosions for breakfast, assassinations for lunch, and kidnapping and other horrendous events that we hear about in the news every day for dinner.
>
> (Al-Anbārī, 2014, 145)

Among the violent events he witnesses and documents, there is a major explosion in Tayaran Square, targeting daily workers. Sura, a reporter who covers the violence targeting women in prisons and other topics, assists the narrator. She is surprised that the narrator left Copenhagen to come back to Iraq:

> This is a country that needs to confront itself. Other places in the world enjoy music, love, gardens, and evenings by the beach, while we are here killing each other like African crocodiles. I don't understand how you could leave such places and come back to this ugly country and these rude people who drink blood as if it was wine. Leave; this country is not worth living in.
>
> (Al-Anbārī, 2014, 164)

The failed return to the homeland in the throes of occupation and war is also clearly staged in *Scant Air*. But in the context of lawlessness and the state of exception, the most improbable thing happens to Youness: he gets kidnapped by militia and deported by British forces. Youness decides to go back to his hometown, Basra. He lands in Kuwait; from there, he rents a private taxi without even telling his family. We accompany him on this land journey as the driver crosses the long, dusty road from Kuwait to Basra. One cainnot help but remember here the iconic return of Ismail (Ismāʿīl) in *The Lamp of Umm Hashm*, from England to Egypt. As Ismail travels back to his neighborhood, his disappointment grows along the way. More than half a century separates the two novels. The scale of the shock and desolation is far greater in the case of Youness; the city of Basra is devastated by a military occupation.

The land journey by car, crossing through Iraq's southern border, reveals the devastation and marks of military occupation and its checkpoints. Youness observes,

> the cab that took me from Kuwait to Basra looked like a little toy next to the gigantic American tanks. The road, which was already in poor condition, was cracking under their heavy weight, while the sky was the theater for all kinds of warplanes.
>
> (Ḥallāwī, 2009, 205)

Youness feels like he is entering a foreign land, not his home country. Everything on the roads belongs to U.S. occupying forces, including soldiers, equipment, and mechanisms. They all contribute to a defamiliarization in reverse: "The American military caravan on the road to Basra was advancing toward the city where I was born, where I and my ancestors grew up. That felt very strange and irrational. It is now an occupied city" (Ḥallāwī, 2009, 209). As the taxi makes its way through the roads of old Basra, Youness realizes that the places he sees resemble only slightly those he left 20 years prior. He muses:

> How these places were crowded with people. They are now deserted, empty, and covered with sadness and defeat. No carriages, no vendors, no horns, no pedestrians, except for the ghosts of a few women cloaked in black abayas with their bare footed kids walking behind them, while British patrols watched the streets leading to the market of old Basra.
>
> (Ḥallāwī, 2009, 218)

The returnee does not recognize his city and its landmarks; it is disfigured by years of neglect, dust, and the accumulation of dirt. Religious and sectarian slogans and giant posters of clerics with their turbans, beards, and abayas make the space look even stranger to Youness. He doesn't fail to notice the overwhelming presence of the color black infiltrating the landscape: from black flags, to black turbans, and black signs. The biggest irony occurs when he decides to go out on a stroll. Visiting the places of his childhood despite the warnings of his family, Youness is mistaken for a foreigner and immediately kidnapped by a gang who sell him to another militia for his English language skills needed in interpreting and blackmailing activities. This leads to the British forces' punishment of Youness. For not having cooperated with them, as a Swedish citizen, he is deported back to Sweden and banned from returning to Iraq for ten years.

In *Namiq Spencer and I* and *Scant Air*, the two main characters keep the homeland in their hearts. When an opportunity arises, they make the reverse journey back to Iraq. But it is with disappointment and bitterness that they face the harsh new realities of occupation and violence; their feelings of loss and helplessness are absolute. Ironically, but not surprisingly, they are doomed to be pushed back again from a country torn by war and occupation, and where violence caused directly or indirectly by the West keeps on proliferating. Both narratives are a clear indictment of the waging of wars by western colonial powers, as well as the local and sectarian violence that was unleashed in Iraq in the context of the rise of sectarianism and extremism. Regarding their failed returns, the narrators in both novels adopt a meditative and contemplative stance on their migration, their lives in exile, and their marginality. They formulate an indirect critique and condemnation of the circumstances and the implied actors who contributed to the descent of their homeland into an abyss of destruction, leading to more migration in the first decade of the twenty-first century. At this juncture of the height of the sectarian violence, Ali Badr's novel *The Musician of the Clouds* depicts the most recent wave of migration caused by the fear and terror of Islamist militia tightening their grips on all aspects of life in Iraq. In the case of Nabil, the alienated musician, no return is envisaged in this novel. This indicates the degree of deterioration of conditions in Iraq, beyond any possibility of considering a return.

In previous novels of migration, in the postcolonial context, the return of the migrant was staged as the opportunity to help formulate the national narrative, negotiating a transition to modernity that could reconcile local tradition with western values. Today, the context of migration, as it is staged in recent Iraqi literature, comprises part of a global mass migration movement. It is nevertheless framed by the conditions of neo-colonial wars and post-occupation violence. It seems that the returnee's task is daunting, and impossible in most cases.

Conclusion

The discussion and analysis of recent Iraqi novels of migration demonstrates a shift in the aesthetics and politics of writing migration in Arabic. With these new narratives, readers move from a postcolonial to a global perspective, marked by a general increase in not only worldwide mobility but also the particular case of Iraq, due to perennial violence that devastates culture and forces Iraqi migrants out of their homeland. The shift is also illustrated in the new geographies of migration shown in these novels to reflect new uncharted territories as well as in the reshaping of more diffuse relationship patterns. The continuum of violence in the new global wars nullifies the relevance of political commitment and a meaningful return to the home country in these novels. This is symptomatic of a cultural and political deterioration, in clear contrast to the postcolonial context of the twentieth century.

Notes

1 All translations from the three novels are mine. Shākir al-Anbārī was born in 1957; Janān Jāsim Ḥallāwī in 1956 and ʿAlī Badr in 1964.

2 *Harraga*, meaning "those who burn" in Algerian Arabic, referring to those who burn their citizenship documents before crossing, thus burning their past.

3 See the chapter on the war deserter, "The Iran-Iraq War and the Bare Life of the War Deserter," in Masmoudi (2015).

References

Agier, M. (2016) *Borderlands: Towards an Anthropology of the Cosmopolitan Condition*. Cambridge, UK: Polity Press.

Al-Anbārī, S. (2014) *Anā wa-Nāmiq Spencer*. Beirut; Baghdad: Manshūrāt al-jamal.

Badr, ʿA. (2016) *ʿĀzif al-ghuyūm*. Milan: Manshūrāt al-Mutawassiṭ.

Blasim, H. (2009) *The Madman of Freedom Square*. Manchester: Comma Press.

Ḥaqqī, Y. (1944) *Qindīl Umm Hāshim*. Cairo: Dār al-maʿārif.

Hassan, W. (2003) *Tayeb Salih: Ideology and the Craft of Fiction*. Syracuse, NY: Syracuse University Press.

Ḥallāwī, J. (2009) *Hawāʾ qalīl*. Beirut: Dār al-ādāb.

Idrīs, S. [1953] (2017) *al-Ḥayy al-Lātīnī*. Beirut: Dār al-ādāb.

International Organization for Migration. (2019) *Glossary on Migration*. Available at: www.iom.int/glossary-migration-2019 (Accessed: 13 February 2021).

Masmoudi, I. (2015) *War and Occupation in Iraqi Fiction*. Edinburgh: Edinburgh University Press.

Ṣāliḥ, Ṭ. (1966) *Mawsim al-hijra ilā al-shimāl*. Beirut: Markaz al-ahrām.

Sellman, J. (2018) A Global Postcolonial: Contemporary Arabic Literature of Migration to Europe. *Journal of Postcolonial Writing*, 54(6), 751–765.

Sellman, J. (2016) The Ghosts of Exilic Belongings: Maḥmūd al-Bayyātī's Raqṣ ʿalā al-māʾ: aḥlām waʾrah and Post-Soviet Themes in Arabic Exile Literature. *Journal of Arabic Literature*, 47(1–2), 111–137.

Epilogue

Maria Elena Paniconi

This volume is a collection of eight articles previously presented as papers during the annual conference of the Italian Society for Middle-Eastern Studies (SeSaMo – Società per gli Studi sul Medio Oriente) held in Catania, Sicily, in May 2016. The conference, called "Migrants: Communities, Borders, Memories, Conflicts", invited scholars and researchers to launch a multidisciplinary investigation of the phenomenon of migration with reference to the Mediterranean Basin and to predominantly Muslim societies. It is no coincidence, however, that the then-mayor of Lampedusa, Giuseppina Maria (Giusi) Nicolini, was asked to make the opening speech – a choice that gave a global rather than merely Mediterranean quality to this academic event.

Indeed, with its migratory background and tens of thousands of migrants landing on the island of Lampedusa, Sicily has historically been a land of emigration and immigration. It is also a privileged observation point from which to investigate the changes that have taken place in the Mediterranean migratory experience over the past few years. And, more specifically, the island of Lampedusa (a sort of "stone raft" stretching between the Sicilian and Tunisian coastlines) has become a true global icon of the emergency situation of immigration via the Mediterranean. In 2016, 181.436 people landed on Italian shores, while shipwreck victims the same year numbered 4.700 (Colucci, 2018, 174–175).[1]

Starting from the year 2011 – in the wake of the Tunisian Revolution – and in the following years, the island became one of the main centres of the Mediterranean migratory crossroads. The island's inhabitants have been actively welcoming refugees since then, and local fishermen have retrieved countless bodies from the sea. A date that stands out indelibly in the mind of the people of Lampedusa is 3 October 2013, when 368 people lost their lives (Leogrande, 2015). The retrieved bodies were laid on the Favaloro pier, used as an open-air morgue; later on, 111 coffins were set out in the hangar of the Lampedusa airport. In her opening speech, Giusi Nicolini chose to dwell on the tragedy of 3 October 2013 in the hopes of making sense of the real, concrete dimension of the act of rescue and refuge. An act performed by her fellow citizens that, in the highly polarised media debate that always

DOI: 10.4324/9780429027338-10

follows the news of landings or shipwrecks, ends up stealing realism from the numbers reported above.

Thus, starting from 2011 and in the wake of the political upheavals that followed on the southern shore of the Mediterranean, Italy became known as a touchstone for the inadequacy of migration laws: from the systems for the containment or turning away of migrants (even forcing them to return to politically unstable and dangerous areas) to the creation and fragmentation of increasingly hostile "frontiers" (Mezzadra, 2013). A case in point of this normative inadequacy is the Dublin Regulation, suspended exceptionally in 2015 due to the migration crisis, and only by some of the signatory countries. This agreement compels aspiring asylum seekers to lodge an asylum claim only in the state they arrive in, no matter their long-term migratory project. Indeed, several studies show that for most migrants, Italy is actually more of a "first stage" within a migration trajectory aimed at Northern European countries (Colucci, 2018, 187).

The results of these unjust and dated agreements are manifold: from the progressive militarisation of borders (Mezzadra, 2013, Leogrande, 2015) to the way Europe and Italy constantly pass the buck to one another. Europe accuses Italy of being unable to manage migratory flows, while Italy complains of "being abandoned" in this management. From the Italian micro-observatory, we also find that migrants began leaving Italy after 2016, in many cases starting a second wave of "onward migration" that saw them leaving the Italian regions where they had settled (often integrating into the workforce), headed for London, Switzerland or Germany. Due to the Covid-19 pandemic (a completely unpredictable event at the time this book was planned), undocumented arrivals in Italy decreased by 80 percent during the first wave, although this phenomenon pertained only to the route from Tunisia, while departures from the Libyan coast hardly varied.[2] The repercussions of the pandemic further jeopardised the already precarious conditions of undocumented workers also with regard to employment, with cases of salary loss, job loss, labour exploitation and an increase in on-the-job discrimination.[3]

The Literary Imaginary as a Space for Negotiating a New Migrant Subjectivity: Trajectories and Borders

As a central element of today's reality and closely connected to its economic, environmental and political instability, the impact of the migratory phenomenon has become increasingly clear on our perception of the self and of what we perceive as "other" from the self. As stated by Censi, based on Nordin et al. (2013), the very nature of works of fiction offers readers the chance to experience a transcultural encounter, inviting them to identify with perspectives, experiences and subjects belonging to unfamiliar cultural backgrounds. However, the mechanism of identifying with fictional characters enables us to break down the effect of "otherness" at times stirred up by the media, by reading academic papers (whether sociological, statistical or historical in nature) or by actual encounters with migrants. Thus, the performative, "poietic" (from the Greek word *Ποίησις*, "to make out of nothing") power of a work of fiction that tackles topics such as displacement, exile, and voluntary or forced migration fosters a type of emotional awareness of the migratory phenomenon in readers. For readers who potentially identify with the story that unfolds, the literary imaginary becomes a space to negotiate and restructure the migrant identity in its complexity and multiple implications, which range from the boundaries dictated by the act of migration to the psychological repercussions of migration on the people who live through it, to the contradictory experiences of the people who endure someone else's – parents or familiars – migratory project, to the risks of lies and nostalgia entailed in the processes of reconstruction of the domestic imaginary.

This volume presents a collection of critical studies on literary works centred on these and other human phenomena connected to migration and to the experience of migrating subjects at different moments along their journey. We have chosen to do so without taking on an alternate perspective to that of "migrant literature", using this expression as a macro-category that, compared to Arabic literature, would also include the Arabic literature of the diaspora, finding its raison d'être in the migration, displacement, emigration, exile or diaspora experiences shared by the authors. Instead, the selection criteria for the works to be analysed consisted in their inclusion of some of the abovementioned themes, as well as of a narrative structure of the multiple identities of the migrant. In the wake of studies by Thomas Nail (Nail, 2015) and Étienne Balibar (Balibar, 2020), we believe that, being political in nature, the subjectivity of migrants and refugees has been historically denied and/or "underrepresented". A potential risk of adopting the perspective of "migration literature", as it has been presented until now, or of "diasporic literature", as it has been presented for instance by Waïl Hassan (Hassan, 2017), who included in the idea of "Arab diasporic novel" novels from Argentina, Australia, Brazil, Britain and nine other countries, is that of creating a secondary literary canon for literature produced by migrants, separate from what is produced by non-migrants or residents and, thus, by extension, by subjects of national and monocultural affiliation.

From the perspective of the themes discussed, the first element that all the narratives studied in the eight chapters collected here appear to have in common is how migration (whether voluntary or forced in nature) maps out a trajectory in the space both outside and within the self. Migrants have to cross frontiers and spatial boundaries, and their perception of time is inevitably marked by the migratory event: there is always a "before" and an "after" migration. Here, the migrants' bodies and their relationships with identity, on the one hand, and with external space, on the other, are at the heart of several reflections (see Chapters 2 and 5) because they represent both the first detector of personal change and a repository for migration politics in the public sphere. In actual fact, the bodies of migrants recount the private aspects of a regulatory, and therefore public, dimension – an act that does not restrict itself to disciplining the movements of individuals, but often reaches their most intimate sphere (see Chapter 3).

The two novels written in the first person, *Taytanikāt Ifrīqiyya* by Abū Bakr Khāl and *Mudun bi- lā nakhīl* by Ṭāriq al-Ṭayyib (see Chapter 1), capture the trajectory of migration as it is being carried out. The story of the migration as it unfolds is, perhaps, a direct consequence of the type of migration described here: forced in both cases. The first novel recounts an escape from the Eritrean War in Tunisia via Libya, while the second novel is the story of a 20-year-old's escape from an abnormal drought that has struck the rural area in Sudan where he lives. In both cases, the first-person narration presents itself as a *necessary* story, almost a "redeeming" practice intent on recreating, in the formation of a potential audience, a "community" that makes up for the original one the character has lost.

The bodies of migrants are also at the heart of narratives that seize upon their act of crossing several boundaries – whether political frontiers between countries, natural boundaries between regions or intraregional passages between rural areas and metropolises. The bodies of migrants often pass through these realities, while also experiencing marginalisation upon encountering their new world. In *Mudun bi-lā nakhīl*, 20-year-old Ḥamza thus describes his arrival in the "enormous city" of Omdurman from the village he is escaping from:

> God! What will I do in this enormous city? I feel lost. I feel as if I were in the middle of a vast and boundless sea: everyone must swim here, myself included, for I will sink to the bottom if I do not. [...] Where can I find work? I ask myself. I need to find something, anything. Otherwise, I will not survive, nor those I left behind in the village.
>
> When I finally succeed in crossing the street, the hope of finding a job once again takes hold of me. Yet whether calmly or rudely, whether indifferently or with a certain degree of surprise, the shopkeepers all give me the same answer.
>
> (Eltayeb, 2009, 25)

Ḥamza sees these shopkeepers as the "gatekeepers" of a world from which he seems, without fail, to be excluded. In *The Location of Culture*, Bhabha claims that national communities should be redefined starting from the perspective of those who, like Ḥamza, are on the fringes of the "national community" that has built its narrative by relegating minority and dissimilar elements to these very fringes. It is interesting to note that although Ḥamza must cross several frontiers (intra-African and then intra-European), his migratory experience will turn out to be a story of perpetual exclusion and marginalisation. In 1992, forestalling the publication of *The Location of Culture* by two years, Ṭāriq al-Ṭayyib uses the character of Ḥamza to write about the encounter between "the Western Metropole" and post-colonial history. An encounter that, according to Bhabha, should be read as the "indigenous or native narrative internal to its national identity" (Bhabha, 1994, 244).

Several narratives, on the other hand, do not illustrate migration as it is happening so much as its result, capturing the situation of the migrating characters after some time. The life of less privileged migrants, labourers in contemporary urban contexts, is often depicted via a map of their exclusion or invisibility. The labourer-migrants of an undefined country in the Gulf described by Muḥammad al-Bisāṭī in *Daqq al-ṭabūl* (see Cristina Dozio in Chapter 3) live on the fringes of the economic and social life of the country. Their bodies are crossed by rules and regulations aimed at restricting their freedom of movement and even their free sexual activity. Dozio emphasises how al-Bisāṭī exploits a *topos* used at length in the language of the experimental Egyptian novel of the late 20th century: sexual impotence as an icon of political subordination. In al-Bisāṭī's novel, specifically, this condition is an eloquent metaphor for the "master's control over every aspect of their worker's life" (Chapter 3, 61) and, albeit within the ironic framework of a grand satire, should be read as a clear accusation against the social inequality underlying the economic system of certain Arab countries.

Survival Strategies and Coping Mechanisms

The theme of the marginality of the migrant's life also features in the three novels analysed by Ikram Masmoudi (Chapter 8): Shākir al-Anbārī's *Anā wa- Nāmiq Spencer*, ʿAlī Badr's *ʿĀzif al-ghuyūm* and Janān Jāsim Ḥallāwī's *Hawāʾ qalīl*. The main characters' *teloi* seem to be the reification of a migration trajectory that takes them from Iraq to the "fringes" of urban life in several European cities. The protagonist of Jāsim Ḥallāwī's novel *Hawāʾ qalīl*, a character often at the limits of self-parody, claims to only feel close to his Swedish travelling companions on weekends, when they are brought together by an alcoholic stupor to which the protagonist happily abandons himself (Chapter 8, 169). In his study "At the Borders of Citizenship: a Democracy in Translation?", Balibar states that borders make up the "transindividual relationship" (Balibar, 2010, 316). In the narrations analysed, the migrant subject often takes shape as an inter-subject, reifying a surrounding network of co-protagonists of migration: travelling companions, ancestors or the first family members to face the challenges of migration. Thus, migrants attempt to "blend" the boundaries of their own selves with those of other migrants in an intersubjective experience that emerges clearly, for example in the generational memoir (see Shahbazi, Chapter 5) or in the storytelling (see Paniconi, Chapter 1) interwoven by the refugees in Abū Bakr Khāl's *Taytanikāt Ifrīqiyya*. Here is how Sellman explains this tendency to create, on the part of migrants or migrant communities, a "transindividual" identity:

> I suggest that the notion of the transindividual takes on a heightened significance in recent Arabic literature of forced migration because it so

> often stages individual narratives and *in relation to* larger modes of legal and social belongings [...]
>
> (Sellman, 2018, 760)

The tendency to "rebuild" networks of individuals through the (at times imaginary) narration of the events experienced before, during and after the completion of the migration project takes on an "immortalising" and almost sacred role in Khāl's novel, where the first chapter is a succinct version of the unfolding of the fate of the protagonist and of the "mythological" figure of Malūk, a Liberian migrant who will perish at sea and whose fate is revealed in the very first pages (Chapter 1). Ultimately, the opportunity to merge and mingle the "boundaries" of the self with those of other migrants is the first of many strategies of survival, negotiation and endurance dictated by the unstable condition of being a migrant.

The prismatic identity of the migrant and the repercussions (both short and long term) of displacement on the migrant subject is analysed by Martina Censi (Chapter 2) in her work on two novels by Ḥanān al-Shaykh centred precisely on migrant identities, notably female. The characters differ greatly as to social class, national and gender identity, type of migration project. Al-Shayk's novels, like the family memoir by Iraqi-Canadian journalist Leilah Nadir (Chapter 5) and the novels by Jordanian-American Laila Halaby (Chapter 6), expose a demystification of the romantic ideal of "exile", as well as the false universalism and false neutrality hidden behind concepts and practices of "multiculturalism" and "assimilation" (Uberoi and Modood, 2015). This demystification is the result of a painstaking exploration of the intersection between provenance, race and class – aspects often hard to distinguish between and of which the migrant becomes aware *through* the storytelling. In actual fact, this identity "prism" encompasses *all* migrant experiences. What some consider to have been an "unproblematic assimilation" for a character in the memoir proves, in the eyes of his daughter, "the result of his social location as a middle-class, educated Christian Iraqi" (see Shahbazi, Chapter 5, 88).

The only exception to the demystification of exile can be found in Waciny Laredj's writing, analysed by Jolanda Guardi from a decolonial perspective, as exile is elected as a place of creativity, as the only possible expression of the self and as a support for the expression of collective and cultural memory, refashioned by the Algerian author in the intertextual layers of works belonging to the Mediterranean and Muslim-Arab tradition (Guardi, Chapter 4).

The complexity inherent in the migrant identity, as well as the awareness of non-neutrality of irenic or consolatory narratives, lead several authors to focus on and develop actual "coping" (that is, "surviving") mechanisms for migrant life in their works. For example, the "hometactics" analysed by Shima Shahbazi (Chapter 5), the salvation-exile just mentioned in Laredj (Chapter 4), the ironic reappropriation in a feminist vein of the old racist stereotypes found in Laila Halaby's novels and revisited in Sara Arami's study (Chapter 6). In the absence of consoling narrations, the ironic reappropriation of old racist stereotypes or the dwelling on self-Orientalism appear to be the last "allies" for migrants constantly searching for themselves and, as mentioned by Censi in the introduction to this volume, not completely free from the stylistic features produced by Orientalism, which is (and was) a formidable mechanism of construction of the Islamic-Arab imaginary.

Theoretical Approaches and Narrative Techniques

The narrative and (see Chapter 7) visual and media materials analysed in this volume have been interpreted in light of several theoretical references. Among these, the ones most cited and present in the critical discourse are indubitably the theories that draw on "positionality", intended both as an approach in the analysis of photographs and visual materials (Azoulay, 2021) and as an approach in the study of the literary phenomenon. Another transversal element is the use of discourse analysis applied by the authors of the various essays to the literary *topoi*, to the tropes that make up the raw canvas of the meanings and narrative strategies employed in the works of fiction, memoirs and media texts analysed here. Also transversal is the resuming of the reflection of border studies, symbolic "places" where migrant individuals and families were segregated.

The abovementioned theoretical approaches help highlight an increasingly global and post-national aspect of migration, which often takes shape as a migration from a global south towards the "metropolis" and as a potential repetition of the power imbalances between migrant and non-migrant, citizen and resident. The parodic rewriting of classic works of the *Nahḍa* and of the 20th century viewed as the cornerstones of the imaginary of migration literature (such as *Qindīl Umm Hāshim* by Yaḥyā Ḥaqqī or *Mawsim al-hijra ilā al-shimāl* by al-Ṭayyib Ṣāliḥ) is proposed by Masmoudi (Chapter 8) as an interpretation of three contemporary Iraqi novels, albeit more to emphasise the discontinuities with the *Nahḍa*'s "progressive" and linear narrative than to underscore continuity. Roula Salam (Chapter 7) points out how several Syrian narrators (such as Samar Yazbik, Nabīl Mulḥim and ʿAbd Allāh Makṣūr) use deliberately defamiliarising narrative techniques to offer an alternate portrayal of the identity of Syrian refugees compared to the prevailing one. For example, Samar Yazbik's *Bawwabāt arḍ al-ʿadam* (The Crossing: My Journey to the Shattered Heart of Syria), which includes a memoir, poetic texts and excerpts from prison narratives, describes a country ravaged by war and described materially as a foreign-Syria.

The alienation experienced by readers is twofold. On one hand, the pre-war image of Syria is defamiliarised and shown in all its true destruction; on the other, we have a defamiliarisation of the current image of the "Syrian refugee" as it has been constructed by the prevailing visual culture. The human body, placed at the centre of attention by the narrative realism of Yazbik and of the other authors analysed by Roula Salam (Chapter 7), is portrayed in its most perturbing dimension: fleeting and potentially "abject", a category used in the wake of Kristeva (Chapter 7, 143–145) to explain the reification – by means of the body – of the "land of forced migration". The wounded and segregated body, "scandalous" in its mortality, reifies the condition of the refugee (whether due to war or other reasons) – a dimension where space and time collapse in "naked" bodies, almost devoid of humanity and indubitably removed from the narrative of the mainstream media by the authors' realism.

To sum up, the works examined in this volume have the potential to open a new narratology of the migrant subject, moving beyond the theoretical limitations suggested and implied by the category of "migrant literature" – a label often rejected by the authors themselves (Guardi, Chapter 2) – and imagining a politics and a cultural identity that do not relegate migrants to the fringes but, rather, place them in the very heart and at the foundation of the community.

Notes

1 Source of the data quoted by Colucci (Colucci, 2018): UNHCR.
2 Sources: UNHCR and IOM, www.ispionline.it/it/pubblicazione/fact-checking-migrazioni-e-covid-19-27058, [consulted on 20th October 2021].
3 Interview with Fabio Perocco, "Coronavirus e migrazione. L'impatto di una crisi sanitaria", www.meltingpot.org/Coronavirus-e-migrazione-l-impatto-di-una-crisi-sanitaria.html#.YYgkz2DMJPY, consulted on [20th October 2021].

References

Azoulay, A. (2001) *Death's Showcase: The Power of Image in Contemporary Democracy*. R. Danieli (trans.) Massachusetts: MIT Press.

Azoulay, A. (2012) *Civil Imagination: A Political Ontology of Photography*. London: Verso.

Balibar, É. (2010) At the Borders of Citizenship: A Democracy in Translation? *European Journal of Social Theory*, 13(3), 315–322.

Balibar, É., Wallerstein, I. (2020) *Razza, nazione, classe. Le identità ambigue*. Trieste: Asterios Editore.

Bhabha, H. (1994) *The Location of Culture*. London: Routledge.

Colucci, M. (2018) *Storia dell'immigrazione straniera in Italia*. Roma: Carocci.

Eltayeb, T. (2009) *Cities Without Palms*. Translated by Kareem James Palmer-Zeid. Cairo: The American University in Cairo Press.

Hassan, W.S. (ed.) (2017) *The Oxford Handbook of Arab Novelistic Tradition*. Oxford: Oxford University Press.

Leogrande, A. (2015) *La frontiera*. Milano: Feltrinelli.

Mezzadra, S. (2013) *Border as Method, or the Multiplication of Labor*. Durham: Duke University Press.

Nail, T. (2015) *The Figure of the Migrant*. Stanford (CA): Stanford University Press.

Nordin, I.G., Hansen, J., Llena, C.Z. (eds) (2013) *Transcultural Identities in Contemporary Literature*. Amsterdam: Rodopi.

Sellman, J. (2018) A Global Postcolonial: Contemporary Arabic Literature of Migration to Europe. *Journal of Postcolonial Writing*, 54(6), 751–765.

Uberoi, V., Modood, T. (eds) (2015) *Multiculturalism Rethought: Interpretation, Dilemmas and New Directions*, Edinburgh: Edinburgh University Press.

Index

ʿAbd al-Majīd, Ibrāhīm, *al-Balda al-ukhrā* (The Other Place) 6, 53–4, 58–9, 60, 65
Abdelrazek, Amal Talaat 4
ʿAbd Allāh, Dārā, *Al-waḥda tudallilu ḍaḥāyā-hā* (Loneliness Pampers Its Victims) 143–5
Abū Julayyil, Ḥamdī: *al-Fāʿil* (A Dog With No Tail) 54
adab al-mahjar 3, 4
adaptability 89, 90, 91–2, 93, 95
ʿAdnān, Etel 29
agency 2, 89, 94, 109–10, 112, 118
Aghacy, Samira 63
Agier, Michel 130, 157, 162
Ai, Weiwei 129
al-Anbārī, Shākir 155; *Anā wa-Nāmiq Spencer* (Namiq Spencer and I) 151–3, 154, 155, 156–8, 162, 163–5, 170–1, 173, 179
Al-Andalus 72, 74
al-Aʿraj, Wasīnī *see* Laredj, Waciny
al-Asad, Bashar 134
al-Asmar, Aziz 133
al-Aswānī, ʿAlāʾ, *Jumhūriyya ka-anna* (The Republic of False Truths) 54–5
al-Bisāṭī, Muḥammad 56; *Daqq al-ṭabūl* (Drumbeat) 52, 53, 55–9, 60–6, 179; *Ḥadīth min al- ṭābiq al- thālith* (A Conversation From the Third Floor) 59; *Ṣakhab al- buḥayra* (Clamor of the Lake) 56
Alcoff, Linda 90
Alexandria 21
al-Fārābī 165
Algeria/Algerian 13, 69, 70, 71–2; black decade 74, 75; culture and identity 71–4; exile from 75, 76–7; Independence 72; politics 75; terrorism 75; *see also* Laredj, Waciny
Algerian War of Independence 75
al-Ghīṭānī, Jamāl, *Waqāʾiʿ ḥārat al-Zaʿfarānī* (The Zafarani Files) 62
al-Ḥāj Ṣāliḥ, Yāsīn, *Al-khalāṣ am al-kharāb? Sūriyā ʿalā muftaraq ṭuruq (*Deliverance or Destruction? Syria at a Crossroads) 134
al-Ḥakīm, Tawfīq, *ʿUṣfūr min al-sharq* (Bird of the East) 4, 12
al-Hussein, Riyadh 133
alienation 14, 20–1, 42–3, 53–4, 55, 155, 159, 162, 165, 168, 173, 181
al-Khamīssī, Khālid, *Safīnat Nūḥ* (Noah's Arch) 13
Alkhateeb, Rafat 129
Allen, R. 65
al-Sammān, Ghāda 29
Al-Samman, Hanadi 33–4, 40–1, 48
al-Sanʿūsī, Saʿūd: *Sāq al-bāmbū* (The Bamboo Stalk) 6, 52–3, 60, 65
al-Shāmī, Leila 134–5
al-Shaykh, Ḥanān 29–30, 31–2, 180; *Innahā London yā ʿazīzī* (This Is London, My Dear) 28, 30, 32, 33–4, 36–7, 40–4, 47–8, 49; *Intiḥār rajul mayyit* (Suicide of a Dead Man) 30; *Misk al-ghazāl* (The Gazelle's Musk) 28, 30–1, 32–3, 34–6, 37–40, 42, 44–7, 49
al-Ṭayyib, Ṭāriq 25; *Mudun bi-lā nakhīl* (Cities Without Palms) 15, 16–21, 24–5, 178–9
Amin, Samir 104
Amsterdam 21, 75, 76–7
amulets 21, 23, 25
ANT theory 138–9
Anzaldua, Gloria 84, 85, 91

Arab American writers 3, 4; women 103, 104, 105, 108–9, 117
Arab British writers 3, 95
Arabian Nights 63–4, 70–1, 94, 116
Arab novel 12–15; identity 31–3, 42–3; of emigration 65–6; as intercultural narratives 120
Arab Spring 126
Arami, Sara 180
Arendt, Hannah 133
Arrighi, Giovanni 104
assimilation 85–9, 91–2, 93, 94, 95, 96
Assmann, Jan 71
asylum seekers 6, 13, 31, 126, 127, 128, 153; policies and agreements 100–1, 125, 126, 176; representations of 123, 125, 127, 145; *see also* refugees
Australia 85, 96
Ayyūb, Dhū-al-Nūn, *Duktūr Ibrāhīm* (Doctor Ibrāhīm) 12
Azoulay, Ariella 127, 129, 131, 132, 181
Aztecs 74

Badawi, Muhammad Mustafa 12
Badr, ʿAlī 155; *ʿĀzif al-ghuyūm* (The Musician of the Clouds) 151, 155, 159–62, 165–7, 173, 179
Baghdad 92, 93, 95, 98, 99, 100, 162; escape from 156, 157, 161; idealization 94; return to 151–2, 170, 171–3; violence 151, 157–8, 159, 171
Bakhtin, Mikhail 136, 137
Balibar, Étienne 1, 177, 179
Barad, Karen 92
Bashīniyya, Mawlid 72
Bauman, Zigmunt 130
Baʿalbakī, Laylā 30
Beck, Ulrich 48
Bedouins 33, 34, 37, 38, 45, 54, 120
Behdad, Ali 85–6
Beirut 30, 35
Beirut Decentrists 29
Belgium/Belgian 16, 20, 159, 160, 161–2, 165–7
belonging 3, 83, 85, 128, 165, 168, 169, 180; alternative forms of 1, 2, 38, 47, 48; and assimilation 86–7, 95; multiple 30, 118, 120; second-generation anxiety 96
Bencheikh, Jamel Eddine 70
Berlin 152
Bhabha, Homi 2, 34, 42, 49, 178–9
Bhattacharjee, Srimatha Nath 106
Bildungsroman 14–15
biracial identity 95
Blāsim, Ḥasan 123, 137, 139, 145, 153; *Majnūn sāḥat al-ḥurriya* (The Madman of Freedom Square) 13
body, the: and the concept of home 90–1; and gender relations 60–2, 105–14, 115, 165, 166; horror of 142–5, 181–2; and identity 29–30, 39, 40–2, 44–6, 128; media images 129–30; and political issues 65–6; and storytelling 62–4
border crossing 18, 19, 20, 24, 57, 63, 86, 87, 89, 91–2, 96, 101, 154
borderlands 6, 13, 96, 153, 157, 168, 170
Boreham, Paul 129, 130
Borges, Jorge Luis 136
boundaries: cultural 135, 142; digital 132; and lines of contact 129; of the self 179, 180; social 35, 39, 40–1, 60, 112; spatial 35, 39, 40–1, 125, 132, 177, 178
Bourdieu, Pierre 71
Brazil/Brazilian 163, 164–5, 170, 177
Britain/British 3, 33, 43, 87, 92–5, 100–1, 131, 145, 172, 173, 177; *see also* London
Brussels 159, 160, 161–2, 165–7
Butler, Judith 42

Cacciari, Massimo 128, 129–30
Cairo 20, 21, 30, 56, 159
Canada/Canadian 87, 88, 93, 94, 98, 100, 132
canon: collective memory 71; exclusion of female authors 29; of migrant literature 3, 20, 177; of modern Arabic literature 12; Western 142
cartoons 129, 134
Casey, Edmund 141
Casini, Lorenzo 4, 12
Censi, Martina 63, 176, 180, 181
censorship 38, 124, 135, 146
Cervantes, Miguel de 71; *Don Quixote* 70, 72
Childers, William P. 70
Chouliaraki, L. 132–3
circular plots 21–2, 24
citizenship 8, 14, 15, 38, 48; multi-tier 2; spaces outside of 6, 62, 168
class 5, 31, 34, 35, 36, 38–42, 47, 49, 55, 62, 96, 105–6, 141, 180; and

assimilation 88, 93, 94; discrimination 138; elite 4
climate crisis 8, 15, 16–17
colonialism: discourses of 154; and the other 42, 44
coloniality of power 101
colonial mimicry 42, 43
Colucci, Michele 175, 176
Comic4 Syria 127
coming-of-age narratives 14–15
community: lack of in Europe 14; marginalisation of migrants 168, 178, 182; of migrants 22, 24, 179; transnational 57–8, 62, 65
Connor, Phillip 126
consumerism 44, 54, 63
cooke, miriam 29, 134, 140
Copenhagen 151, 152, 157–8, 163–4, 170–1
Covid-19 pandemic 176
Cresswell, Tim 132
crisis (term) 126
Cuauhtemoc 74
cultural practices 92–3, 132

dance 57, 58, 96, 108, 115, 134, 164
Darrāj, Faysal 57
Darraj, Susan Muaddi 104–5
Dawes, James 14, 15
decolonial theory 74, 100
Deleuze, Gilles 84
Delisle, Jennifer Bowering 97–8
Denmark/Danish 151, 152, 155, 157–8, 163–4, 170–1
desert 45; authenticity 33, 35–6; crossings 13, 16, 18, 22, 24; urbanization 33, 36, 46–7, 58–9
detention 21, 24, 156
developmental paradigm 14, 15, 25
diaspora 48, 93, 162; second-generation 96; stories and memory 116, 117; view of women 105–6, 113
diasporic literature 3, 7, 48, 177
Dīb, Thā'ir 127
dichotomous pairs 75, 76
discrimination 89, 115, 138, 156, 176
disguise 41–2
dispossession 37–8, 39, 42
Dozio, Cristina 179
Dragostinova, Theodora 126
dress 39, 40, 41–2, 112, 113, 114, 116, 117; stereotypes 94–5, 108, 109
drought 17
Du Gay, Paul 2

East–West encounters 4, 5, 12
Egypt/Egyptian 16, 20, 21, 30, 53–6, 139; 2011 uprisings 54, 55; influence on Islam in Algeria 72; literature 53–6, 65, 179; *see also* al-Bisāṭī, Muḥammad
El-Ariss, Tarek 40, 43
Elayyan, Hani 5–6, 53, 60
El-Enany, Racheed 4, 12
Ellis Island 85
Elmeligi, Wessam 5
Eritrea/Eritrean 16, 18, 19, 22
Eritrean civil war 22, 178
escape-plot novels 21
Eurocentrism 88
Europe: as discursive construction 12–13; idealization 4, 5, 6, 31, 48, 155, 159, 160, 165; metropolises 4, 6, 8, 29, 31, 32, 34, 43, 47
European Union (EU) 126
exile 70, 76, 77, 152, 157, 170, 173, 177; idealization of 6–7, 180; as metaphor 13; modernist view 62; psychological 74, 75; *see also manfā*
expats 44, 46, 52, 53, 57

Facebook 127, 141–2
Fadda-Conrey, Carol 4
Fāḍil, Yūsuf: *Ḥashīsh* 13
family history 93, 96–7, 99–100
fantasy 42, 62, 65, 99
fate, preordained 24
Fischer, Susan Alice 34, 47
Fisher, Dominique 70
folktales 117
folk wisdom 72–3
food, and homeland 61, 91, 96
forced migration, literature of 6, 13–14, 15, 24–5, 31, 62, 153, 181; Iraq 154–62, 163–75; Syria 123, 124, 125, 134, 136–45, 146
Fotografiska 130
France/French 4, 16, 19–20, 52, 56, 69, 75
Francīs, Ghādī 126–7
Freedman, Jane 126
Friedman, Susan Stanford 120

gender relations 63–4, 65; and the body 60–2, 105–14, 115, 165, 166
Germany 152, 176

Ghana 22
Gharrafi, Miloud 4, 5
Giusi Nicolini, Giuseppina Maria 175–6
globalization 3, 6, 28, 32, 33, 62, 137, 153, 165
Goodnow, Katherine 127, 130, 145
graffiti 132, 133, 134
Gramsci, Antonio 127
Grosfoguel, Ramòn 74
Greece/Greek 71, 131, 142, 160, 177
Guardi, Jolanda 42, 180, 182
Guattari, Félix 84
Gulf countries: expats 44, 46, 57; landscape 33, 35–6; migrant workers 56–8, 59, 60–4, 65–6; migration to 5–6, 30–1, 52, 53–6; social control over sexuality 60–2; spaces 32–3, 35, 36, 37, 38–9; storytelling 62, 63–4, 65
Gulf War 97

Habermas, Jürgen 128
Ḥaddād, Fawwāz, *Al-mutarjim al-khāʾin* (The Unfaithful Translator) 135–6
Hage, Ghassan 130
Halabi, Zeina 6–7, 13
Halaby, Laila 180; *Once in a Promised Land* 103, 107–10, *111*, 112, 116–17, 118, 120; *West of Jordan* 103, 105, 106–7, 110–16, 117–20
Halasa, Malu 132, 143, 144
Hall, Stuart 2, 118
Ḥallāwī, Janān Jāsim 155; *Hawāʾ qalīl* (Scant Air) 151, 155, 158, 162, 167–9, 172–3, 179
Ḥaqqī, Yaḥyā, *Qindīl Umm Hāshim* (The Lamp of Umm Hashim) 4, 12, 154, 159, 163, 164, 172, 181
harraga novels 6, 13–14, 153; *see also* forced migration, literature of
Ḥasan, Mahā 136
Hassan, Waïl S 3–4, 12, 16, 30, 154, 177
Heidegger, Martin 84
hermeneutic horizon 90
hijab 91
Hirsch, Marianne 97
home 85, 86–7, 90; and the body 90–1; second-generation confusion 96
homeland 90; desire to return 5, 93; failed return 170–3; fear of return 98; impossibility of return 99–100; interconnection with host land 117–20; second-generation nostalgia 96, 98–9
homemaking 86, 87, 89, 91, 93, 96, 100
hometactics 86, 88–9, 90, 91, 92, 93, 95, 100, 101
homosexuality 29, 37, 39, 40
Huggan, Graham 130
Human Rights Law 14–15
human rights literature 25; and *Bildungsroman* 14, 15
Ḥusayn, Ṭāhā, *Adīb* (A Man of Letters) 4, 12
Hussein, Saddam 90, 98, 100, 101, 154, 156, 158, 159

Ibrāhīm, Ṣunʿ Allāh: *Dhāt* (Zaat) 54
idealization: of Europe 4, 5, 6, 31, 48, 155, 159, 160, 165; of the Middle East 94; of migratory experience 6–7, 49; women and national culture 106, 107
identity: biracial 95; and the body 29–30, 40, 41–2, 90–1; changes in 19–20, 30, 44–5; community-based 24; crisis of 4, 36; cultural 5, 13, 71, 84, 127, 142, 182; effects of migration 8, 28, 41, 63; fixed understanding of 1, 2, 3, 28, 49; gendered 29, 63, 90, 91, 141; and language 77; in literature of forced migration 6, 13, 15, 18–20, 23, 24, 123–4, 136–7, 138, 139, 140, 141, 142, 146, 177, 181; loss of 18–19; in modernist literature 13, 14, 15, 24, 151; multiple 18–19; multiplicitous 84, 87, 91; relationship with space 28–9, 32, 36, 37, 47–8; and stories 117; transcultural 2, 4, 28, 34, 40, 41, 43, 44, 46, 48; transindividual 24, 179–80; transnational 2, 3, 4, 84, 85, 90, 91, 92, 93; unified 91
ideologies, failure of 13
Idrīs, Suhayl, *al-Ḥayy al-Lātīnī* (The Latin Quarter) 4, 163, 164
illegal immigration 19–20
illegal jobs 21
imaginary, the 74, 76, 95; collective 15; literary 177, 181; nationalist 12; Western 94–5
immigration policies 19–20, 85–6, 100–1, 126, 158, 176
impotence 61, 62, 63, 179
incest 106, 110–12
indigenous civilizations 74
inequality 35, 49, 153, 179
infidelity 21, 37, 44–6, 63, 106, 107–8, 109

intercultural narratives 120
inter-subjectivity 24, 179
intimate terrorism 84–5, 91
Iran/Iranian 98; exilic identities 88; second-generation diaspora 96
Iran-Iraq War 97, 155, 156, 158
Iraq/Iraqi 36, 42, 43, 44, 48, 139; 2003 invasion and occupation 83–4, 87, 90, 159, 162, 172–3; Baath regime 83–4, 87, 88, 89–90, 155, 156, 158; literature of migration 145, 151–3, 154–5, 156–62, 163–9, 170–4; second-generation diaspora 96; second-generation life writing narratives 83–4, 86–90, 91, 92–101; sectarian violence 151, 159; *see also* al-Anbārī, Shākir; Badr, ʿAlī; Ḥallāwī, Janān Jāsim; Nadir, Leilah
Iraq War 89–90, 152, 155, 159
Ireland, C. 127
irony 21–2, 24
Islam 58, 69, 71–2, 85, 161, 162, 170; socialization 91; women 91, 104
Islamism 70, 75, 159, 161, 162, 173
Israel/Israeli 115, 116, 119–20, 131
Italian Society for Middle-Eastern Studies 175
Italy/Italian 16, 20, 21, 175–6

Jackson, Elizabeth 141
Jebeyli, Claire 29
jihadism 139; *see also* terrorism
Jordan/Jordanian 103, 107, 117–18, 120, 139

Kahf, Mohja 104, 124, 134
Kamāl, Dunyā: *Sījāra sābiʿa* (Cigarette Number Seven) 55
Kanafānī, Ghassān: *Rijāl fī al- shams* (Men in the Sun) 5
Katrak, Ketu 120
Khāl, Abū Bakr: magical realism 25; *Taytanikāt Ifriqiyya* (African Titanics) 15, 16, 17, 18, 19, 21–5, 178, 179, 180
Khalīfa, Khālid 126; *Lā sakākīn fī matābikh hādhihi al-madīna* (No Knives in the Kitchens of this City) 134
Khayat, Sarah 133
Khūrī, Ilyās, *Sīnālkūl* 63
Kimak, Izabella 105–6, 107, 113, 114
Kinopolitics 24
Kolb, David 136
Král, Françoise 118
Kristeva, Julia 142, 143, 144, 182
Kurdi, Aylan 129
Kurds/Kurdish 143, 155, 156, 158
Kuwait/Kuwaiti 52–3, 156, 172

Laghtīrī, Musṭafā, *Layla Ifrīqiyya* (An African Night) 13
Lampedusa 131, 175–6
language 22, 42, 69, 70–1, 74, 77, 78, 97, 163–4, 173; multiple 142; second-generation diaspora 96
Laredj, Waciny 69, 78; *Al-laylā al-sābiʿa baʿd al-alf*: *Raml al-māya* (The 1007th Night) 71; *Ḥārisat al-ẓilāl*: *Dūn Kīshūt fī al-Jazāʾir* (The Shadows' (she) guardian: Don Quixote in Algeria) 69, 71, 72–4, 75, 76, 77; *Kitāb al-amīr* (The Book of the Emir) 69–70; *Shurafāt baḥr al-shamāl* (The North Sea's Balconies: Amsterdam Rains) 69, 75–7
Latour, Bruno 15, 16, 136, 138–9
Lau, Lisa 103–4
law enforcement agencies 13
Lebanese civil war 29, 30, 35, 40, 63
Lebanon/Lebanese 4, 29, 30, 35, 40, 46; *see also* al-Shaykh, Ḥanān
Lens Young (photography project) 131–2
Leogrande, Alessandro 175, 176
Liberia/Liberian 22–3
Libya/Libyan 16, 18, 19, 176, 178
Lindsey, Ursula 56–7, 62, 63–4
Lohman, Jack 127, 130
London 30, 31, 33–4, 36–7, 40–1, 42–3, 44, 47–9, 92, 96, 100, 145, 152, 176
loneliness 37, 168, 169
loss, sense of 3, 17, 21, 28, 86, 131, 173
Luffin, Xavier 19, 22
Lugones, Maria 85
Lynx Qualey, M. 62

Madood, T. 180
Maghreb 6
magical realism 25
Mahjar literati 3–4
Majaj, Lisa Suhair 4
Maksūr, ʿAbd Allāh 181; *Ayyām Bābā ʿAmrū* (Baba Amro Days) 136, 137–9, 140; *ʿĀʾid ilā Ḥalab* (Returning to Aleppo) 136, 137–9, 140
Maldonado-Torres, N. 74
manfā 69, 75, 76, 77, 78; *see also* exile

Marfleet, Philip 127, 130, 131, 145
marginality 25, 29, 34, 56, 84, 87, 133, 141, 173, 178, 179
marriage 60–2, 106–9; and assimilation 88, 95
masculinity 60–1, 62, 63
masks 18, 19
Masmoudi, Ikram 179, 181
McFayden, Gillian 127, 128
Mediterranean: culture 70, 73; migration 6, 13, 22, 153, 175, 176
memoir (genre) 87
memory 75, 76; bodily 90; collective 71, 75; cultural 71; second-generation 95–6; *see also* nostalgia; postmemory
men, Arab, orientalist view of 108, 109
mestiza consciousness 84, 85
metropolises 162, 178–9, 181; European 4, 6, 8, 29, 31, 32, 34, 43, 47
Mexico 84
Mezzadra, Sandro 13, 176
migration: contemporary importance 28; forced 6, 13; to Gulf countries 5–6, 30–1, 52, 53–6; inter-cultural dialogue 70; in modernist literature 3, 6, 14, 15, 24, 62, 151; as plague 17, 18; post-national aspects 14, 181; romanticized view 6, 141, 151, 154, 163, 180; of students 12, 13; terminology 126; undocumented 6; *see also* asylum seekers; exile; forced migration, literature of; *manfā*; refugees
migration literature 3–7, 12–15, 28, 66, 78, 151, 152–5, 173–4, 176–82; *see also* forced migration, literature of
migratory journeys 16, 22–4; backwards movement 24; planning 17
Mikhail, Mona 53–4
Million, Dian 85
miscarriage 108–9, 112, 117
modernist literature: concept of identity 13, 14, 15, 24, 151; depiction of migration 3, 6, 14, 15, 24, 62, 151
Modood, Tariq 180
Mokhtari, Rachid 70
Morocco/Moroccan 5, 13
motherhood 37, 106, 108–9, 112–13
Moya, Paula 92
Mulḥim, Nabīl, *Bānsyūn Maryam* (Maryam's Boarding House) 136, 138–9, 140, 181
multiplicitous selves 84–5, 86, 91
Muses 71
museumification 131, 142
music 23, 38, 57, 65, 76, 96, 159, 160, 162, 169, 171; theory 165, 166
Muslim Brotherhood 72
mysticism 87, 88
mythology 71, 72, 73, 180

Nadir, Leilah, *Orange Trees of Baghdad* 83–4, 86–90, 91, 92–101, 180
Nahḍa (Arab Renaissance) 5, 12, 154, 181
nahḍawī novels 12, 13, 14, 15, 24
Nail, Thomas 1–2, 15, 18, 24, 177
names, multiple 18–19
Naṣr Āllāh, Emily 29
Naṣr Allāh, Ibrāhīm: *Barārī al-ḥummā* (Prairies of Fever) 6
National Liberation Front (FLN) 75
Netherlands 16, 20, 21, 75, 76–7
networks 2, 138–9, 179, 180
9/11 9, 103, 108, 110
nomads 33, 84, 128
Noman, Asthana 104
Nora, Pierre 71
Nordin, Irene Gilsenan 2, 28, 32, 34, 48, 176
North Sea 76, 164
nostalgia 5, 61–2, 76, 77, 95–6, 177; genealogical 97–9
Nyman, Jopi 2–3, 15, 28, 43, 48–9

Ogata, Sadako 127, 130
Omdurman 20, 21
One Thousand and One Nights 63–4, 70–1, 94, 116
orientalism 4, 44, 45, 94, 104, 108, 119, 181; depictions of refugees 125, 127, 128, 129; view of Arab men 108, 109; view of Arab women 103, 108, 112; *see also* re-orientalism; self-orientalism
Ortega, Mariana 84–5, 86
Other, the 30, 35, 42, 44, 45, 52, 69–70, 71, 77, 127, 144, 145
Ouyang, Wenchin 14, 134, 136, 137

Pakistan/Pakistani 60
Palestine/Palestinian 100, 107, 117, 118, 119, 120, 131, 139; refugees 145
palm trees 17–18, 21
Pan-Arabism 13, 53
Paniconi, Maria Elena 179
Paris 4, 56
patriarchal discourses 104

patriarchy: depictions of refugees 140–1; model of masculinity 63; roles and depictions of women 103, 104, 105, 106, 109, 112–13, 115; social organization 29; Western 100–1
Philippines/Filipino 62
political crisis 13
polyphonic narrative 29, 34–5, 83–4, 87
Port Said 21
postcolonialism 7, 43, 49, 62, 127, 128, 141; novels 3, 4, 15, 152–3, 154, 163, 164, 173; shift to global context 6, 31, 151, 152, 153, 157, 162, 164–5, 173–4
postmemory 97, 98
postnationalism 14, 123, 128, 137, 146, 181
Post-traumatic stress disorder (PTSD) 168
prison 20, 59, 70, 75, 77, 133, 138; Iraq 156, 157, 171; narratives 140, 142–5
Prometheus 73
Puumala, Eeva 128, 129, 130

Qabbānī, Nizār 124

Rabinowitz, Dan 145
racism 88, 89, 130, 154, 158, 160, 167, 180–1
Ramaḍān, ʿAbbān 75
rationality 88
refugees 6, 31; Arab-Syrian representations 123, 124, 125, 134, 136–45, 146, 181; artistic representations 124–5, 129, 130–1, 145–6; infrahuman trope 123; Iraqi representations 154–62, 163–75; media representations 123, 124–5, 127, 129–30, 145–6; obstacles to seeking asylum 100–1; selfies 132–3; terminology and hierarchy 125–6, 127–8, 130, 145; *see also* asylum seekers; forced migration, literature of
re-orientalism 103–4; *see also* self-orientalism 103–4
return: failed 170–3; fear of 98; hope of 5, 93; impossibility of 99–100
romanticism 94, 104; depiction of migration 6, 141, 151, 154, 163, 180
Rome 21
Rothberg, Michael 71
rozas 112, 113, 114, 116, 117

Said, Aleya 53–4
Said, Edward 2
Sakr, Rita 123, 137, 139–40, 145
Salaita, Steven 4
Salam, Roula 181
Ṣāliḥ, al-Ṭayyib, *Mawsim al-hijra ilā al-shamāl* (Season of Migration to the North) 5, 151, 152–3, 154, 155, 163, 164, 170, 181
Saudi Arabia 30, 32, 53, 54
Saʿīd, ʿAbbūd, *Afham shakhṣ bi-l-Faysbūk* (The Smartest Guy on Facebook) 141–2
Scandinavia 155, 162, 168; *see also* Denmark; Sweden
sea crossings 6, 13, 22–3, 153, 175–6
seasonal work 19, 21
second-generation 95–6, 97
self-esteem 89
selfies 132–3
self-orientalism 103–4, 105, 106, 108, 109, 164, 181
Sellman, Johanna 5, 6, 13, 15, 31, 62, 139, 153, 162, 168, 179–80
sexuality: homosexuality 29, 37, 39, 40; social control of 60–2, 63; women's 39, 43, 44–6, 105–6, 107–12, 113–14, 161, 166
Shahbazi, Shima 179, 180
Shakir, Evelyn 3, 108
Shalan, Jeff 12
shaming 60
shipwrecks 175–6
silence: and alienation 168; Syrian culture of 124, 134, 146; of women 104, 109, 110, 115–16
simultaneity of geography 120
Sīrīs, Nihād 126; *Al-ṣamt wa-l-ṣakhab* (The Silence and the Roar) 134
Slaughter, Joseph 14–15
smuggling 18, 21, 22, 40, 156, 160–1, 162
social media 127, 141–2
social practices 54, 92–3
solitude 35, 37, 39, 74, 77
Soueif, Ahdaf, *1964* 14, 15
space: interaction with 32–3, 35, 36; relationship with identity 28–9, 32, 36, 37, 47–8; representation of 58–9; and social control 59
Spain/Spanish 70, 71, 73, 74
Spoke (magazine) 130
sponsorship system 52
stereotypes 88, 105, 123, 128, 180–1; of Arab men 94, 109, 163; of Arab women 95, 107, 110, 112

storytelling 22–4, 63–4, 114–15, 116–17
students, migration of 4, 12–13, 92, 153, 154
subaltern narratives 124, 125, 127, 128, 134, 135, 136, 137, 139, 146
subjectivities: female 107; of migrants 15, 24, 31, 47, 63, 153, 154, 177
sub-Saharan African literatures 6
Sudan/Sudanese 5, 16, 20, 21, 22, 58, 135, 152, 154, 178
suicide 5, 77
superstition 88
Sūriyā tataḥaddath (Syria Speaks) (anthology) 132, 140, 143, 144
surveillance 59
Ṣuwayliḥ, Khalīl 126
Sweden/Swedish 130–1, 155, 158, 167–9, 173, 179
Switzerland 176
Sydney 96
Syrian civil war 124, 130, 136, 138, 140, 155
Syria/Syrian 59, 157, 170; culture of silence 124, 134, 146; identity 123–4, 125, 128, 135, 142, 146; literature and art 4, 123, 124, 125, 126–7, 128, 133, 134–5, 136–45, 181; migration to 155, 156; photographs 131–3; popular culture 133; *see also* refugees

Ṭāhir, Bahā', *Bi-l-amsi ḥalamtu bi-ka* (Last Night I Dreamt of You) 14, 15
Tāmir, Zakariyyā 126
Taylor, Jason deCaires 131
terrorism 75, 77, 100, 108, 138, 139, 170
theft 21, 59
torture 24, 139
tragedy 24, 77
transculturality 2, 32, 34, 48; identity 2, 4, 28, 34, 40, 41, 43, 44, 46, 48; imagery 45; literature 2, 30, 32, 176; space 38
transnationalism: community 57, 58, 62; families 97; identity 2, 3, 4, 84, 85, 90, 91, 92, 93; literature 29, 30, 83; spaces 56
transvestitism 29, 33, 40
Tunisia/Tunisian 16, 18, 19, 24, 139, 175, 176, 178
Turkey/Turkish 39, 131, 132, 140, 160, 161, 166, 167

Uberoi, Varun 180
undocumented workers 5, 176
United Arab Emirates (UAE) 52
United Nations High Commissioner for Refugees (UNHCR) 130, 158
United States 103, 106–9, 110, 112, 113, 114, 117–20; aesthetic standards 44, 46; Arab-American women writers 104, 105; border 84; immigration 85–6
urbanization 33, 36, 46–7, 58–9
'Usayrān, Laylā 29

Wallerstein, Immanuel 104
Wannūs, Sa'd Allāh, *Ṭuqūs al-ishārāt wa-l-taḥawwulāt* (Rituals of Signs and Transformations) 1994
Weiwei, Ai *see* Ai, Weiwei
Wennman, Magnus 130–1
whiteness 95
Wilson, Erin 127
Wilson, Janet Mary 23
women: in Arab countries 29, 35, 36, 37–40, 104, 105; orientalist view 103, 108, 112; sexuality 44–6, 105–6, 107–12, 113–14, 115, 166; storytelling 63–4, 114–15, 116–17
Wright, Terence 129, 141

xenophobia 85, 151, 160, 162, 168, 169

Yain-Allah, Ayman 129
Yassīn-Kassab, Robin 134–5
Yazbik, Samar 126–7, 136, 142; *Bawwābāt arḍ al-'adam* (The Crossing: My Journey to the Shattered Heart of Syria) 140–1, 181–2; *Taqāṭu' nīrān, min yawmiyyāt al-intifāḍa al-sūrīyya* (A Woman in the Crossfire: Diaries of the Syrian Revolution) 134
Yelles, Mourad 70
Yaḥyā, Yūsuf Abū, "*Anā sūrī*" (I Am Syrian) 134
Yuval-Davis, Nira 2

Ziyād, Ṣālih 12

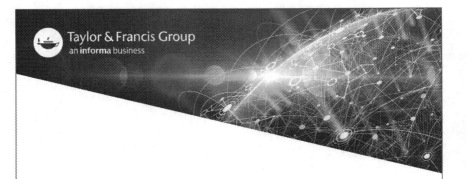